The
JEWISH HOLIDAY
KITCHEN

The
JEWISH HOLIDAY KITCHEN

Joan Nathan

SCHOCKEN BOOKS
New York

*To all the women of valour who have passed down these recipes
And to my daughter, Daniela, who will inherit them.*

First published by Schocken Books 1979
Copyright ©1979 by Schocken Books Inc.

Library of Congress Cataloging in Publication Data
Nathan, Joan.
  The Jewish holiday kitchen.

  Bibliography: p.
  Includes index.
  1. Cookery, Jewish. I. Title.
TX724.N37   641.5'67'6   79-64114

Drawings by Debbie Insetta
Designed by Janet Sutherland

Manufactured in the United States of America

CONTENTS

ACKNOWLEDGMENTS

The seed for this book was planted during my stay in Jerusalem from 1970 to 1972. It germinated during the academic year of 1975–76, when I was fortunate to be studying at the John F. Kennedy School of Government at Harvard University, on a fellowship from the Smith Fund. I am especially grateful to three professors I met there who encouraged me to study Jewish food within the context of an ethnic society. Wilma Wetterstrom's course on nutrition and socio-cultural systems directed my approach to Jewish cuisine. Daniel Patrick Moynihan allowed me to deviate in his course on ethnicity and politics to write a paper on ethnicity and food, which has formed the basis for the introduction to this book. Folklorist Dov Noy, on sabbatical from Hebrew University, Jerusalem, encouraged my exploration into the folklore surrounding Jewish food and introduced me to the concept of seasonal and life cycles.

A *Jewish Holiday Kitchen* cookbook that tries to be in some way comprehensive cannot be written without the assistance of the many Jewish cooks, around the United States and abroad, who have inherited treasured family festival recipes. Thus, I thank the following people: Claire Ackerman, Max Baskies, Dorothy Battist, Lisa Benaroya, Mercedes Bensimon, Debbie Berger, Rosette Bishop, Alice Broch, Marian Burros, Irma Cardozo, Eva Lubetkin Cantor, Kadem Cohen, Michel Cohen, Sarah Cooper, Ava Ehrlich, Elaine Grossinger Etess, Mrs. Coleman Falk, Michel Fitoussi, Elaine Frank, Judy Stacey Goldman, Charles Guggenheim, Helen Harrison, Leon Hirschbaum, Rabbi Richard Israel, Shoshanna Israeli, Bobbie Jellinek, Madelline Kamman, Felicia Lamport Kaplan, Jacob Licht, Alex Lichtman, Ada Baum Lipschitz, Frances Luzzatto, Jane Mesirow, Vicki Mittenthal, Lilly Modiano, Fran Monus, Eva Nadelstern, Ariane Nahor, Ruth and Emily Nathan, Irene Pletka, Moria Rafiakh, Phyllis Richman, Jane Rogul, June Rogul, Sultan Levy Rosenblatt, Irene Robinson, Delle Sacks, Nadav Safran, Chaya and Beryl Segal, Mohtaran Shirazi, Rose Siegel, Macie Fain Silver, Liliane Sivan, Mozelle and Pearl Sofaer, Ginette Spier, Bruno and Lisl Stern, Olga Stern, Mark Talisman, Rosalyn Talisman, Jack Turkoff, Annie Simonian Totah, Jack Tulkoff, Sam Weinberg, Bertha Weiss, Ben Wertleb,

Eveline Moos Weyl, Heidi Wortzel, Sally Wolfson, Gisella Warburg Wyzanski, and Wendy Simon Zinn.

Many people helped test recipes for this book. In particular I want to thank Sarah Wattenberg and all the young girls of our neighborhood in Chevy Chase, who either helped cook or watched my baby so that I could cook, research, and write.

I am appreciative of the time Professor David Altshuler, chairman of the Jewish Studies Department at George Washington University; Dr. Molly G. Schuchat, cultural anthropologist; and Mickey and Mordecai Feinberg spent reading the text of this book. They generously shared with me their religious, historical, and anthropological expertise.

Special thanks to Karen Dobkin, Michael Janeway, and Anthony Spinazzola of the Boston *Globe*, Marian Burros and William Rice of the Washington *Post*, and Leonard Fein of *Moment* magazine for encouraging me to write the kinds of articles that, in part, could eventually be incorporated in this book. And, of course, it was my editors, Seymour Barofsky and Beverly Colman, who helped me to execute the writing of this cookbook.

Whenever I needed technical information, I turned to the indefatigable and extraordinarily knowledgeable staff of the Library of Congress' Hebraic Section. Without the assistance of Myron Weinstein and Feiga Zylberming, this book could not have been written.

The pictures taken by the late Edward Fitzgerald, Judith Licht, Judith Shepard Rosenfeld, Dan Scheuer, and my husband, Allan Gerson, add the life necessary to a cookbook about people.

Important thanks go to my in-laws, Morton and Paula Gerson; my parents, Ernest and Pearl Nathan; my aunt Lisl Regensteiner; and my cousin Dorothy Regensteiner, all of whom graciously shared with me those Jewish roots and recipes that have made up my own culinary heritage.

A very special note of appreciation is due to my husband, Allan Gerson, who—always in good spirits—was willing to play the role of quality controller in tasting all the recipes in this book. Last, but certainly not least, I want to thank my daughter, Daniela, who patiently played at my feet during her first year of life and considerately awaited the manuscript's completion before taking her first steps.

INTRODUCTION

Eighty-four-year-old Ada Baum Lipsitz of Boston would never think of making her weekly hallah without first separating some dough, reciting a blessing over it, and then burning it in the oven, in accordance with the biblical commandment. Seventy-nine-year-old Rose Siegel of Washington, D.C., breaks each egg into a separate bowl to check that there is no drop of blood, which would make the food *tref*. To Ada Baum Lipsitz and Rose Siegel, and all observant Jewish women of any age, these acts are as automatic as setting the table before a meal. But, for second- and third-generation assimilated Americans like myself, they are fast becoming relics of the past. Yet, these seemingly innocuous and ostensibly eccentric rituals carry within them the legends and traditions of the Jews. With the help of people throughout the country, I have tried to piece together some of the folklore and foods of our people.

Like many Jews of the 1970's, I have become passionately involved in discovering my roots. As a food writer, my explorations have not been confined to assembling family genealogies; rather, whenever testing a recipe, I have attempted to discover the origin of the dish and of the ingredients. These recipes often unfold the backgrounds of the people who have passed them down.

When I lived in Israel from 1970 to 1972, I often daydreamed about the early Israelites, my ancestors. Driving through the sand dunes of Beersheba and the hills surrounding Jerusalem, I tried to visualize the lives the nomadic Israelites led. Ancient olive trees still abound there. The other foods mentioned in Deuteronomy—wheat and barley, grapes, figs, pomegranates, honey made from bee nectar, date jam—are still produced in abundance. In the marketplace of Jerusalem's Old City, they have altered only slightly in form over the past two thousand years.

As I traveled from Mount Sinai back to Jerusalem, layers of civilizations and thousands of years unwound like a newsreel before me at each fork in the road. In Jerusalem the modernity is most startling. The Bedouin's tented existence, where everyone shared the same pot, has gradually been replaced. Jerusalem's fast-food restaurants are light years away from the nomadic feasts in the desert.

My quest for culinary roots began in Jerusalem in 1970. It spurred me to write, together with Judy Stacey Goldman, *The Flavor of Jerusalem* (Boston: Little, Brown, 1975), in which we tried to portray the ethnic groups and food of the Holy City. My search has continued in the food columns I have been writing for the Boston *Globe* and, occasionally, the Washington

Post. More often than not, my stories have centered around octogenarian immigrants whose culinary knowledge and folk history have been passed on by word of mouth from generation to generation.

ANCIENT FOOD TRADITIONS

Before delving into the holiday recipes we use in this century, let us go back to ancient Palestine to see where some of these festival dishes may have originated and to examine the dietary laws which have always differentiated Jewish foods from those of other peoples. Despite the wanderings of the Jews throughout millennia, their foods still have the ring of that ancient authenticity. Holidays and festive occasions may not have originally come with gefilte fish, latkes, hamantashen, baklava, or blintzes. Yet, these modern dishes are the offspring of ancient symbols, combined with ingredients available during the great Diaspora.

Hunting and gathering societies of the ancient Middle East subsisted on berries, grains, insects, and other foods found in the woods, fields, and desert. The everyday diet of these nomads was rather sparse: birds' eggs, yoghurt, sheep or goat milk, wild-bee honey, wine, olive oil, lentils, fresh or dried dates and figs, pomegranates, wild melons, cucumbers, sesame seeds, garlic, onions, and grain from barley and wheat. They ate most of these foods as they found them. Some, such as oil, were pressed, and others, such as yoghurt, were fermented. Only occasionally did they kill a wild animal as a dietary supplement. Naturally, the seasons greatly influenced the foods they ate.

In ancient Palestine, the first grain planted and harvested or the felling of an animal large enough to feed many people provided an occasion for jubilation and festivity, among both Jews and Gentiles. Both peoples offered sacrifices to God—sometimes in gratitude, sometimes in fear, and sometimes as an expression of regret for sin. The Jews, however, recognizing more strongly God's presence in nature, showed a concern for monotheism as well as an ethical and moral basis in their sacrifices. The laws of sacrifice in Judaism are strictly governed, both as to the manner of sacrifice and the disposition of the food afterward. (The sacrificial object—animal, grain, or fruit—was sometimes eaten by the priests after parts of it were burned, depending on the type of sacrifice.)

Ceremonial foods thus performed two major functions for the ancient Israelites. They served as a means of expression of the relationship between nature and God, and as a unifying economic bond between the tribe of Levi (priests) and the rest of the Israelite people.

For Jews, then, foods have deep symbolic value. Each act of dining, from the preparation of food to the grace after meals, is carefully prescribed by Jewish law.

THE JEWISH HOLIDAYS

For many people of all ethnic groups, holidays are the last ties binding them to their family and their traditions. Whether or not they have adopted standard American daily fare, they turn to traditional, ethnic food for the holidays. This is even more true for the Jews, given the importance of our dietary laws and the table-centered rituals involved in the Sabbath and holidays. Judaism is a religion based on the combination of belief, practice, and piety. Many of the commandments require some sort of accompanying physical action for fulfillment. The symbolism and inherent qualities of food are just some of the means by which the lofty ideals of Judaism are transmitted to everyday living. One can see that even where some of the more stringent commandments have been forgotten, the festive holiday get-togethers are scrupulously and lovingly perpetuated.

If we look at each Jewish holiday, we can see how closely connected feasting and fasting are to jubilation and penitence. Moreover, the times of the year in which these occasions occur show that account has been taken of the seasonal abundance of certain foods.

The celebration of Rosh Hashanah, the New Year, always includes honey and a new fruit for a sweet year ahead. At Sukkot, the fall harvest festival, families eat their meals for one week in a specially constructed booth, covered with branches or bamboo sticks and decorated with small jars of wine, flour, and oil, among other things. At Hanukkah, foods are cooked in goose fat, abundant in winter. Many pastries are eaten at Purim, the last festival before Passover, when the yearly store of flour must be used up. At Passover, for eight days dishes prepared with unleavened bread and eggs, abundant in the spring, are eaten. Josephus describes the event in ancient Israel whereby hundreds of thousands of newborn lambs were sacrificed at the Temple in Jerusalem at Passover. On Shavuot, the feast of the first fruits and the time of the receiving of the Torah, milk products are traditionally eaten, probably accounted for by the small amount of meat available at the time of newborn animals, the good pasturage, and the fact that in early times the laws of ritual slaughter had not been fully explained. The Sabbath is usually marked by two symbolic loaves of bread, wine, and fish, and other special foods for a special day. Cooking is not allowed on this day, and thus women may share in the Sabbath rest.

Jewish seasonal festivals often predate the national historic events they commemorate. Today, therefore, each festival possesses more than one significance. For example, Passover was a harvest celebration even before it came to represent the Exodus from Egypt.

The three major seasonal festivals are Passover, marking the beginning of the barley harvest, in the springtime; Shavuot (the Feast of Weeks), marking the end of it, seven weeks later; and Sukkot (the Feast of Booths), celebrating the harvesting of the grain at the commencement of autumn. Historically, all three festivals have become associated with the Exodus from Egypt—Passover representing the release from bondage; Shavuot, the giving of the Torah at Mount Sinai and the completion of the Covenant between God and His people; and Sukkot, the sojourn of the Israelites in the wilderness on their way to the promised land. The three festivals thus represent a covenant between God and the Jews. In ancient times, they were marked by pilgrimages to the Temple in Jerusalem and special offerings of food to God in thanksgiving.

THE LIFE CYCLE

In addition to the seasonal cycle of festivals, there are meaningful events in the individual Jewish life. Days of rejoicing for births, bar and bat mitzvahs, and weddings have particular twists in the symbolic foods used. Foods can be used to symbolize fertility, prosperity, good luck, and immortality—all the good things that one wishes another. Birth and death have their special foods, such as eggs and bagels—symbolizing the circle of life—and lentils. Fatty foods augur a rich and good life; thus, golden chicken soup is served at weddings. Fish symbolizes fertility and prosperity; it is eaten on Friday night and served at weddings and at Rosh Hashanah.

KASHRUT

All religions have special days devoted to feasting or fasting. Judaism, however, has a complete written code of religious dietary laws governing every single act of eating. Today these laws are often dismissed as merely ancient sanitary precautions. The Torah includes no rationale for the laws. Throughout the centuries, various hygienic and theological reasons have been suggested. But whether the reason was satisfactory or left questions unanswered, there has always been a core of the faithful who followed this proscription because it is a commandment of God. No reason is necessary.

A number of principles of *kashrut* are mentioned in the Bible. These have been codified and elaborated upon throughout the centuries. The rules and the rabbis' commentaries are listed in the *Shulhan Arukh*, the standard code of Jewish law. The following are some of the major regulations governing food.

"Whatsoever parteth the hoof, and is wholly cloven-footed, and cheweth the cud...that may ye eat" (Leviticus 11:3). Both these conditions limit the kinds of animals Jews may eat. Permissible species include ox, sheep, goat, hart, gazelle, roebuck, antelope, and mountain sheep. Prohibited are, in addition to pork, such foods as horsemeat, camel, rabbit or hare, and whale steaks.

No signs to identify permissible fowl are given in the Torah. Rather, the Bible enumerates twenty-four species of impermissible fowl: birds of prey may not be eaten; edible fowl have in common a projecting claw, a crop, and a gizzard or stomach that can be peeled readily of its inner lining. But local tradition determines which are kosher. Some Yemenite Jews will not eat geese because they are of both land and sea. Yet geese were eaten by East European Jews.

"These may ye eat of all that are in the waters: whatsoever hath fins and scales in the waters, in the seas, and in the rivers, them may ye eat" (Leviticus 11:9). A clean fish must have both fins and scales, and the scales must be detachable from the skin. For this reason, sturgeon, famous for caviar, whose scales are not removable unless the skin is also removed, is not considered kosher. Swordfish in its adult stage lacks scales and is not considered kosher. Shellfish, such as shrimp and oysters, lack fins and scales and are scavengers. They are not kosher.

Much anthropological discussion has ensued on the arbitrariness of Jewish dietary laws, especially concerning the exclusion of shellfish and pork in the diet. British anthropologist Mary Douglas thinks that the exclusion of some animals was arbitrary and reinforced the concept of exclusiveness of the Jews. "Moses forbade most delicious meats. The lawgiver sternly forbade all animals of land, sea or air whose flesh is the finest and fattiest, like that of pigs and scaleless fish, knowing that they set a trap for the most slavish of senses, the taste, and that they produced gluttony." Douglas feels that the dietary laws in general and the avoidance of eating pig—the pagan delicacy—in particular made of the Jews an exclusive people, one set apart from its neighbors. She also states that it was only after the pigs defiled the Temple at the time of the Maccabees that this animal came to be singled out. Columbia University anthropologist Marvin Harris offers an economic reason for the exclusion of pigs to the Jews. In the ancient Middle East, the Jews wandered in the hot desert where pigs, although delicious, would have been difficult if not impossible to maintain. Thus, the rabbis cleverly forbade them, as they did not fit into the economic system. Though there may be some truth in both Douglas' and Harris' interpretations of the prohibition of pork, probably no one will ever know the real reason.

Before eating permissible meat, the animal must first be slaughtered. A limb torn or cut from a living animal is forbidden. An animal not slaughtered, but that dies of itself, is prohibited. Only select animals, thoroughly tested, are used. What is most important to the Jews, however, is the fact that to the present so many have adhered to this prohibition. Moreover, many who do so may not observe any other facet of *kashrut.*

Another Jewish distinction is the way in which animals are slaughtered. The rules for slaughtering spring from ethical principles and are also designed to reject the sacrificial practices of paganism. "Thou shalt kill thy herd and thy flock, which the Lord hath given thee, as I have commanded thee, and thou shalt eat within thy gates, after all the desire of the soul" (Deuteronomy 12:21). All animals and birds require *shehitah*, the ritualistic slaughtering. The method of slaughter is prescribed by tradition. Each knife must be twice as long as the width of the animal's throat and extremely sharp and smooth. The *shohet* (the slaughterer) must sever the major portions of the animal's trachea and esophagus without grazing its spine. Further, the knife must be drawn gently across the throat without hesitation or pressure. Even a fraction of a second's delay makes the killing invalid.

Before and after each kill, the *shohet* must check the condition of the blade and, when necessary, sharpen it on a fine, smooth stone. He is required to view the incision to make certain that the throat has been cut sufficiently. If the blade is nicked, or if any hair clings to it, the animal is ruled ritually unfit. After the carcasses are removed from the slaughtering ramp, the lungs are cut open and checked for abnormalities. Later, the lungs are removed and examined for discolored areas and other symptoms of disease. If they show no irregularity, the *shohet* assumes that the animal is healthy and pronounces the meat fit to eat. If he suspects some disorder but cannot spot it, he blows air into the lungs. If the lungs hold air, the animal is kosher; if they don't, it's *tref,* unfit.

The *shohet* follows a tradition dating back three thousand years to the meat sacrificed at the Tabernacle in Jerusalem when he says, "Blessed art Thou, O Lord our God, King of the Universe, who has commanded us in koshering."

After slaughtering, the *shohet* rejects cattle with certain types of adhesions, cuts, and bruises. Only the forequarters of the approved cattle are used because of the cost of butchering the hindquarters.

In the Bible there is an absolute prohibition against the consumption of blood. "Therefore I said unto the children of Israel: No soul of you shall eat blood. . . . Ye shall eat the blood of no manner of flesh. . . whosoever eateth it shall be cut off" (Leviticus 17:12, 14). Thus, the blood must be extracted from the meat through salting or broiling. This prohibition against the eating of blood was the result of a deliberate, reasoned enactment of the early Israelites against the pagan practice of drinking blood. To the Jew, blood is sacred, a gift of God. "I have given it [the blood] to you upon the altar to make an atonement for your souls" (Leviticus 17:11). Blood is thus also a means of atonement. It wards off future harm if the pascal blood is smeared upon doorposts and lintels. It expiates sin when dashed upon the side of the altar. This superstition might even be behind the original circumcision rite.

After all the blood is removed by soaking in cold water for half an hour, the meat is then salted for one hour with coarse kosher rather than fine-grained salt (which would dissolve instead of drawing out the blood). Then the salt is shaken off and the meat washed three times so that no blood remains.

The excessive use of salt in Judaism recalls the salting of sacrifices in the Tabernacle. Salt, a pure preservative, was always used, whereas honey and leaven—both in a state of fermentation—were not. With the destruction of the Temple, the home table is now as much God's table as the altar was. On the one hand, the salt recalls the purity of God and the Temple. On the other, this white condiment could ward off evil spirits. For a symbol of permanence, purity, and a good omen, it is understandable that newborn babies were once sprinkled with salt.

Before a meal is begun, salt must be set on the table. After the blessing, salt is always spread on bread.

Some people feel that salt is not needed on the Sabbath because no harm will come to a family if it celebrates the day of rest. Bread and salt are the traditional offerings to new homeowners, securing the family against evil spirits.

Fish does not need to be made kosher, but some people, probably out of superstition, even salt fish.

Another dietary law prohibits cooking or eating meat and milk together. "Thou shalt not seethe a kid in its mother's milk" (Deuteronomy 14:20), the basis of the prohibition, prevented the ancient Hebrews from participating in pagan customs of animal sacrifice. It was also a way of helping digestion. Two separate sets of utensils must be provided for the preparation, serving, and storing of milk and meat dishes. The utensils must be washed separately. Traditionalist Jews may have two sinks, and two sets of sponges, mixing bowls, and dishes, or two sets of blades and bowls for mixers and food processors. Between a milk and a meat meal, one must merely rinse out the mouth or eat a morsel of bread. For this there is no waiting requirement. Between a meat and a milk meal, however, where digestion is more difficult, Dutch Jews wait one hour, Germans three, and East Europeans six.

Neutral or *pareve* foods, such as fish, eggs, and vegetables, may be used with either milk or meat. Originally, all Jews used olive oil as the main cooking oil, causing no problems at dairy *(milchig)* and meat *(fleishig)* meals. Later, North and East European Jews had little access to olive oil or even vegetable oils. They depended on butter or meat fats for cooking. Since butter, a dairy product, cannot be eaten with meat, and since lard, a pork fat, is forbidden to Jews, chicken and other poultry fats have always figured importantly in a number of European Jewish cuisines. Jews could not even eat *pareve* foods outside the home for fear that they were çooked in a forbidden fat. Thus, cooking agents became one way of separating the Jews from the Gentiles.

Certain packaged foods are marked with symbols such as Ⓤ or Ⓐ, to indicate that a Jewish organization has approved them as kosher. There are a number of different symbols in the various parts of the country.

As we can see from this brief introduction to Jewish holidays and the dietary laws, much of Jewish communal life centers around the dinner table. By scrutinizing each act in the kitchen, the Jew is forever aware of his separateness and his oneness with God. Food, then, has great representative value for him.

In religious homes, no fire for domestic use is lit on the Sabbath, because of the commandment: "Ye shall kindle no fire throughout your habitations upon the sabbath day" (Exodus 35:3). This means that it is not permissible to smoke, cook, or in any way burn anything. Cooking is considered one of the thirty-nine types of work forbidden on the Sabbath. For this reason, Sabbath candles are lit just before sunset.

In ancient times (and today, too), fires made before the Sabbath could burn until they went out naturally. Thus, slow-cooking dishes such as cholents and kugels were devised for this arrangement. With modern gas and electric stoves, however, there is less of a problem, and warm foods can be eaten throughout the rest day. A tin, asbestos, or aluminum sheet shaped to cover two burners and the dials of a stove was devised. Many intricate rules surround the definition of cooking with this warmer. For example, the food should have been partially cooked before the Sabbath starts. A coffee urn can be plugged in before the Sabbath falls and kept plugged in throughout the day. Or previously boiled hot water can be simmered on the tin throughout the day.

Having to do without certain ingredients has given the Jewish people the opportunity to experiment with the properties of foods. It would be no surprise to learn, for example, that a Jew discovered that egg whites beaten stiffly and combined with egg yolks, sugar, and some kind of flour, with perhaps a dash of lemon, produced a fluffy sponge cake, without leaven, to be eaten at Passover. The world's greatest long-simmering stews might have all orig-inated in the Sabbath cholent cooking in overnight ashes. And how many festive dishes have been created out of meager ingredients! Take gefilte fish, for example. The Talmud suggests that Jews eat fish on Friday night. East European Jews created this delicacy when they removed the bones (so that the Jew would not pick, or *"borer"*) and stretched precious fish, so expensive to these poor people, with breadcrumbs, onions, and eggs, and poached it in broth. The leftover broth could then be used during the week as a soup, with potatoes. The Jews, unlike the French and the Chinese—who created masterful cuisines based on last-minute stir-frying and cream sauces—had to create a holiday-oriented cuisine preparable in advance.

During the nineteenth century, German Jews were the leaders in most Jewish communities throughout the United States. The earlier Sephardic families had mostly integrated into American life and never constituted the numbers the Germans did. German cuisine first influenced the mainstream of American Jewish life. The earliest cookbooks in English in which Jewish recipes were included stemmed from the tradition of the German forebears, most of whom were adherents of Reform Judaism, which by the mid-nineteenth century had pronounced *kashrut* incompatible with the enlightened spirit of the age. Side by side with recipes for Passover or Friday night were dishes for oysters, crab, and the like. The earliest American cookbook was Esther Levy's *Jewish Cookery Book;* first published in Philadelphia in 1871, it was kosher. In *Aunt Babette's* non-kosher cookbook of 1889, however, appeared Easter dishes for Passover—almond tortes, krimsel, schalet—but no gefilte fish. The third well-known cookbook, especially in the South, was the *Twentieth Century Cookbook,* published in 1897 in Montgomery, Alabama, by C. F. Moritz and Adelle Kahn. It did not even boast a Passover section, but included an occasional Jewish recipe such as Purim Puffs, basically a doughnut cooked in chicken fat rather than the lard prescribed for doughnuts in the same book. The most important cookbook, however, was the *Settlement Cook Book,* which, to this day, has influenced American Jewish women who want the recipes their parents used to make. Published in 1901 by Mrs. Simon Kander to raise funds for the Settlement House in Milwaukee, it offered basic German recipes but also included those of the poor Russian immigrants helped by the Settlement House. Thus, gefilte fish, matzah balls, kreplakh, kugel, and kichel finally worked their way into a major American cookbook. In all three cookbooks, however, the Jewish and general recipes are of distinctly German flavor. Many latter-day synagogue cookbooks are considerably more universal.

At the time these books were published, Jewish immigrants from Russia did not yet need cookbooks to reproduce recipes. Neither did they think of abandoning *kashrut* for distinctly American foods. East European Jews lacked culinary influence even as late as the 1930's, as a look at the *Tempting Kosher Dishes, Prepared by World Famous Manischewitz Matzah Products* of 1931 shows. There were recipes for salmon loaf, tuna loaf, and other fishes, but not one for gefilte fish. (Today Manischewitz sells over 150,000 jars of gefilte fish a year.) Yiddish was the East Europeans' language, and the only way food might have been described to them was, perhaps, in the stories of Sholom Aleichem. Recipes were handed down by word of mouth and by watching. The Russian influence was felt later in the mass-marketing of such items as gefilte fish, matzah balls, rye bread, and borscht.

About the time of World War I, mass-marketing of food came into existence. Italian, German, and Jewish foods, all eaten until then by ethnic groups only, slowly became available to all Americans. Today, "You don't have to be Jewish to love Levy's rye bread" or the Hebrew National advertisements are reminders of how times have changed. Gefilte fish, borscht, matzah, and of course bagels are all marketed for both Jews and non-Jews. Indeed, Manischewitz wine is sold to a primarily non-Jewish clientele. This coming of age of Jewish and all ethnic foods makes of Jewish holiday cooking a different phenomenon from what it was a hundred years ago. Ethnic food is a matter of public pride rather than something hidden in the home. Major publishers have Jewish cookbooks on their lists, and almost every sisterhood has published a cookbook. Since the late 1950's, people have been desperately trying to record their culinary roots. Cookbooks and mass production of food are a far cry from the biblical foods of the desert, but somehow there are unifying threads—the holidays and *kashrut*.

I have read hundreds of folktales and scanned popular cookbooks in three of the great Judaica collections in the United States—Harvard University, the New York Public Library, and the Library of Congress—for clues to the customs and backgrounds of foods and recipes used by Jews in this country. Some of the most interesting revelations have come from nineteenth-century Christian cookbooks. (At the back of this book is a list of the major works consulted.) I have also tried to visit some of the centers of American Jewry and have interviewed people to see which recipes have regional popularity and from which area they come.

Fortunately for me, too, my aunt Lisl Regensteiner, an excellent cook, found a well-worn book of favorite recipes my grandmother compiled as a young bride almost a hundred years ago in Augsburg, Germany. While German fare seems to have been eaten during the week, Jewish recipes were used for the holidays, despite the Enlightenment, which pervaded my not-very-religious family. My mother, Pearl Gluck Nathan, also a whiz in the kitchen and a splendid hostess, born in Manhattan of immigrant parents from Cracow and Hungary, learned to cook via the *Settlement Cook Book* and by watching her maternal grandmother prepare holiday recipes, which she has passed on to me. More faithful to the world depicted by Sholom Aleichem and American immigrant food, post–1900, is my mother-in-law, Paula (Peshka) Gerson. She still cooks as did her mother in Zamosc, Poland, a small city near the Russian border.

This is an American Jewish holiday cookbook. Its more than one hundred fifty recipes come from Central and East European Jews, as well as those Sephardic Jews from Spain and Portugal who came here either via Holland and Latin America or after sojourns in the countries of the Ottoman Empire. Where appropriate, I include the native name of the dish; many of the Sephardic foods have Ladino names.

Seasonal recipes such as a Lebanese stuffed zucchini with apricot sauce at Rosh Hashanah or a Polish stuffed cabbage at Sukkot have stories behind them. The vignette preceding each recipe might be a description of a hallah baker, the origin of pomegranates, or an interview with a cook who provides us with a link to our culinary roots. We live in such an international environment today that a Russian Jewish family living in Chicago should feel no qualms at including a Hungarian cabbage strudel from Staten Island at Sukkot or, at Passover, an Austrian chocolate soufflé roll whose creator escaped the Holocaust and set up what many consider to be Boston's finest pastry shop. The recipes—all of which I have personally tested and tasted— are sensational, and no dish is included that I would not be proud to serve in my own home. The ingredients are all natural, and often meats, fruits, vegetables, and grains are healthily combined in one holiday dish.

Since the Sabbath is the basis of holiday cuisine in general, recipes can often be used for several holidays, e.g., the three different hallah recipes. Don't be afraid, for example, to try a prune-and-meat tsimmes for Purim, although it is listed for Sukkot. Moroccan couscous is traditionally served at Rosh Hashanah. Try it for Friday night sometime.

A properly set Seder table (photo: Providence-Journal Bulletin)

Many of the dishes I give are suitable at different times of the year. In modern America—with our ability to grow, transport, and store food almost without regard to season or distance—procuring the ingredients will generally cause no problem. However, if you attempt to accord your holiday menus more closely with those of our ancestors—choosing, for instance, lamb and egg dishes in spring, fresh fruits and milk products in summer, grains and squashes in fall, and fried foods in winter—you may find yourself adding an extra ingredient to your feasts: a heightened awareness of the order of the world and of our place in nature.

All recipes are labeled as (P) = *pareve;* (M) = *milchig* (dairy); or (F) = *fleishig* (meat). Variations on recipes are also indicated where applicable, often telling of the twist of lemon or sprinkle of pepper one cook prefers to another. In some instances the original recipes called for hours of pains-taking cutting and slicing, not to mention simmering and sautéing. Wherever possible, I have shown how modern cooks can cut their cooking time—without affecting the authenticity—by using a wondrous food processor, blender, or mixer.

Since American Jewish brunch fare has become extremely popular for Jews and non-Jews alike, I have included, for Shavuot and the Sabbath, scrumptious recipes worthy of the finest brunch. There are also menu sugges-tions for the two Seders, the Sabbath, and Rosh Hashanah. Recipes on these menus that appear in the book are indicated by the symbol ★. I have tried to confine myself to using recipes most suitable to our holiday cooking in present-day Jewish America.

In sum, in this book I have attempted to answer the many questions Jewish and non-Jewish friends and readers have posed to me and which I have often asked myself: "Why do Jews eat fish on Friday night?" "Why potato latkes?" "Why can't we make our own matzot for Passover?" The recipes and their stories will provide all our families with a wealth of delicious holiday foods.

Better is a dinner of herbs where love is,
Than a stalled ox and hatred therewith.

Better is a dry morsel and quietness therewith,
Than a house full of feasting with strife.

Proverbs 15:17; 17:1

The
SABBATH

THE SABBATH

It is a sign between Me and the children of Israel for ever; for in six days the Lord made heaven and earth, and on the seventh day He ceased from work and rested.

Exodus 31:17

More than Israel has kept the Sabbath, the Sabbath has kept Israel.

Ahad Ha-am

Every European language has a word for the Sabbath, the day of rest. Although no one knows its real origin, the concept of one day of the week different from all the others has been part and parcel of religions since earliest times. Many primitive sabbaths were market days, when normal village routines were suspended while everyone was away selling wares at a central depot. Some groups determined their sabbaths by the phases of the moon. Not every sabbath occurred every seven days; it could come once every four, five, or even ten or fifteen days.

Whatever the origins of such special days, the Jews took a unique approach to the Sabbath. The fourth commandment received on Mount Sinai explains the meaning of the Jewish Sabbath. The Bible says that it commemorates the respite taken by God after His six days' labor of creation. "On the seventh day He stopped and was refreshed." "Refreshed" meant a combination of physical rest and spiritual replenishment. An entire cuisine, therefore, had to be created that could be cooked in advance of the Sabbath. The bustle on the Friday preceding the Sabbath insures quiet and rest for the entire family, including the constantly working mother.

If no fire could be kindled, how could food be cooked? Candles and fires could be lit Friday afternoon and left to continue to burn. Thus, long-cooking foods such as cholent and kugel were invented early on, because they would start cooking under a strong fire and later cook slowly in the ashes as the fire went out.

Since the Sabbath is a special day, festive foods have to be prepared. The feast must include wine, two loaves of bread, salt, and fish or meat. The elevation of one day in the week means three special meals: Friday evening, Saturday midday, and Saturday late afternoon before dusk. On this one day, families are together with no interruption. At leisure, people can savor their rest and their food. For this reason the *seudah shelishit*, the third meal of the Sabbath, is extremely important. If one knows that it is a religious obligation to eat no less than three meals on the Sabbath, he will eat just enough at each meal to satisfy his hunger. And by savoring the Sabbath food, he will enjoy this day into his innermost parts. The third meal is usually a light milk meal. (In Judaism a meal without bread is no meal. Each meal must begin with the blessing over the bread. Thus, the early morning pre-synagogue sustenance which some people have to tide them over until the second meal is not a meal. It usually consists of a cup of coffee and a small piece of cake.)

For the rich it was never a problem to fulfill the talmudic injunction of preparing three meals, but for the poor—and the majority of people have always been poor—this was a difficulty to be surmounted with imagination and inventiveness. Originally designed for the Sabbath, such foods as hallah, gefilte fish, petcha, cholent, and kugel are the basis of most Jewish holiday fare.

Today, most Jews do not celebrate the Sabbath as did our ancestors. The great majority of those who *do* observe only light candles, make *kiddush*, and celebrate the culinary side of Judaism. Most people, however, religious or not, are aware of the special feeling of that one day in the week.

Sabbath eve in [Grandmother's] house began not on Friday, as is customary, but on Thursday afternoon.

Immediately after dinner, Etel Neha, the perennial maid, dragged into the kitchen the two sacks of flour already waiting for her, and emptied them into two large troughs, one to be used for the Sabbath loaf, the hallah, the other for bread for the coming week.

Grandmother then rubbed a handful of the flour between her fingers, sniffed it, tasted it, and reiterated her eternal complaint that the miller was cheating her and that the flour wasn't as fine, sweet, and pure as it once was.

This ritual over, she gauged the amount of flour in the troughs and decided it was excessive for a week's needs. She then took a handful and threw it back in the sack in order to cut down on expenses. From her righteous expression, one might have gathered she had just salvaged a fortune.

Then she took half a handful from the sack and threw it back into the trough, remarking, "Well, in honor of the Sabbath, so be it...."

Etel Neha rolled up her sleeves and began pouring water into the flour. Grandmother helped her with the leavening and recited prayers that the baking prove successful.

All Thursday evening the kitchen smelled of dough and yeast. The oven blazed and Etel Neha performed herculean feats with pokers, lid-lifters, and ladles, Grandmother assisting. The breads, hallahs, rolls, poppyseed cakes, egg cookies, and assorted pastries emerged from the oven in impressive profusion.

At midnight the women retired. At dawn they were already up and about. After praying at the women's synagogue, Grandmother was back in her kitchen preparing the prescribed dish for Friday—stewed meat and hot white bread. The dish never varied on Fridays—it might have been prescribed by law. And had it been so, it was a wise law; as far as I was concerned, this combination contained the essence of paradise.

But Grandmother was reluctant to give me a piece of the wyskrobek—a loaf baked from the last scrapings of dough and one I coveted above every-thing else. It belonged by custom and tradition to Haim the water-bearer, who kept the huge water barrel in the vestibule filled.

I. J. Singer, OF A WORLD THAT IS NO MORE

I. J. Singer and perhaps his younger brother, Isaac Bashevis, were not the only youngsters who craved wyskrobek on Friday afternoon. Chaya Segal, from the Ukraine and now living in Providence, Rhode Island, recalls with relish how she raced home from school on Friday at noon to taste the turnovers or strudel her mother made from the scrapings of leftover hallah dough.

To make the turnovers, a wad of leftover hallah dough would be rolled out, spread with a tablespoon or so of prune or strawberry jam, and then folded over like a turnover before the cookie was placed in a medium oven. If there was more dough left than usual, her mother would make a strudel. She would roll out one strip of dough, spread it with jam, cover it with another strip, and bake it in a medium oven for about 20 minutes.

With the hallah aroma permeating the house, it was no wonder that small children could not wait for the Sabbath dinner to taste the Friday treat! Try your own wyskrobek and continue this tradition in your own home.

MENUS

FRIDAY NIGHT

Seattle Sephardic
Hallah★
Fish with Plum Sauce★
Sakau (Eggplant and Meat
   Casserole)★
Fresh Fruit
Egg Cookies

Old New York Sephardic
Hallah★
Cold Spicy Fish★
Fassoulia
(String Bean and Meat Stew)★

Green Salad
Fruit Cup with Sherbet

Minsk
Hallah★
Gefilte Fish★
Friday Night Brisket★
Kosher Dill Pickles★
Potato Kugel★
Carrots
Hot Fruit Compote★
Mandelbrot★

Henrietta Szold, Baltimore

Hallah★
Chopped Chicken Liver★
Fish with Lemon Sauce★
Rice
Salad
Chocolate Cream

Hungarian

Hallah★
Chicken Noodle Soup
Chicken Paprika★
Rice
Cucumber Salad★
Apple Strudel★

SATURDAY

Desayuno (Sephardic Saturday Morning Meal)

Cheese- or Vegetable-filled
  Burekas or Sambusak★
Huevos Haminadav
  (Hard-boiled Eggs)★
Zucchini Fritada★ or Spinach
  Soufflé★
Cheese
Melons and Grapes
Yoghurt★
Cookies
Turkish Coffee

Moroccan Main Meal

Pain Petri★
Carrot Salad★
Eggplant Salad★

Dafina★
Fresh Fruit
Ghouribi (Sugar Cookies)★

East European Main Meal

Hallah★
Cholent★
Pineapple Noodle Kugel★

Seudah Shelishit

Hallah★
Herring in Sour Cream★
Fresh Fruit

Seudah Shelishit

Hallah★
Petcha★
Compote

HALLAH
(Sweet Egg Bread for the Sabbath)

And the Lord spoke to Moses, saying: Speak unto the children of Israel, and say unto them: When ye come into the land whither I bring you, then it shall be, that, when ye eat of the bread of the land, ye shall set apart a portion for a gift unto the Lord. Of the first of your dough ye shall set apart a cake for a gift; as that which is set apart of the threshing-floor, so shall ye set it apart. Of the first of your dough ye shall give unto the Lord a portion for a gift throughout your generations.

Numbers 15:17–21

And they gathered it [manna] morning by morning, every man according to his eating; and as the sun waxed hot, it melted. And it came to pass that on the sixth day they gathered twice as much bread, two omers for each one; and all the rulers of the congregation came and told Moses. And he said unto them: "This is that which the Lord hath spoken: Tomorrow is a solemn rest, a holy sabbath unto the Lord. Bake that which ye will bake, and seethe that which ye will seethe; and all that remaineth over lay up for you to be kept until the morning."

Exodus 16:21–23

Ada Baum Lipsitz of Boston believes she was "born making hallah." She has been making the sweet twisted loaf once a week for the last seventy-four years. From the age of ten, she started making hallah each Friday morning before going to school. While she was in class, her father would punch down the dough (her mother was an invalid) and store it in a cool place until the young girl returned. With the advent of the freezer, Mrs. Lipsitz makes at least four loaves each Monday and sometimes fights insomnia by making additional loaves throughout the week.

Watching Mrs. Lipsitz make bread is quite an experience. She never measures the ingredients exactly, just takes a pinch of this and a handful of that. Her fingers, usually in pain with arthritis, miraculously spring back to life as she kneads the dough.

Before shaping the dough, Mrs. Lipsitz tears off a piece about the size of an olive, recites a blessing over the bread, and puts it into the oven. This piece of kneaded dough is a symbolic contribution of a loaf given to the priest in the days of the Temple, as commanded in the Bible. Mrs. Lipsitz believes, too, that the act is symbolic of the creation of Adam on Friday; he is like dough which God kneaded and "separated" from the earth. Adam was the "heave offering" defiled by Eve. As expiation, all women are commanded to separate a heave offering from the dough.

After separating the portion, Mrs. Lipsitz braids the bread with deftness and alacrity. She then sprinkles sesame or poppy seeds on top, symbolic of manna (which resembled white coriander seed).

When the hallah comes out of the oven, shiny and sweet-smelling, Mrs. Lipsitz always reserves two loaves for her family's Friday night dinner table and two loaves for each of the other Sabbath meals. At each meal these loaves are covered with a white cloth so they will not feel shamefully ignored because the *kiddush* is not recited over them.

In ancient times the number of loaves of bread served at a meal corresponded to the number of dishes served. And since ancient times Jews have made the whole week's bread on Friday; with no preservatives, at least the Sabbath loaves would be fresh! During the week one communal dish and one loaf were served. On Friday night there were two dishes and two loaves. Later, these two covered loaves came to represent the double portion of dew-covered (thus the cloths above and below) manna given to the Jews on Friday in the desert during their forty-year Exodus from Egypt.

After the lights are kindled and the *kiddush* recited, one of Mrs. Lipsitz' sons gives thanks for letting the family taste of the bread from the earth. He then cuts a portion large enough to last throughout the meal. After breaking off a piece of bread, dipping it in salt, and tasting it, he distributes a morsel to each member of the family, who repeats his act.

Twisted white hallah, rich in eggs and sweetened by sugar or honey and raisins, was originally much different from Mrs. Lipsitz' robust loaves. The original was unleavened or only occasionally leavened. The pita bread of the Arabs today is more similar to the original Friday night loaf. To this day, Jews in the Middle East do not use the definitely Germanic hallah.

10 cups unbleached white flour (maybe more)	½ pound *pareve* margarine, melted
2 tablespoons salt	2½ cups warm water
½ cup raisins (optional)	7 eggs at room temperature
½ cup sugar	Sesame seeds
2 heaping tablespoons yeast	

1. Preheat oven to warm (140°).

2. Mix the flour, salt, and raisins in a large bowl, making a well in the center.

3. Add ¼ cup sugar to the well, cover with the yeast, and top with the remaining ¼ cup sugar.

4. Mix the yeast with the sugar in the well.

5. Melt the margarine and add warm water slowly, mixing well.

6. Add the margarine mixture to the yeast mixture and work in well with your hands.

7. Set aside 1 egg plus the yolk of another. The Orthodox way is to break each egg individually into a cup, lest blood be found, in which case the egg is *tref* (not kosher).

8. Add the remaining 5 eggs (plus the white of the separated egg) individually to the bread dough, kneading well after each addition, until all the flour is absorbed (about 10 minutes). As you knead, you may have to add more flour, so have some handy. You can divide the dough into about 4 parts and knead it in a food processor, using the steel blade.

9. Cover the bowl first with waxed paper smeared with margarine, then with a towel, and put in a warm oven for ½ hour.

10. When the dough has almost doubled in size, punch it down and knead thoroughly and briskly for about 10 minutes.

11. Cover with the greased paper and towel and let rise for 15–20 minutes more in the warm oven, until it is almost doubled again.

12. Remove once more, punch down, knead again for 5–10 minutes. Re-cover and let rise once more for 15–20 minutes in the warm oven.

13. Turn the dough onto a pastry board and knead thoroughly. Using a knife, cut the dough into 4 pieces. Then divide each piece into 6. Add a little flour, and knead each portion, and shape it into a ball. Cover the pieces not being worked on with a moist paper towel.

14. With the palm of your hand, roll out the balls into long ropes about 9″ in length. Continue until all 6 balls are shaped into ropes.

15. Place all the ropes side by side, touching at one end. Pinch that end to seal well. Bring the extreme right rope over the next three; then bring the extreme left over three. Continue until the bread is completely braided. When no more can be braided, pinch the ends to seal together. Shape to the size of the pan. Braid the remaining 3 loaves.

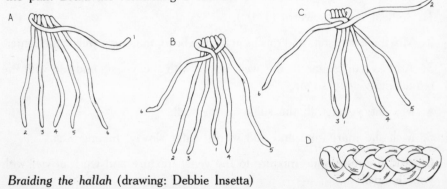

Braiding the hallah (drawing: Debbie Insetta)

16. Brush with the egg yolk mixture that was set aside, making sure you get into all the cracks. Sprinkle with the sesame seeds.

17. Place the bread in greased and floured 4½" x 10" pans or other rectangular bread pans.

18. Place in warm oven for 20 minutes.

19. Raise the oven temperature to 200° for 15 minutes.

20. Raise it to 275° for 15 minutes.

21. Finally, raise the oven temperature to 375° for 10–15 minutes, until the bread is golden brown. The baked hallah freezes well.

Makes 4 loaves. (P)

For a holiday round-shaped hallah recipe, see p. 65

BERCHES
(My Great Grandmother's Potato Hallah)

Birkat Adonai hi ta-ashir. *(The blessing of the Lord, it maketh rich.)*
Proverbs 10:22

Berches is the Judaeo-German oblong loaf of twisted bread eaten on the Sabbath. Unlike the traditional sweet hallah we know in this country, berches is often a bread with a slightly sourdough taste and a crunchy crust. My father ate this as a child in Augsburg, Germany, and so did Jews I have interviewed who lived as far away as Budapest. This particular recipe is that of my great grandmother, Rose Bernheim, of Augsburg.

A popular explanation of the name "berches" is that it is a corruption of the Hebrew word *"birkat"* (blessing) from the above verse in Proverbs. Both *birkat* and *ta-ashir* are words derived for the twisted form of bread. *Taatscher* is a corrupt form of *tartcher* and a diminutive of *tart* or *torta* ("twisted" in Italian). The above verse is still engraved on knives used on the Sabbath to cut the hallah.

Berches, like Berges in Northern Germany among non-Jews, was the bread offered to Berchta, or Perchta, the Teutonic goddess of fertility. In ancient times women would offer their hair to her. When this practice became obsolete, it was replaced by a symbolic offering of the hair in the form of a loaf of intertwined braids. It is a moot point as to whether or not berches was indeed a Jewish version of this practice. (Other scholars say the twisted loaf rather represents interlocked arms.)

Another reason for braiding the hallah is to get the hump effect to

21

represent the twelve loaves of show bread *(lehem hapanim)* that were in the Temple. There are those who are careful in braiding the dough so that at least six humps will show in each loaf. The two loaves represent the separate commandments regarding the Sabbath: *zakhor*, remember, and *shamor*, watch.

Note: If you need this hallah for Friday evening, start the dough about eight o'clock Thursday night to let it rise overnight. Finish the next morning.

1	pound bread or unbleached all-purpose flour (4 cups)	4	medium, cooked, mashed potatoes (about 1½ cups), still lukewarm
1	yeast cake or 1 package dry yeast		2½ teaspoons salt
½	cup lukewarm water		Poppy seeds

1. Place the flour in a large bowl, making a well in the middle. Stir in the yeast and ½ cup water. Add to the well a small amount of the flour, about 3 tablespoons. Cover and let the "starter" stand in a lukewarm place until doubled in size (about 30 minutes).

2. Add the potatoes, salt, and more lukewarm water if needed. Knead the dough about 10–12 minutes or until it separates from the bowl and is as hard as possible. Alternatively, divide in thirds and whirl in a food processor, using the steel blade. Put the dough in a greased bowl, and cover with a cloth. Place in a medium-warm, draft-free spot, and let stand until the dough has doubled (about 8 hours).

3. Next morning, place the dough on a floured wooden board and split into 2 parts. Make a long loaf of one part and divide the other into 3 pieces. Roll the 3 pieces into long ropes as thick as a thumb and braid them. Place the braid on top of the long loaf, pinching down to attach. Cover the hallah and let rise once more for about 1 hour.

4. Preheat oven to 350°.

5. When ready to bake, baste the top with water and sprinkle with poppy seeds.

6. Bake 45 minutes to 1 hour or until the hallah is nicely browned and sounds hollow when tapped with the knuckles.

Makes 1 large loaf. (P)

COLD SPICY FISH
(Pescado Helado)

We remember the fish, which we were wont to eat in Egypt for nought.
Numbers 11:5

*There dwelt men of Tyre also therein, who brought in fish, and all manner of
ware, and sold on the sabbath unto the children of Judah, and in Jerusalem.*
Nehemiah 13:16

Fish has always been a mainstay of the Jewish diet. Jewish history tells us
how, during their long journey in the Sinai to the promised land, the Israelites
longed for the fish first tasted in Egypt. Later, at the time of Nehemiah, so
much sea fish was sold in Jerusalem that the gate nearby was called "The
Fish Gate."

From earliest times fresh seafood markets surrounded the Sea of Galilee.
During the Roman period, fresh fish for the Sabbath was in such demand that
the Romans imposed a high tax for the right to fish in the lake.

Eating fish symbolizes the hope of redemption for Israel and reminds us
of the mercies of God. In Genesis, God blesses man and fish several times,
creating a mystical triad. He urges them to "be fruitful and multiply." From
this, fish came to symbolize fertility and immortality. The defeat of the
Leviathan, the great monstrous fish mentioned in Job, is used as the symbol
of glory to come in the Messianic Age, when good will triumph over evil. At
that time the Leviathan will be caught and the flesh given to the faithful.

In folk traditions, a woman who ate a fish found inside a larger fish
would become pregnant. A virgin should be married on the fourth day of the
week and have intercourse on the fifth day, when the blessing of the fish is
pronounced. For Moroccans, the seventh day of the wedding feast is "fish
day," when the groom sends the bride a plate of fish—which her mother
throws at the groom's feet. After he takes a bite of the fish, the bride steps
over a fishnet and symbolically becomes pregnant. In Sarajevo, Yugoslavia,
after the wedding-ring ceremonies, relatives arrive carrying fish, the heads
decorated with flowers and the bellies garnished with tinsel. The bride then
hops over each fish in the hope that she soon will become pregnant. To this
day, North African Jewish women wear fish amulets around their neck.

Although the Talmud does not command the eating of fish on Friday
night, it is nevertheless strongly suggested. From talmudic times, Orthodox
Jews have been eating fish, meat, and wine on Friday night and at each of
the other two meals of the Sabbath. The Talmud describes the joy of eating
fish on the Sabbath. "Wherewith does one show his delight therein? . . . With
a dish of beet, a large fish, and cloves of garlic."

The talmudic combination of fish, garlic, and beets is today most often found in eating gefilte fish—but not always. Jews throughout the world eat variations of fish recipes on Friday night.

The same delights of a spicy fish can be found elsewhere, however. A recipe which is a possible carryover from as far back as the Middle Ages is for the following cold spicy fish. Handed down in the Sephardic family of Emily Nathan, it may have originally been used in Spain as an appetizer on Friday night or to start holiday meals. The dish may very well have been served the first Friday night that Emily's forebear, Abraham De Lucena, spent in New Amsterdam, when twenty-three Sephardic Jews established a settlement in 1654. There have been subtle changes in the recipe throughout the years to adjust to special tastes. The tomato juice and cayenne pepper were probably later additions, picked up when Emily's ancestors were in Brazil prior to their arrival on this continent.

Note: Have the fishman cut a whole fish through the backbone into steaks about 3″ wide. The backbone must be left in the fish. Ask for several fish heads with the eyes left in. This is essential for natural jell.

1 4½-pound striped bass, rockfish, pickerel, yellow pike, or any firm fish	6 cups (or more) tomato juice
	1 bay leaf
	1 medium onion, sliced
Coarse salt	2 tablespoons lemon juice, or to taste
1 teaspoon cayenne pepper, or to taste*	

1. Rub the fish steaks with coarse salt and about ½ teaspoon cayenne and let stand.

2. Bring to a boil enough tomato juice to cover the fish skeleton and heads. You can put the heads in a cheesecloth, if you like, to extract after the fish is done. Some people, however, like to eat them.

3. Season with bay leaf, onion, lemon juice, and the remaining ½ teaspoon cayenne. There should be enough cayenne to make it sharp and hot.

4. Simmer, covered, for 15 minutes.

5. Then add the steaks to the liquid, bring to a boil again, and simmer, covered, until fish is done (about 12–15 minutes, or until it flakes easily with a fork).

6. Remove fish steaks and heads (if desired), place in a bowl, and pour the liquid over. Add onions if you like. Let cool and refrigerate overnight.

Serves 6–8 as an appetizer. (P)

*Cayenne pepper can be omitted and about ½ cup fresh parsley added, as served in Turkey.

FISH WITH PLUM SAUCE
(Pescado con Abramela)

Seattle's Pike Street Market is famous for its fresh salmon. One of the most popular shops is the City Fish Market, owned by the Levy brothers, Sephardic Jews from the island of Marmora.

Today, there are over three thousand Sephardim in Seattle, with two synagogues. The older Bikur Holim congregation is from Marmora and Fikirdayi, the newer, from the island of Rhodes.

On a recent trip to Seattle, I visited the Bikur Holim synagogue and stopped to talk with Lisa Benaroya, the wife of the rabbi. She is one of the prime movers behind their *Sephardic Cooking*, one of four Sephardic synagogue cookbooks in this country. (The others are in Los Angeles, Atlanta, and Deal, New Jersey.) While talking about the special recipes from her native Marmora, she fed me biscochos (egg cookies), which she deftly molds each week for her grandchildren.

Although I am quite familiar with Sephardic cooking, the unusual combination of ingredients described in Mrs. Benaroya's recipes intrigued me, especially the Friday night fish dishes. We have all heard of the typically Greek fish with lemon sauce. But what about fish poached in rhubarb and tomatoes, greengage plums, or sour (unripe) grapes? These are favorite recipes of this picturesque Seattle community.

Eager to try these tantalizing dishes, I hurried down to the City Fish Market and spoke to Jack Levy. "Try the white salmon," he insisted. "It is less expensive and tastier than the red." Living in the East, fresh salmon—red or white—is so prohibitively expensive that either fish seemed a steal. Try making the following fish with plum sauce with salmon, snapper, sole, or rockfish for your Friday night meal.

6-7 greengage plums, peeled and diced	1 teaspoon sugar
	Salt and pepper to taste
4 tomatoes, peeled and diced	2 pounds salmon steaks, red
1 tablespoon fresh parsley	snapper, or sole fillets (salted
Juice of 1 lemon	and drained)

1. Combine the plums and tomatoes in a saucepan. Simmer, covered, until soft (about 20 minutes). Do not overcook.

2. Remove from heat and add parsley, lemon juice, sugar, salt, and pepper to taste.

3. Preheat oven to 400°.

4. Let mixture sit until lukewarm and then add the fish.

5. Bake in oven, uncovered, 15–20 minutes. Serve cold as an appetizer or as a main course with rice.

Serves 4–6 as a main course and 6–8 as an appetizer. (P)

To make the fish in rhubarb sauce, simmer 2 cups sliced rhubarb, ½ cup tomato sauce, 3 tablespoons oil, 1 teaspoon sugar, salt to taste, and ½ cup water, covered, for about 30 minutes, or until the rhubarb is tender. Then add the fish and proceed with Steps 3–5 above.

GEFILTE FISH

On an enormous silver platter a great fish reposed in a bed of parsley; it was complete and perfect from head to tail, with eyes of carrots and capers, and gleaming scales of gelatin.

"Why, it's the most wonderful thing I ever tasted!" a lady once said, and Mother beamed. "It's not a bit like gefüllte fish," the lady continued. Mother stiffened; that was not the comment she wanted at all: her fish was the apotheosis of gefüllte fish.

Someone asked Mother how it was made; she began a rather vague explanation about chopped carp and whitefish and egg, but Father took over.

"Made?" he said. "You might as well ask how a salmon is made. Every Friday morning the gefüllte fish swarm down the Hudson in schools of thousands and tens of thousands. The orthodox Jews stand on one bank with nets, and the reform Jews on the other bank with poles—they don't think nets are sporting. Of course the orthodox side catches twice as many as——."

"Dan," Mother said, and she motioned to the maid to pass the cucumbers. These were always served with the fish; they were cut in long, thin, spaghetti-like strips and soaked in a wonderfully pungent thin white sauce.

Felicia Lamport, MINK ON WEEKDAYS, ERMINE ON SUNDAY

Surely no holiday food is more Jewish than gefilte fish. Yet it was not eaten until the late Middle Ages.

When the Jews migrated to East Europe, fresh fish was hard to come by. And, they wanted just a little bit for their Friday evening meal—to enjoy the delights of the Sabbath. Since nearly all the Jews were extremely poor, they learned to invent dishes for people of limited means. During the week their diet consisted of potatoes, salted herring, onions, and dark bread. Fresh fish was reserved for the Sabbath. Living near the North Sea, they could use pike, carp, buffel, or other inexpensive freshwater fish. But these fish spoil quickly.

A fish stretcher—gefilte fish—was therefore concocted so that all the members of the family could have at least a small taste for the Friday meal. The women learned to scrape the flesh away from the skin and bones, to add chopped onions, seasoning, and bread or matzah crumbs. Egg was added and the fish poached in much the same way kneydlakh is. The fish broth could be used again for a *milchig* dish of fish chowder during the week.

There may be an additional reason for eating gefilte fish. On Friday nights Jews are not supposed to *"borer,"* to pick meat from the bones of meat or fish while eating. Gefilte fish eliminated this messy process.

To locate the earliest-written gefilte fish recipe, I pored through over five hundred books on fish in a collection donated to Harvard University in 1915. I found not one recipe from anywhere in the world remotely resembling gefilte fish.

Elsewhere, in Mrs. Hertz's German cookbook of 1867, I saw a resemblance to gefilte fish. And in the first American Jewish cookbook, the *Jewish Cookery Book*, published by Esther Levy in 1871, there is a fishcake.

Leon Hirschbaum, a Jewish-cookbook buff in Brooklyn, sent me the earliest recipe for gefilte fish in English. It is for stewed codfish balls. (Codfish was substituted for the freshwater fish of East Europe and the recipe was probably brought by an immigrant to England.) The 1874 book is entitled *The Easy and Economical Book of Jewish Cookery*, written by Mrs. J. Atputel, cook to the Baroness Lionel de Rothschild.

Stewed Fish Balls with Egg Sauce

Take 2 pounds of cod and free it from all the bones; chop it and season it with pepper, salt, grated nutmeg, and a little of the rind of a lemon chopped fine, parsley and marjoram, a little soaked bread, with the water drained from it. Mix well together with an egg, make them into nice-sized balls the size of an apple. Slice in the stew-pan a large onion, 3 tablespoonfuls of salad oil, let it fry, add a teacupful of boiling water, let it boil up, put in the balls. When done beat in a basic 3 eggs, strain the juice of 2 large lemons, with a little dried saffron and a little chopped parsley. Stir and mix it all well together, dish them up by first taking out the balls, then strain the sauce over them. Garnish with parsley; 3 or 4 tomatoes added to the balls is a great improvement and makes it a pretty dish.

ZAMOSC GEFILTE FISH

Carp in Poland had a fine clean taste, never "muddy." It was poached, sautéed au bleu, or baked—the latter version sometimes stuffed with a farci made of the carp's milt and liver, mushrooms, truffles, parsley, seasonings, eggs and bread crumbs. The stuffed fish would be sewn up with cotton thread, wrapped in a sheet of buttered white paper and baked in a moderately hot oven. Karp po Zydowsku, "in the Jewish style," was popular all over Poland. Diced carrots, chopped onions, chopped celery, diced celery root, and chopped parsley root would be simmered in salt water and butter, and season-ings (bay leaves, cloves, peppercorns, salt) would be added. Before the vegetables were done, the thick slices of carp were put on top and left steam-ing for another half-hour. The carp was served hot, or cold with an aspic made of the strained sauce some housewives would put into additional fish heads.
Joseph Wechsberg, GOURMET Magazine (February 1975)

Joseph Wechsberg's mouthwatering description of gefilte fish is unfortunately a dish of the past. Today, most people buy bottled brands. Good cooks, however, insist on preparing the homemade variety for Friday night and the holidays. My mother-in-law, Peshka, is a case in point. She uses her mother's recipe, handed down orally, from Zamosc, Poland. Her only concession to modernity is making individual patties rather than stuffing the filling back into the skin as described by Wechsberg. In addition, her filling is less elaborate.

When I asked Peshka for her recipe, two of her sisters-in-law were present. Inevitably, a dispute arose. They all agreed that the rule of thumb is one pound of fat fish to one pound of thin. They also preferred the Polish custom of adding a little sugar. (Lithuanians say sugar is added to freshen already unfresh fish. Needless to say, Lithuanians do not add sugar to their gefilte fish.) Peshka, Chuma, and Rushka disagreed, however, on season-ings. Chuma insisted on more salt than is called for in Peshka's recipe, and Rushka explained that a little almond extract would do the trick. They both took me aside and promised to show me the "real" way to make gefilte fish. I have used their two suggestions as variations on Peshka's basic recipe. Make your fish Lithuanian or Polish, with sugar or without, but just remember— it's the carrots and horseradish that really count!

Stock:

4	stalks celery, cut in 4″ slices		Bones of fish (and heads, if desired)
2	onions, quartered		
6	carrots, sliced on the bias	1	tablespoon salt
8	cups water, or enough to cover bones with 1″ to spare (use less rather than more)	½	tablespoon freshly ground pepper
		1	tablespoon sugar

Fish:

3	pounds carp	1	teaspoon sugar
1½	pounds whitefish, pickerel, or rockfish	½–1	cup matzah meal
		¾	cup water
1½	pounds yellow pike or buffel	1	teaspoon almond extract (optional)
4	onions		
2	tablespoons salt, or to taste	1¼	teaspoons pepper
4	eggs		

Note: The ratio of fish can be adjusted according to taste and availability. The less carp and the more whitefish, the more delicate the flavor and the lighter the dish. Each fish market will have its own suggestions for the most flavorful and economical mix. Today most markets will grind the fish for you and give you the heads, bones, and skins in a separate package.

1. Place all the stock ingredients in a large kettle with a cover. Bring to a boil, then partially cover and reduce heat to simmer. While waiting for the pot to boil, begin preparing the fish.

2. In a wooden bowl, add to the ground-up fish all the other ingredients listed under *Fish*, carefully chopping and blending. Wet your hands and form the fish into fat, oval-shaped patties, carefully sliding each into the simmering stock.

3. Cook slowly for 2 hours. Allow to cool slightly in the pot and carefully remove all the patties, placing them on a platter. After the fish has been removed, strain off the vegetables and loose pieces of fish. This stock should then jell when chilled; however, if it does not, simply add a package of unflavored gelatin.

4. Serve the chilled gefilte fish with the jellied fish stock, horseradish, and of course the carrot.

Makes 24 large patties. (P)

HENRIETTA SZOLD'S STEWED FISH WITH LEMON SAUCE

Henrietta Szold, founder of Hadassah, was known for her scholarship, translations, leadership ability, and a number of other laudable activities. Expertise in cooking was not one of them. Yet she knew how to cook, and in her exacting way typed out many of the favorite family recipes, which one of her nieces kindly shared with me.

One recipe was for strudel calling for a "supperplateful of sugar and cinnamon" and a quart of flour. Her "liver for entreé" is known to us as chopped liver. A most interesting recipe was for ganef, a barley- and farina-filled stuffing for the back of a goose.

An especially tasty dish is a stewed fish with lemon sauce which was usually served as a main course on Friday nights. This particular recipe is not typically German (their Friday night fish was usually sweet-and-sour). I was surprised to find it cited as well by a number of other German Jewish women from old Baltimore families. Confused by this coincidence, I searched for an answer.

An old friend of the Szold family told me that Baltimore's German Jewish community was extremely close-knit. Although few of the women actually cooked themselves, they all guided their Irish maids in the kitchen. *The Settlement Cook Book*, first published in 1901, was then the rage in the German Jewish circles. One hostess must have served this boiled fish with lemon sauce on a Tuesday or Friday (fish market days) and then passed the recipe on to her friends. To this day, many German Jewish families of Baltimore, including the remaining Szolds, serve stewed fish with lemon sauce on Friday night, the second night of Passover, and special occasions.

1 4-pound rockfish, striped bass, sea trout, salmon, or halibut, cleaned, cut in steaks, with the head and tail still attached	1 teaspoon white peppercorns
	1 teaspoon ground ginger
	Salt and pepper to taste
	2 tablespoons butter or *pareve* margarine
Salt	
2 quarts water (about)	2 tablespoons flour
1 medium onion, sliced	2 cups fish bouillon
2 carrots, sliced	2 egg yolks
2 stalks celery with leaves, sliced	Juice of 1 lemon
6 large sprigs parsley	

1. Clean the fish and let stand in salt several hours. (Some Jewish cooks feel that stewed fish has a better taste if it is salted when it is cleaned and allowed to stand awhile. Then, before stewing, the salt is rinsed off.)*

2. Place the fish in a flat wide dish or fish poacher and cover with water. Remove the fish and add the onion, carrots, celery, parsley, peppercorns, ginger, salt, and pepper. Bring to a boil to make a court bouillon of all the ingredients but the fish. After the court bouillon has simmered until flavorful (about 15–20 minutes), pour enough of it over the fish to come halfway up the fish. Bring the bouillon to the boil, reduce the heat, and simmer the fish 10 minutes for each inch of thickness. Let simmer until the fish is soft or white (about 20 minutes). A large fish might take longer.

3. Remove the fish. Skin and bone it and set aside.

4. Make a velouté sauce by melting the butter or margarine, adding the flour, cooking 2 minutes, and then pouring in the fish bouillon. Stir thoroughly until smooth. Add some of the hot sauce to the well-beaten egg yolks, and pour the mixture back into the sauce; beat carefully. Add the lemon juice to make the sauce creamy. Don't let the sauce boil again or the eggs will curdle.

5. Pour the sauce over the fish and garnish with lemon slices and chopped parsley.

Serves 4–6. (M or P)

Note: The court bouillon can include lemon, more or less celery, onions, or carrots. Some recipes call for sugar and vinegar as well. Interestingly enough, this dish is almost identical to a Sephardic fish with lemon sauce, also served on Friday nights.

---

*It is really not necessary to salt fish in this way. Very religious Jews might feel, however, that fish should be treated as meat and salted. Also, there is a Jewish superstition about salting food to keep away the evil eye.

CHICKEN SOUP WITH MATZAH BALLS

Chicken soup, prepared and eaten on Shabbat and holidays, was made by cooking all of the chicken parts and innards, excluding the head and lungs, in a pot of water, with onions, carrots, and salt. The feet of the chicken were added to the soup to give it a rich flavor. When cooked in water, the skin of the feet came off, settled on the bottom of the pot, and gave the soup a nice color and rich flavor. If an extra piece of meat or chicken were available, it would be added to the soup. Often the skin from the neck of the bird was filled with fat, flour, raw chopped potatoes, cooked potatoes, or cooked grains. Each end was sewn together and the neck was cooked in the soup. The heart was also added to the soup. In the summer, various fresh vegetables, such as parsley root or parsley leaf, might be added. Some women added millet or other grains, or even something special, such as farfl, lokshn, or cooked rice. If extra ingredients were added to the basic soup, they would be added from the onset of the cooking.

Amy Snyder, Columbia University Master's thesis
on the cooking of a Jewish lady from Lagev, Poland

Soup:
2 beef bones	2 large stalks celery, sliced
2 quarts water	Salt and pepper to taste
1 back and bones of chicken	2 sprigs parsley
1 quarter chicken	
2 tablespoons instant chicken- soup mix	**Matzah Balls (Kneydlakh):**
2 carrots	3 large eggs
2 medium onions, quartered	¾ cup matzah meal
	Salt and pepper to taste

1. Simmer beef bones in water, covered, for 1 hour.

2. After 1 hour, add the chicken bones, the quarter chicken, and the instant chicken-soup mix.

3. After 10 minutes more, skim, and add carrots, onions, celery, salt and pepper, and parsley. Cover and simmer slowly for 50 minutes.

4. Before beginning the matzah balls, have a bowl of cold water handy to wash your hands.

5. Breaking the eggs individually into a glass bowl, beat them until they are frothy.

6. Add a little less than ¾ cup matzah meal and salt and pepper to taste, and mix thoroughly. Let stand for 15 minutes.

7. Wet hands. Take 1 heaping teaspoon of the matzah-meal mixture and roll in your hands to make each ball.

8. Bring the soup to a rapid boil and remove the cover.

9. Drop the matzah balls into the soup and continue cooking, covered, over medium heat about 20 minutes.

Makes 12. Soup serves 6. (F)

CALVES' LIVER SOUP

This soup, handed down on the German side of my family, was served on Friday nights. It is a good example of how the German Jews changed a rich cream of liver soup to adhere to the dietary customs. The non-Jewish equivalent includes cream and butter. My grandmother used palmin, a coconut oil employed before margarine was invented.

½ pound calves' liver	2 tablespoons flour
3 tablespoons *pareve* margarine	1½ quarts beef or chicken broth
Salt and pepper to taste	2 egg yolks, beaten
½ teaspoon dried tarragon (optional)	1 teaspoon cognac (optional)
1 small onion, diced	Croutons made from 3 slices toasted bread
1 tablespoon chopped fresh parsley	

1. Lightly broil and slice the liver. Then sauté it in 1 tablespoon of margarine for 10 minutes. Add salt, pepper, and tarragon to taste. Remove from pan.

2. In a heavy saucepan, sauté the onion in the 2 remaining tablespoons of margarine. When the onion is golden, add the parsley and the liver. Cover and simmer over low heat 5 minutes.

3. Add the flour, mix thoroughly, and slowly add the beef or chicken broth. Let simmer, covered, a few minutes.

4. Before serving, strain the soup through a cheesecloth and whip in the mixed egg yolks and cognac.

5. Serve with toasted croutons.

Serves 4–6. (F)

VEGETARIAN CHOPPED LIVER

The dairy restaurant is an American Jewish phenomenon, perhaps a precursor of many of today's health-food restaurants. New York abounds in dairy restaurants. Perhaps the most famous is Ratner's, now located only on Delancey Street. It boasts an endless array of pickles, bagels, onion rolls, bialys (flat onion rolls from Bialystock), herring, borscht, chopped hard-boiled eggs with fried mushrooms and onions, and much more. Salads include mock chopped liver made from cooked millet, green beans, or eggplant. Eggplant is also an economical replacement for meat as in eggplant schnitzel, for caviar in eggplant caviar, and for chopped liver in this Friday night vegetarian dish.

1 medium eggplant	2 hard-boiled eggs
¼ pound *pareve* margarine	Salt and pepper to taste
1 medium onion, minced	

1. Slice eggplant in ¼″ circles. Sauté it in margarine until golden on both sides.

2. Sauté half of the minced onion.

3. Grind the eggplant, fried and raw onions, and eggs in a food grinder or processor.

4. Add salt and pepper to taste. Refrigerate. Remove from refrigerator ½ hour before serving.

Makes 2 cups. (P)

EGGPLANT

There is a saying in the Middle East that, until a woman knows how to prepare 101 eggplant dishes, she is not ready to marry. At the beginning of the Middle Ages, Arab, and possibly Jewish, merchants brought the eggplant with them from the East. Since that time it has been the most versatile vegetable in the eastern Mediterranean. It has been known for centuries as far north as Russia and Bulgaria.

It is probably fair to say that Jerusalem has become the eggplant capital of the world, with each immigrant bringing his favorite recipe. There are pickled eggplants and eggplant salads spiced with tomatoes, green peppers, and onions. There is baba ghanouj with tahina (sesame-seed paste) and moussaka with ground meat. Soups are filled with eggplants, and so are cakes. There is even a restaurant in Tel Aviv that boasts over seventy different eggplant recipes on its menu. Try these two Israeli eggplant salads, which must be made a day or two in advance to heighten the taste.

ISRAELI EGGPLANT SALAD

Note: The first two steps of this and the following eggplant and tomato salad are identical and therefore it is a good idea to make both at the same time. They go well together as hors d'oeuvres with bread or crackers.

Vegetable oil for frying	3 tablespoons mayonnaise, or
1 medium eggplant, unpeeled	to taste
Salt to taste	Juice of 1½ lemons
½ large onion, sliced in thin rings	Pepper to taste
1 clove garlic, minced	

1. Pour about 2″ of oil in a heavy frying pan and heat to 375°.

2. Divide the eggplant in half and cube the flesh into ½″ squares. Sprinkle with salt and deep-fry half the eggplant at a time. When it is golden, remove to a glass or ceramic bowl. Add the onion rings.

3. Blend in the garlic, mayonnaise, lemon juice, and salt and pepper to taste. Adjust seasoning. Let sit overnight and serve with hot bread.

Makes 3 cups. (P)

EGGPLANT AND TOMATO SALAD

Vegetable oil for frying	3 tablespoons water
1 medium eggplant, unpeeled	2 tablespoons catsup
Salt to taste	1 clove garlic, minced
½ large onion, sliced in thin rings	Pepper to taste
3 tablespoons tomato paste	

1. Pour about 2″ of oil in a heavy frying pan and heat to 375°.

2. Divide the eggplant in half and cube the flesh into ½″ squares. Sprinkle with salt and deep-fry half the eggplant at a time. When it is golden, remove to a glass or ceramic bowl. Add the onion rings.

3. Add the tomato paste, water, catsup, garlic, salt, and pepper to taste. Let sit overnight before serving.

Makes 3 cups. (P)

GREEN PEPPER AND TOMATO SALAD

Crisp fresh salads are of late culinary vintage. With little or no refrigeration and often impure water available until the twentieth century, ordinary people did not risk eating fresh vegetables that couldn't be peeled or shelled. Cucumber, beet, or cabbage salads were about the only ones used in East Europe, with cooked salads featuring eggplant or broiled peppers in many Mediterranean countries. Lettuce, the base of most salads we eat today, had to be cleaned in sterilized water and eaten immediately. Tomatoes were considered inedible in the raw state and were only used in purées.

Taboos surrounded many of these foods, especially the tomato. Until about 1900, many people believed the red fruit to be poisonous like its relative, the deadly nightshade.

It seems that Jews were especially superstitious about the tomato. One Jewish lady from Poland relates how she feared buying this new blood-red fruit. Grown by Gentiles in fields surrounding her *shtetl*, tomatoes seemed to grow on crosses. In time, however, these fears were dispelled.

Today, tomatoes are an indispensable part of everyday cuisine. The following is a Hungarian salad.

2	green peppers	¼	cup white vinegar
2–3	tomatoes	2	teaspoons sugar
1	red onion	½	cup olive or vegetable oil
Salt to taste			

1. Remove ribs and seeds from the green peppers and cut lengthwise into slices.

2. Slice and remove seeds from the tomatoes.

3. Slice thin the red onion.

4. Combine the salt, vinegar, and sugar, and slowly add the olive oil. Pour over the green peppers, tomatoes, and onion, arranged tastefully in a glass bowl.

Serves 6. (P)

HUNGARIAN CUCUMBER SALAD
(Uborkasalata)

2 medium or large cucumbers
1 teaspoon salt
Pinch of sugar
¼ cup white vinegar

Dash of garlic powder
½ cup water
Sweet paprika
Black pepper

1. Peel the cucumbers and slice them paper-thin. Sprinkle with salt and let stand, for 30–60 minutes, with a plate and a 5-pound weight on top. Squeeze out water.

2. Combine the sugar, vinegar, garlic powder, and water. Add the cucumbers and marinate for a few hours. Serve sprinkled with paprika on half the salad and black pepper on the other half.

Serves 4–6. (P)

Note: Instead of garlic powder, a thinly sliced onion may be used.

GERMAN-STYLE CUCUMBER SALAD

2 cucumbers
1 teaspoon salt
2 tablespoons mayonnaise
1 teaspoon mustard

¼ teaspoon garlic powder
Salt to taste
1 tablespoon fresh dill (optional)

1. Peel the cucumbers and slice them paper-thin. Sprinkle with salt and place in a colander for ½ hour. Wash off the salt with cold water and press to extract the remaining liquid.

2. Mix the mayonnaise and mustard and add to the cucumbers. Sprinkle with garlic powder, salt to taste, and fresh dill. Mix well. Chill.

Serves 4–6. (P)

CHOPPED CHICKEN LIVER

For the king of Babylon standeth at the parting of the way, at the head of the two ways, to use divination; he shaketh the arrows to and fro, he inquireth of the teraphim, he looketh in the liver.

Ezekiel 21:26

Before Nebuchadnezzar approached the Land of Israel, he stood at the parting of the ways and, using means of divination, determined which way he should go—to Jerusalem or to the capital of the Ammonites. Archaeologists have found models of livers at Megiddo and Hazor dating back as far as 1400 B.C.E.

One might assume that the ancients thought the liver to have a life of its own, that it was the soul of man. The reason might be in its shape or in the fact that it contains so much blood, which is life itself. In prayer Jews often say, *"Nefesh habasar bedam hu,"* "The life of the flesh [Hebrew soul] is in the blood."

With blood considered the seat of life, it is easy to understand how it became an object of sacred awe. Because of the liver's excess blood, salting does not suffice in koshering; fire is also needed.

Whatever the ancient origins, chopped chicken liver has become a Jewish specialty, and every mother has her own version. Here is my mother's, coarsely chopped in a wooden bowl with a hand chopper. Some people prefer a smoother pâtélike consistency. Grated egg yolk may be served on top, delicatessen-style. Onion and pepper may be omitted. Although not traditional, tarragon is a pleasant herb to add to this dish.

½ pound chicken livers	2 hard-boiled eggs
½ cup chopped onion	1 teaspoon Worcestershire sauce
½ cup chopped celery	Salt and freshly ground pepper to
2 tablespoons chicken fat or	taste
pareve margarine	

1. Broil the livers* lightly and quickly, and then sauté them with the onion and celery in chicken fat or margarine until the onions are golden (about 5 minutes).

*According to *kashrut,* liver must be cut open across its length and width and placed with the rent part downward over the fire, so that the fire will draw out all of the blood. Before broiling, it is washed and lightly salted. It must be broiled until it is edible and then washed 3 times so that the blood is rinsed off. It must be broiled with a forked utensil or over a grate so that the blood is consumed by the fire or drained off. After it is koshered, it can be sautéed.

2. Place in a wooden chopping bowl and chop with the eggs until smooth. Or you can place in a food processor, using a plastic blade, and spin for a few seconds until the mixture is well blended and fairly smooth. Do not overblend.

3. Add Worcestershire sauce and salt and pepper to taste. If the mixture seems dry, add additional chicken fat or margarine.

Makes about 2 cups. (F)

FRIDAY NIGHT BRISKET

You could smell the roast all over the house, it had so much garlic in it. A roast like that, with fresh warm twist, is a delicacy from heaven. And when you consider that we had some fresh dill pickles, and a bottle of beer, and some cognac before the meal and cherry cider after the meal—you can imagine the state our guest was in.

Sholom Aleichem, "Tit for Tat"

In the ancient world, garlic was known as an aphrodisiac and the phrase "to eat garlic" was therefore a euphemism for sexual intercourse. Since a husband is supposed to fulfill his marital obligation to his wife—at least on Friday night—rabbis have suggested that more garlic and less salt be used in dishes at the Sabbath meal. Thus, Jews became known as "garlic eaters."

Foods can be divided into two categories—those that "chill" the body and therefore have a quieting effect on procreative powers, and those that "heat" the body and awaken sexual desires. Salt is in the first category; garlic and onion in the second.

Early in history, Jews became addicted to garlic. In the desert they mourned the garlic, onions, leeks, and melons they had eaten in Egypt. Manna in the desert contained all the flavors found in the world except those of onion and garlic. These last two were excluded, as they were considered harmful to pregnant women.

The Romans, too, considered garlic an aphrodisiac. At their festival of Ceres, Cerealia, garlic was eaten. Serbians still use garlic as a remedy against witches and demons, and the custom is prevalent among Jews in Northern Europe of using garlic to avert the effects of the "evil eye."

The following dish, loaded with garlic, is a typical Russian Jewish recipe for brisket. Serve it next Friday night and see the results!

1	4-pound brisket	6	carrots, chopped
6	cloves garlic	4-5	stalks celery with leaves,
Salt and pepper to taste			chopped
Paprika to taste		1	cup water, tomato juice, or
2	tablespoons vegetable oil		tomato sauce
2	large onions, chopped	1	envelope dried onion soup

1. Preheat oven to 325°.

2. Rinse the meat with water. Pat it dry. Rub the meat on all sides with crushed garlic and then sprinkle with salt, pepper, and paprika.

3. Heat the oil in a heavy-bottomed casserole and brown the meat on all sides.

4. Add the onions, carrots, and celery. Cover with water or tomato juice and sprinkle with the dried onion soup.

5. Cover and bake in the oven 3 hours. Before serving, remove cover and brown ½ hour more. This dish is best prepared a day in advance so the fat is easily skimmed off and the brisket reheated.

Serves 6–8. (F)

CHICKEN PAPRIKA

A Hungarian Jew is Hungarian—especially in the kitchen—except for two basic ingredients. Goose fat or, now, *pareve* margarine or vegetable oil replaces suet or lard. A dollop of sour cream does not adorn such favorites as Hungarian goulash, stuffed cabbage, or chicken paprika. But poppy seeds and paprika still decorate many dishes, and salads are flavored with vinegary dressings. Chicken paprika with rice and cucumber salad or green pepper and tomato salad are typical and typically delicious Hungarian Friday dinner dishes.

2 large onions, minced	1 hot pepper, or a few sprinkles of crushed red pepper
2 tablespoons chicken fat (or vegetable oil)	1 large, plump fryer cut into pieces
2 green peppers, sliced	Salt to taste
2 tomatoes, quartered (optional)	2 cups long-grained white rice
2 tablespoons paprika	

1. In a Dutch oven, sauté the onions in the chicken fat or vegetable oil until golden brown. Add the green peppers and brown slightly. Add the tomatoes, paprika, and hot pepper, mixing well and making sure the paprika does not burn.

2. Salt the chicken and add it to the above. Mix and cover. Let the chicken render its own juices, simmering until tender (about 50 minutes). You may have to add water.

3. When the chicken is cooked, move it to one side of the Dutch oven, or remove to a warm plate, and add the rice. Mix with the gravy; add water if

the gravy does not cover the rice by about 1″. Add salt to taste. Cover and simmer about 20 minutes, until the rice is cooked.

Serves 4–6. (F)

Hungarian non-Jews would serve this dish with sour cream. I serve it with plum preserves and it is delicious!

STUFFED CHICKEN

Poultry has always been a typically Jewish main course for Friday night. This chicken, with a stuffing of bread and green peppers under the skin, is a superb Russian dish.

4 medium onions, chopped	1 small loaf white bread with
½ cup vegetable oil	crusts removed
1 green pepper, chopped	2 eggs
4 stalks celery with leaves,	1 cup *pareve* cornflake crumbs
chopped	8 chicken breasts
2 tablespoons minced fresh	3 cloves garlic
parsley	1 teaspoon paprika
Salt and pepper to taste	

1. Sauté the onions in ¼ cup oil. Add the green pepper, celery, parsley, and salt and pepper to taste. Continue cooking until pepper is soft.

2. Wet the bread in water and squeeze out water.

3. Mix in the eggs and then fold in the cornflake crumbs and onion mixture.

4. Preheat oven to 350°.

5. Wash and dry the chicken breasts and rub with garlic. Sprinkle with salt, pepper, and paprika.

6. Stuff the filling under the skin of each breast and brush the top with the remaining ¼ cup oil.

7. Place in a 9″ × 13″ or similar casserole and bake uncovered in the oven 30–45 minutes or until golden brown.

Serves 6–8. (F)

Note: The leftover stuffing can be placed in foil and cooked alongside the chicken.

FASSOULIA
(String Bean and Meat Stew)

This string bean and meat casserole, coming from the heyday of Sephardic Jewry, is probably one of the oldest Jewish recipes in this country. Handed down through the generations of the New York Nathan family, whose first relatives landed on American soil in 1654, it probably came with them in oral form during their flight from Spain via Brazil, where they picked up the allspice. Every other recipe I have ever seen for this dish—known as fassoulia in Arab countries—includes tomatoes, which makes me think this recipe antedates the others. After the Nathans' departure from Spain, tomatoes were introduced to the Old World from the New. Jews who stayed in Spain or fled to the various parts of the Turkish Empire added the new fruit. By the time the Nathans might have added tomatoes, the recipe had become such a symbol of their past that it remained pretty much intact.

Given the fact that Nathan ancestry includes poets Emma Lazarus and Robert Nathan, Supreme Court Justice Benjamin Nathan Cardozo, and Annie Nathan Meyer, founder of Barnard College, consider yourself in good company if you serve the following recipe. Try it in the original Nathan form or with the later addition of tomatoes. Both ways, it has become a family favorite in my home (and we are no kin to the Sephardic Nathans).

3 pounds lean brisket, chuck, shoulder steak, or breast deckel	½ teaspoon whole allspice, or to taste
1 clove garlic	1 teaspoon salt
Salt and pepper to taste	2 cups water
2 tablespoons vegetable oil	12 small onions
4 whole black peppercorns	2 pounds fresh string beans

1. Rub the brisket with garlic and season well with salt and pepper. Brown in a little oil.

2. Place peppercorns and allspice in a cheesecloth and add, with 1 teaspoon salt, to the meat.

3. Simmer covered in 2 cups of water, with the onions, for 2½ hours or more. Let stand and skim off the fat.

4. Remove the tip ends and string the beans if necessary. Add to the meat and simmer slowly, covered, ½ hour more, or until tender.

Serves 6-8. (F)

MOROCCAN MEATBALLS
(Kofta)

When we think of meatballs, it is most often in terms of the Italian or Swedish variety. As did so many other foods, however, meatballs originated in the Middle East. Arab and Jewish merchants and later the Crusaders spread the word to Europe of how easy and tasty it is to combine ground lamb, beef, or veal with onions, garlic, breadcrumbs, and spices. These balls are then usually simmered in a sauce. By tasting the spices in each meatball, it is easy to discern from which country and even sometimes from which town the recipe came. Iraqi Jews, for example, tend to add turmeric; Greeks use oregano and potatoes; and Persians introduce a combination of turmeric and such novel ingredients as ground nuts, rice, apricots, or prunes. The following recipe comes from Morocco. Its ingredients include cumin, garlic, and breadcrumbs or matzah meal. It is often served on Friday night with a variety of salads.

Meatballs:		Sauce:	
1	pound ground beef	¼	cup vegetable oil
2–3	cloves garlic	Salt and pepper to taste	
Salt and pepper to taste		1	teaspoon cumin
¼	cup matzah meal or breadcrumbs	1	teaspoon paprika
1	egg	⅛	teaspoon crushed red pepper (optional)
1	teaspoon cumin	½	cup water
		Juice of 1 lemon (optional)	

1. Mix all the ingredients for the meatballs. Roll into balls the size of a walnut.

2. Combine the ingredients for the sauce.

3. In a heavy saucepan, bring the sauce to a boil. Add the meatballs and simmer, uncovered, in the sauce until cooked (about 20 minutes).

Makes 18. (F)

CALVES' FOOT JELLY
(Petcha)

Petcha, or calves' foot jelly, is often eaten as a main dish in summer at noon on the Sabbath or, in winter, as an appetizer or with the third meal. Called *drelies* in Galicia, *pacha* in Iraq, and *pilse* in Rumania, it is *fisnoga* in Russia. The Yiddish for foot is *fus*. The Russian for foot is *noga*. Russian Jews combined both these words into *fisnoga*, literally "foot-foot."

What is the custom of eating calves' foot jelly on the Sabbath? In the days of redemption, even the feet—the lower extremities of the body—will be elevated on high. Since the Sabbath affords the faithful a taste of the World to Come, "food made of feet" is eaten in anticipation.

There may also be a more practical reason for eating the calf's foot. It is an inexpensive cut of meat. Jews in East Europe were generally very poor. This delicacy was just one more way of stretching a little bit of meat to be eaten on the Sabbath.

Rose Siegel, originally of Minsk, remembers how her mother prepared fisnoga. In winter she would often leave it in the oven overnight and serve it at noon as a gravy with kasha, followed by a brisket or chicken. In summer she would serve it cold, as it is in the following recipe.

2 large onions, sliced	1½ teaspoons salt
1 cow's or 2 calves' (preferred) feet, cleaned and cut into large pieces	½ teaspoon pepper
	3 hard-boiled eggs, sliced
½ head of garlic, minced	Lemon slices

1. Put the sliced onions in a large soup pot. Add all the other ingredients except the eggs and lemon slices.

2. Cover with water and boil slowly until the meat falls away from the bones (about 3 hours), adding water as needed to keep all the ingredients covered.

3. Turn off the heat and remove the meat. Clear the meat and the jelly-like substance from the bones. Grind the meat and place in the bottom of a deep glass pie plate or bowl. Strain the soup over the ground meat to cover, using about 2 cups liquid. Place the sliced eggs in the liquid; they will fall to the bottom.

4. Refrigerate until firm. Cut into squares and serve cold with lemon slices.

Serves 6–8. (F)

Variation: Some people separate the egg whites and yolks, mixing the whites with the meat and the yolks with the gravy. It can also be served warm, topped with a hot egg sauce made from 6 eggs, water, salt, sugar, and lemon, diluted, after thickening, with a little chicken soup.

DAFINA
(Moroccan-style Cholent)

Go now to the flock, and fetch me from thence two good kids of the goats; and I will make them savoury food for thy father, such as he loveth.

Genesis 27:9

Rebecca's savory venison stew which Jacob fed to Isaac may have been a precursor to hamim ("hot" in Hebrew) or cholent, the long-simmering stew traditionally served at noon of the Sabbath. The original version would have included olive oil, chick-peas or other lentils, meat, water, onions, garlic, herbs, and leeks. Because of the prohibition against lighting a fire on the Sabbath, the hamim, as far back as the second century, was hermetically sealed and placed in a very low oven, originally the remaining hot embers of a fire begun on Friday afternoon and opened at noon Saturday after the morning services. When the Jews left Palestine, they brought this dish with them. With the local ingredients available in different countries, the stew changed character. The lamb changed to beef, tongue, or calves' feet; the beans became white, black, or navy beans. Potatoes, eggs, carrots, and barley were all local changes, as was the addition of rice.

The following recipe for Moroccan dafina (meaning "hidden") came to Casablanca from Spain at the time of the Inquisition. An Egyptian version would include a calf's foot instead of a tongue, and a Brazilian version would have black beans rather than chick-peas.

Hamim is one example of how a Jewish dish influenced the great national cuisine of a country. In Spain, the cocido Madrileno is the finest stew made in the land. Its ingredients classically include chicken, beef, veal, bone marrow, chorizo sausage, a ham joint, blood sausage, fresh pork fat, and salt pork fat. Chick-peas, potatoes, carrots, cabbage, garlic, and leeks are also included. Sound familiar? It is a descendant of dafina similar to the one in the following recipe. Peter Feibleman, author of Time-Life's *Spanish Cookery*, relates that during the Inquisition it was necessary for every Spaniard to show his adherence to Christianity. While Moslems and Jews ate no pork for religious reasons, a "pure" Christian ate pork once a day, preferably in public. Even at home he could be caught off guard, for anyone who came unexpectedly to share his cocido could see clearly from the pork in it that this was the house not of an infidel but of a "pure believer in the True Faith."

Thus, hard-boiled eggs, symbolic of the eternity of life, were quickly replaced by large quantities of pork and pork fat.

It has been suggested by many that New Amsterdam Jews, taking the dafina across the ocean, loaned this recipe to the Pilgrims for—you guessed it—baked beans. Baked beans became, with the addition of salt pork and navy beans, the long-simmering New World stew eaten on Saturday nights.

The following dafina recipe from Morocco is outstanding. The meatloaf—made from ground walnuts, ground beef, cinnamon, and sugar—is a marvelous Moroccan addition. By sealing the stew tightly and cooking for about eighteen hours, the result is a melt-in-your-mouth meat stew. It can be served in three courses. The broth becomes a soup with the addition of thin, vermicelli-like fidellos noodles. Then come the vegetables, and finally the meat course. Having identified hamim and cholent as stews so heavy only Alka-Seltzer and a good long nap could cure them, I was pleasantly surprised at how absolutely savory this stew was. Just follow it with a light fruit dessert rather than a heavy kugel. Try it next Sabbath or for your next dinner party.

1 cup chick-peas which have been soaked in water overnight	1 teaspoon cinnamon
	¼ teaspoon ground cloves
	10 eggs
Salt and pepper to taste	1 beef tongue (optional)
¼ teaspoon turmeric	2 cups rice, uncooked
½ teaspoon mace	½ cup vegetable oil
1 entire head garlic	6–7 yams or sweet potatoes, peeled
1 onion, sliced	
1 4-pound top rib, breast of beef, or brisket	10–12 whole potatoes, peeled
	4–6 dates, pitted
1 pound ground meat	Water
½ cup sugar	

1. Using a large 9-quart casserole with a tight-fitting lid, place the chick-peas on the bottom. Sprinkle with salt and pepper and add turmeric and mace.

2. Place the garlic cloves, onion, and brisket on top of the chick-peas. Sprinkle again with salt and pepper.

3. Combine the ground meat, sugar, cinnamon, cloves, and 2 eggs and form into a meat loaf. Cover tightly with aluminum foil and place next to the meat.

4. If using tongue, place that in with the rest of the meat.

5. Put the rice loosely in a cheesecloth and close tightly. Place on top of the meat. Pour the oil over the rice.

6. Surround the rice with the yams or sweet potatoes, the white potatoes, the dates, and the remaining 8 eggs. Sprinkle again with salt and pepper.

7. Add water up to the top of the potatoes, about ¾ full. Bring to a boil, cover, and simmer 1 hour on top of the stove. Add more water, if necessary, to keep it ¾ full.

8. Preheat the oven to 250° and place the dafina in the oven. Leave overnight or for at least 10 hours. Do not open until ready to serve. Place the vegetables in one dish, the meat in another, the rice in a third, and the broth in a fourth as your soup course.

Serves 8–10. (F)

HUNGARIAN-STYLE CHOLENT

The Jewish rabbi and the Catholic priest in a village of Hungary were very friendly. The priest complained to the rabbi that he could not sleep. The rabbi suggested the solet (cholent) recipe as a cure for insomnia. A few days later when they met again, the rabbi asked the priest how the solet was. The priest replied, "I understand how you fall asleep from this dish, but what puzzles me is: How do you get up?" According to George Lang in his *Cuisine of Hungary*, from which this story is excerpted, barley was added to this soupy stew in Hungary; the closer to the Austrian border, the less barley and the more rice included. The Central European version originated during the Middle Ages in the Rhineland and was called schalet by German Jews. Rice with beans or peas was the basic vegetable in cholent; later, in Poland and Russia, potatoes, barley, and brisket appeared. The amount of meat depended on the wealth of the family.

Each town and in fact each family of Central and East Europe had its special cholent recipe. There were said to be over three hundred varieties. Cholent is basically the hamim or dafina from the previous recipe, carried to East Europe instead of to Spain.

The word "cholent" itself has an interesting history. Cholent and the German *Schalet* come from the old French word *chald*, or the modern French *chaud*, for warm. This, of course, was a translation from the Hebrew *ham*, also meaning warm. Another theory is that the word comes quite simply from the Yiddish *shul ende*, or end of synagogue, since that is when the cholent is eaten. The second explanation sounds more to me like a play on the words of the first.

The cholent was hermetically sealed in an iron pot to retain the juices during its long cooking. A piece of cloth or cheesecloth would be placed around the top of the casserole, or even a dough made from flour and water pressed between the cover and the top of the casserole. After it was sealed, the cholent was either placed in the oven at home or taken to the baker, where each saucepan was marked with the name of the owner. Often there were mistaken identities. The baker locked all the community pots in his oven and allowed the fire to go out. To retain the heat, he often sealed the door with lime.

After synagogue, small boys brought the meal home. Dessert kugels and schalets were also cooked in a similar manner, often inside the cholent pot.

To make carrying permissible on the Sabbath, the entire town (if it was small enough) was surrounded with a string or wire. The *eruv*, that is, the enclosure of the village by wire for the Sabbath, made the village like one household within which carrying is permissible. If the fence broke, the cholents were handed from person to person to the house.

This Hungarian cholent recipe was given to me by Alex Lichtman, the owner of Mrs. Herbst's bakery in New York.

2 cloves garlic, finely chopped	2 stalks celery, quartered
1 medium onion, diced	1 parsley root and greens
⅓ cup chicken or goose fat or	(turnips can be substituted)
vegetable shortening	1 pound breast of beef or
2–3 quarts water	brisket
1½ cups dried small white or lima	2 slices flanken, cut into 3
beans, uncooked	pieces each
½ cup pearl barley	2 unbroken eggs, in the shell
1 smoked beef tongue, fat part	1½ tablespoons salt
1½ tablespoons hot paprika	Pepper to taste
1 large ripe tomato, quartered	Stuffed goose neck (optional)

1. Preheat oven to 250°.

2. Sauté the garlic and onion in the chicken or goose fat or vegetable oil.

3. Using a heavy 5–6-quart casserole, combine the garlic and onion with all the remaining ingredients, starting with about 8 cups of water. Bring to a boil on top of the stove.

4. Cover and bake in the oven 4–6 hours. After the cholent has been cooking about 2 hours, stir, and check if there is enough water. If not, add 2 cups more. If, later, it needs more water, add about ½ cup at a time. Serve in large soup bowls.

Serves 8. (F)

Note: Traditionally this dish was cooked overnight and then eaten at noon the next day. The Orthodox could not open the pot and therefore started with more water than I have in this recipe. I make it in advance, cool it, skim the fat off, and then reheat it.

STUFFED GOOSE NECK
(Toltott Libanyak)

1 whole large goose neck (remove skin from neck and clean inside and out)	1 teaspoon paprika
	½ clove garlic, crushed
	1 cup flour
1 small onion, chopped	1 teaspoon salt
¾ pound goose meat	1 egg
7 ounces goose fat	1 cup chicken broth

1. Grind together any remaining meat from the goose neck, plus the onion, goose meat, and 4 ounces of the goose fat. Grind again.

2. Combine the ground goose mixture with the paprika, garlic, flour, salt, egg, and the remaining 3 ounces of goose fat, which has been melted. Mix well.

3. Fill the skin of the goose neck with the stuffing. Sew the narrow end. Fill with more stuffing and sew the other end. Sew any other openings.

4. Preheat oven to 400°.

5. In a small casserole, place the chicken broth and the stuffed goose neck. Bake uncovered in the oven for about ½ hour, making sure to brown the goose neck on each side. Serve alone or add to the previous cholent recipe. Serve hot or cold. Slice like a sausage.

Serves 6–8 as an appetizer and 4 for a main course (in the cholent recipe it will serve 8). (F)

RICE WITH SOUR LEMON SAUCE AND EGGPLANT
(Riz-au-Hamod with Eggplant)

The following recipe is listed as Egyptian, Syrian, or Lebanese in various Middle Eastern cookbooks. This particular version of rice with sour lemon sauce and eggplant came from Annie Simonian Totah. Her Jewish husband, Sammy, was the number one student at the American University of Beirut and she, an Armenian, number two. The two fell in love, overcoming religious and ethnic differences. Annie learned this recipe from her Syrian-born mother-in-law. It is served on Friday nights.

2 cups rich chicken broth or water	1 tablespoon sugar
1 tablespoon vegetable oil	Dash of cayenne pepper
Salt and pepper to taste	Dash of paprika
2 small garlic cloves, minced	Juice of 2 lemons
2 tablespoons fresh chopped parsley	1 medium or 2–3 dwarf eggplants, thickly chopped
2 stalks celery with leaves, chopped	2 cups uncooked rice

1. In a medium saucepan, place the chicken broth or water. (This chicken broth is traditionally made from the neck, giblets, and wing bones of the chicken.)

2. Add the oil, salt and pepper to taste, garlic, parsley, celery, sugar, cayenne, and paprika. Bring to a boil and add the lemon juice. (For an even more lemony taste, use more lemon juice.)

3. Add the peeled and chopped eggplants. Simmer uncovered until the eggplants are soft (about 20 minutes).

4. Meanwhile, cook the rice. Serve the eggplant over the rice with broiled or roasted chicken and a green salad.

Serves 6–8. (F)

SWEET PINEAPPLE KUGEL

In East Europe, kugel was the official Sabbath dessert at noon. Made of lokshen (noodles) or soaked white bread mixed with beaten eggs, and liberally dotted with raisins, sugar, spice, and shortening, it was baked firm, brown, and fragrant. The kugel was baked inside the iron cholent pot. How? An earthenware, covered pot holding the kugel was placed in the center of the cholent pot. The cholent potatoes or beans were spread out to fill the empty space around this centerpiece. Thus, the main course and dessert were conveniently cooked together. With the heavy main course and the heavy dessert, it is no wonder that Sabbath afternoons were (and for many still are) literally days of rest.

The following pineapple kugel—my husband's favorite—can be prepared for dessert or as a starch with roast or broiled chicken on the Sabbath or any day.

8 ounces broad noodles	1 teaspoon vanilla
6 eggs	1 teaspoon cinnamon
4 tablespoons *pareve* margarine, melted	Vegetable oil
½ cup sugar	Pineapple rings
1 8-ounce can crushed pineapple with juice	Cherries

1. Preheat oven to 350°. Parboil the noodles in salted water. Rinse and drain.

2. Combine the eggs and margarine. Beat well. Add the sugar, crushed pineapple and juice, vanilla, and cinnamon. Mix well. Add the noodles.

3. Grease a 9″ × 13″ baking dish with vegetable oil. Pour in the kugel. Place pineapple rings on top, with a cherry in the middle of each ring.

4. Bake 40–60 minutes, until golden.

Serves 8. (P)

Note: You can decrease the number of eggs, but the result will be less fluffy. To make a *milchig* pineapple kugel, use 3 eggs, ½ pound pot cheese, 1 cup sour cream, and 1 cup milk.

POTATO KUGEL

The potatoes never failed us....For each meal, they looked different and tasted different. Once in a great while she [Tanta Malka] even managed a spoonful of chicken fat to flavor them with. For days afterward the smell of chicken fat would linger with me. And I'd even dream about it in my sleep. But the main stand-by for flavoring and trimming was the onion. There was no limit to its uses and versatility and there was no meal without it. Sliced, browned, or cooked, it was there. But onion or no onion, there was always the appetite. It was like a curse.

Yuri Suhl, ONE FOOT IN AMERICA

In the poorer *shtetls* of East Europe, four eggs would have been a luxury in a potato kugel. The baking powder in the following recipe is an American addition and gives a lightness to this particular kugel.

4	eggs	1½	teaspoons baking powder
8	medium Idaho potatoes	2	teaspoons salt
1	large onion, peeled and cut in	¼	teaspoon pepper
	pieces	¼	cup melted chicken fat or
6	tablespoons matzah meal		*pareve* margarine

1. Preheat oven to 375°.

2. Break the eggs in a medium bowl and set aside.

3. Grate the potatoes and onion in a food processor or by hand. Pour into a large strainer. Drain water and combine potatoes and onions with the eggs. Stir thoroughly and add the matzah meal, baking powder, salt, pepper, and chicken fat or margarine. Turn into a large greased soufflé dish.

4. Bake in the oven 30–45 minutes, until golden brown.

Serves 8–10. (F or P)

EXCITING NOODLE KUGEL

When my mother was just about my age, she edited *Regard thy Table*, put out by the Larchmont, New York, temple. One of her favorite recipes in this charming book is Exciting Noodles, basically a tart noodle kugel with onions and sour cream. It can be prepared in advance and served for Friday or Saturday dinner if you are having a fish or vegetarian meal.

8 ounces medium-wide noodles	1 clove garlic, chopped
1 cup uncreamed cottage or pot	1 cup sour cream
cheese	1 onion, finely minced

Salt to taste	Grated Parmesan cheese
Dash of Tabasco sauce	Sour cream
1 tablespoon Worcestershire sauce	

1. Preheat oven to 350°.

2. Cook noodles until tender. Drain and combine with the cottage or pot cheese, garlic, sour cream, onion, salt, Tabasco, and Worcestershire sauce.

3. Butter the inside of a 1½-quart casserole and insert the mixture. Bake until brown and crusty on top. Serve with grated Parmesan cheese and additional sour cream.

Serves 4–6. (M)

ZUCCHINI FRITADA
(Simple Soufflé)

Saturday breakfast after early morning synagogue is a special meal for the Sephardim. Desayuno—as this meal is called—has a quality all its own. Huevos haminadav (hard-boiled eggs cooked in coffee grinds and onion peels to make the eggs brown) are served with buttery burekas filled with eggplant, spinach, or cheese. Fritada, a low egg soufflé with vegetables and feta or farmers cheese, is another easy dish to prepare. The following is an outstanding fritada recipe from Bulgaria.

1 pound zucchini, grated	Salt to taste (if using farmers
8 ounces farmers or feta cheese	cheese)
2 tablespoons fresh dill (optional)	¼ cup grated Parmesan or
3 eggs	kaskeval cheese

1. Set the grated zucchini in a colander for at least ½ hour. Squeeze out as much water as possible.

2. Preheat oven to 350°.

3. Crumble the farmers or feta cheese and add to the zucchini. Sprinkle with dill.

4. Beat the eggs and add to the above, mixing well.

5. Place the zucchini mixture in a greased 9″ pie plate or casserole. Sprinkle with grated cheese.

6. Bake 45–60 minutes in the oven, until golden brown.

Serves 4. (M)

MARINATED MUSHROOMS

When I lived in Jerusalem, a pre-dawn, post-rain sport was hunting wild mushrooms in the Judean Hills. It was always necessary to include a mushroom expert in the group who could distinguish the poisonous from the edible varieties. When we returned to the city, we would quickly prepare a fresh mushroom omelet for breakfast.

In the United States we are accustomed to eating only one type of mushroom, the white *Agaricus campestris*, which is farmed mostly in Pennsylvania and distributed around the country. We can safely keep the mushrooms in the refrigerator until we decide to use them in a salad, soup, or sauce. It was not, however, always so easy to hunt or to purchase mushrooms.

In the Ukraine, for example, it was the Christian peasants who knew how to differentiate edible from inedible varieties of wild mushrooms. They would go into the forest after a rain in the dark hours before dawn. Since you cannot propagate wild mushrooms, the peasants would hunt for them in the rich dirt of the forest. Then they would sell them in the local marketplace. Housewives would buy large quantities of mushrooms with more texture and richness than our cultivated varieties. They would then string them on a line and air-dry them for later use. The famous mushroom and barley soup usually included not fresh but dry mushrooms, so tasty as flavoring agents. Today, dried mushrooms are extremely expensive for everyday cuisine. With modern marketing techniques, it is more economical for us to use the blander cultured fresh mushrooms throughout the year. The following marinated mushroom recipe is one of the most sought-after hors d'oeuvres at my cocktail and dinner parties.

1 pound fresh mushrooms	1 tablespoon mustard
1 small onion, sliced in rings	1 teaspoon chopped parsley
1/3 cup red wine vinegar	1 tablespoon chopped fresh dill
1/3 cup salad oil	1/4 teaspoon salt
1 tablespoon brown sugar	3 peppercorns

1. Steam the mushrooms for 1 minute.

2. In a saucepan, bring to a boil the onion, vinegar, oil, sugar, mustard, parsley, dill, salt, and peppercorns. Simmer, uncovered, a few minutes.

3. Place the mushrooms in a glass or ceramic bowl and add the marinade. Let marinate in refrigerator at least 24 hours. Serve with toothpicks.

Makes about 2 cups. (P)

KOSHER DILL PICKLES

What would the Lower East Side be without pickles? And what would a kosher deli be without pickles? Although pickles are mass-marketed quite successfully, there is still a nostalgic taste sensation in reaching into a wooden barrel, pulling out a wet, garlic-smelling pickle, and slurping it down, dripping it over the floor and one's chin.

While we lived in Cambridge, Massachusetts, I loved sampling the pickles at Savenor's, the grocer and butcher whom Julia Child made famous on her "French Chef" show. At the entrance to Savenor's, there is a huge wooden barrel filled with pickles twelve months a year. Jack Savenor's brother-in-law, Max Baskies, learned to make the following Polish kosher dill pickles at his mother's knee over fifty years ago. For a smaller quantity, see the recipe on p. 124.

50 pounds pickling cucumbers (Boston or Chicago variety)	1 pound pickling spice
3 pounds kosher salt	3 ounces garlic, minced
15 quarts hot water (about)	1 pint cider vinegar
2 ounces dill	

1. Find an old wooden barrel, preferably one that contained olives from Portugal or Spain.

2. Wash the cucumbers and place them in the bottom of the barrel.

3. Mix the kosher salt (which Max feels makes the best brine) with enough hot water to make the salt dissolve. Add the dill, pickling spice, garlic, and vinegar. Pour the brine on the cucumbers.

4. Add enough hot water to cover, close with a wooden top, and let stand 3 days. Then taste. In the summer the cucumbers pickle faster than in winter. Max uses no sodium benzoate or aluminum sulfate.

Makes about 150. (P)

PICKLED PEACHES

Early Jewish settlers in this country also ate pickles, although a different sort from the kosher pickles described above. Abigail Franks of New York used to write letters to her son David, who was studying in England. She would send him preserved foods—fish, meat, strawberries, apples, and vegetables, including artichokes and cauliflower. In a letter from the year 1736, she wrote:

I have sent you two Caggs of pickles one is a 15 gallon filled with peper and the other ten with Mangoes Peaches and a few peper to fill up the Cask when you receive them take the Peaches and Mangoes from the peper and put fresh vinegar to them and that will take of the strength of the peper.

And here is the earliest recipe for pickled peaches I could find in this country. It is taken from Esther Levy's *Jewish Cookery Book* of 1871.

TO PICKLE PEACHES—Take a quarter of a pound of sugar to one pint of vinegar and scald the peaches, they should not be quite ripe; put them with some mace, allspice, cloves and nutmeg; when boiled take out the spice, and put the peaches in a jar; observe that the vinegar covers them, and put them away in a dry cool place. Pears and plums can be pickled the same way.

UKRAINIAN KAMISH BROIT

This easily prepared zwieback-type cookie was always on hand in Ukrainian Jewish households. It is served at any time for unexpected guests and is perfect on a Sabbath afternoon.

1½ cups all-purpose unbleached flour	4 tablespoons orange juice
½ teaspoon salt	1 teaspoon vanilla
1 teaspoon baking powder	1 cup chopped almonds or walnuts, or half nuts and half raisins or chopped dates
3 eggs	1¼ teaspoons cinnamon
1 cup plus 2 teaspoons sugar	
4 tablespoons corn oil	

1. Preheat oven to 350°.

2. Sift the flour, salt, and baking powder into a bowl.

3. Using a beater or food processor, beat the eggs until fluffy. Add 1 cup of sugar and mix until the mixture turns yellow.

4. Mix together the oil, orange juice, and vanilla. Stir into the eggs, alternating with the flour mixture. Blend in the nuts or nut mixture.

5. Grease two 9″ loaf pans and cover the bottom with a little of the batter. Sprinkle with a little cinnamon and repeat until all the batter and 1 teaspoon of the cinnamon are used up.

6. Bake for 30 minutes. Cool and cut into ½″ slices.

7. Turn up the oven to 400°. Arrange the slices on a baking sheet. Sprinkle

with the remaining 2 teaspoons sugar, to which ¼ teaspoon cinnamon has been added. Brown for a few minutes until golden.

Makes about 36. (P)

MANDELBROT
(Almond Bread)

Particular tea drinkers have always on their 5 o'clock tea tray a special kind of sugar. This is made from the beet and comes in thin oblongs better suited to tiny teacups than are the usual cubes. It is claimed, too, by connoisseurs, that this sugar gives just the right flavour.
New York JEWISH MESSENGER, May 12, 1899

And with this sugar, most probably first brought to these shores by Marrano Jews in the seventeenth century, a sweet is always eaten. Mandelbrot is a typical cookie for Saturday afternoon tea.

1	cup unsalted *pareve* margarine or butter	4	teaspoons baking powder
1½	cups sugar	1	teaspoon salt
4	eggs	1	cup raisins
1	teaspoon vanilla	1	cup grated coconut
½	cup whiskey or brandy	½	cup chopped walnuts
4	cups unbleached all-purpose flour	1	cup slivered, blanched, and toasted almonds

1. Preheat oven to 350°.

2. Cream together the margarine and the sugar.

3. Beat the eggs well and combine with the margarine, vanilla, and whiskey.

4. Combine the flour with the baking powder and salt. Add to the margarine mixture. Mix well.

5. Blend in the raisins, coconut, walnuts, and almonds.

6. Grease and flour three pans approximately 4½″ × 10″ and bake about 30–40 minutes, until done. Serve sliced thin.

Makes 3 loaves. (P or M)

A perfect accompaniment to a fruit dessert. The Mandelbrot keeps very well and is especially good toasted.

PEAR KUGEL

In East Europe, kugel was the official Sabbath dessert after a hot cholent. My in-laws from Poland remember the lokshen kugel mixed with raisins, sugar, spices, and shortening (cocoa butter) and baked until it was firm, brown, and fragrant. The kugel could be baked simultaneously with the cholent. A covered earthenware pot bearing the kugel was placed in the center of the iron cholent pot. The cholent potatoes or beans were arrayed to fill the empty space around this centerpiece. By placing the pudding inside the cholent, the kugel came out moister than it would have had it been baked alone.

The following pear kugel is an unusual dessert recipe I found in the 1947 *Community Cookbook* of Congregation B'nai Israel in Woonsocket, Rhode Island. I was fortunately able to contact Mrs. Coleman Falk, who chaired the writing of this excellent collection of authentic Jewish recipes. During the war years, she and a number of other ladies observed the older members of their community making dishes. Thus, they were able to write down and preserve an oral tradition. The recipe calls for steaming the kugel in water, but it could very well be steamed inside the cholent.

Filling:	Dough:
3 hard pears, pared, cleaned, and sliced	1½ cups flour
½ cup sugar	¼ teaspoon salt
1 teaspoon cinnamon	2 teaspoons baking powder
Pinch of nutmeg	1 teaspoon sugar
Pinch of salt	3 tablespoons butter or *pareve* margarine
½ cup raisins	2 eggs
4–5 prunes, washed, soaked, pitted, and diced	Milk or water

1. Mix all the filling ingredients and set aside.

2. Preheat oven to 250°. Grease a 2-quart soufflé dish.

3. Sift the flour, salt, baking powder, and sugar together. Add 1 tablespoon of butter and the eggs and work into a medium-loose dough with your hands or a food processor. Add a little milk or water if too stiff. If too loose to roll, add a little flour (the softer the dough the better). Knead into a round ball. Roll out about ⅛" thick.

4. Sprinkle the filling mixture all over the dough. Dot with the remaining 2 tablespoons of butter. Fold the outside edges in toward the center, pinching into the shape of a ball. With a wide spatula, transfer to a baking dish.

5. Set this dish into a pan of hot water, making sure the water is lower than the top of the inner pan. Cover the kugel tightly and bake 4–5 hours or overnight. As the water evaporates in the outer pan, add more water so that the kugel will brown slowly and not burn.

Serves 4–6. (M or P)

HOT FRUIT COMPOTE

This is one of those recipes that originated in East Europe as a simple fruit compote, with honey, water, and dried fruits. Transplanted to the United States—where more glamorous ingredients are available—it has become a fancier dish.

4 cups canned fruits, drained, with juice reserved	Juice of ½ lemon
½ pound dried prunes	½ teaspoon cinnamon
½ pound dried apricots	12 dried macaroons, crumbled
¼ cup brown sugar	4 tablespoons *pareve* margarine
½ cup brandy	or butter

1. Preheat oven to 350°. Grease a 2½-quart casserole.

2. Fill the casserole with the drained canned fruits, prunes, apricots, brown sugar, brandy, lemon juice, and cinnamon. Add juice to barely cover the fruit. Cover and bake for 30 minutes.

3. Sprinkle the macaroon crumbs over the top. Dot with margarine or butter and bake 15 minutes more. Serve hot or cold.

Serves 8. (P or M)

CHOCOLATE MOUSSE

It is traditional to serve some sort of kugel, or pudding, on the Sabbath. This pudding is to remind us of the manna, which was covered with dew. It was supposed to be white, like coriander seed. Just as manna was considered a delicacy in the desert, mousse, a rich pudding, has become a dessert delicacy for us. This is one of the creamiest and most easily prepared mousses I have ever tasted.

1 cup semi-sweet chocolate bits	2 medium eggs
¾ cup hot milk	2 tablespoons rum, or your
3 tablespoons hot strong coffee	favorite liqueur

1. Place the chocolate bits in your blender or food processor. Add the hot milk, coffee, eggs, and liqueur. Blend well.

2. Place in an attractive 3–4-cup bowl. Refrigerate a few hours or overnight. Serve alone or with whipped cream.

Serves 4. (M)

HAVDALAH SPICES

The Emperor asked Rabbi Joshua ben Hananiah, "What gives your Sabbath meal such an aroma?" He replied, "We have a spice called Sabbath which is put in the cooking of the meat, and this gives it its aroma." The Emperor said, "Give me some of this spice." He replied, "For him who keeps the Sabbath, the spice works, for him who does not keep it, it does not work."
                                                                    Sabbath 119a

In cooking for the Sabbath and other holidays, we sometimes forget the importance of using real "spice and spirit." Spices form an essential part of the Sabbath in the Havdalah service after sunset. First there is a blessing over the wine, which symbolizes joy; then the spices are blessed. Any aromatic spice or flower will do. Cinnamon and cloves are traditional. The spices symbolize the spiritual riches of the Sabbath and are sniffed before replacing them in the *hadas*, or receptacle. These spices are to cheer the soul—so saddened with the departure of the Sabbath.

ROSH HASHANAH

ROSH HASHANAH

Go your way, eat the fat, and drink the sweet, and send portions unto him for whom nothing is prepared; for this day is holy unto our Lord.

Nehemiah 8:10

The Jewish New Year, the anniversary of the Creation, is a time for self-examination and repentance. It comes ten days before Yom Kippur, the day on which the divine judgment is sealed. The *shofar*—a horn of a ram or one of the four other animals specified in the Talmud, whose tradition in Jewish history stems from the time when God permitted Abraham to substitute a ram for Isaac as a sacrifice—is sounded. Blowing the ram's horn has become a symbol of the complete faith of Abraham and of the Jewish people.

The ancient peoples had no organized New Year, but rather calculated the year from the new moon nearest to the beginning of the barley harvest in spring (at Passover) or to the ingathering of the fruits (Sukkot) in autumn. Rosh Hashanah—the time of the new moon close to the latter holiday—was eventually adopted as the beginning of the festal year. Today it is one of the great solemn days of the Jewish faith.

The Rosh Hashanah table is laden with delicacies representing optimism for a sweet future. Dishes abound with honey, raisins, carrots, and apples—all seasonal reminders of hope for the coming year.

No sour or bitter dishes have a place on this joyous table. Moroccans, for example, will not eat black foods such as olives or eggplants, whose color and possible bitter taste might augur evil for the coming year. Lebanese will not eat salty or lemony foods, and Bulgarians eat only sweet-and-sour foods.

Some East European Jews—those from the Ukraine—will not serve cucumbers, pickles, horseradish, or even walnuts or almonds. The sourness of the first three is obvious, but the reason the nuts are avoided is less so. The total numerical value of the letters of the Hebrew word for walnut, *egoz*, is seventeen, equivalent to the numerical value of the Hebrew word for sin, *het*. Almonds might be avoided because, historically, the almond branch of Aaron's rod included sweet almonds on one side and bitter on the other. As long as Israel walked in the ways of the Lord, sweet almonds were fresh (moist); but when they departed from the right path, the bitter ones ripened. Thus, at the day of judgment the superstitious would avoid all nuts. (In addition, nuts and almonds stimulate an increased flow of saliva, which interferes with the recital of prayers.)

Because of the original harvest-festival character of Rosh Hashanah, it is natural that, for the ancients, the symbolic foods would be chosen from those fruits and vegetables abundant at that time of year.

Rosh Hashanah, Greek style (photo: Edward Fitzgerald)

Both Sephardic and Ashkenazic Jews say a blessing over an apple dipped in honey. "May it be Thy will to renew unto us a good and sweet year." On the second night, another new fruit (a pomegranate when available) evokes, the blessing: "In the coming year may we be rich and replete with acts inspired by religion and piety as this pomegranate is rich and replete with seeds." Either a new fruit of the season is eaten or a new garment is worn on the second night at the *kiddush*, because new fruits and garments rate the Sheheheyanu prayer, the blessing for new experiences.

In addition to the above fruits, Sephardic Jews say blessings over other seasonal foods. Pumpkins, fenugreek, leeks, onions, beets, turnips, gourds, quinces, and zucchini all grow rapidly in the early fall and are considered symbolic of fertility, abundance, and prosperity.

Moroccan Jews dip a date in anise seeds, sesame seeds, and powdered sugar. "As we eat this date, may we date the new year that is beginning as one of happiness and blessing and peace for all mankind."

Most important is the cooked head of a fish or lamb. The head expresses the hope that the New Year will see the Jewish nation redeemed and at the head of the nations of the world, rather than at the tail as small, downtrodden people.

After these symbolic foods are blessed, the meal begins with the blessing over the wine and the round hallah for a full year. The foods selected for the meal are usually colorful and sweet. Carrots, prunes, honey, apples, and sweet potatoes are all present. The carrots, prunes, honey, and apples in the recipes that follow are all seasonal reminders of the hope for a good New Year.

MENUS

German
Berches★
Chicken Soup with Nockerln★
Sweet-and-Sour Carp★
Roast Goose★
Carrots
Cucumber Salad★
Potato Salad★
Plum Pie★
Apple Streusel★

Russian
Four-Hundred-Year-Old Hallah★
Gefilte Fish★
Chicken Soup with Matzah Balls★
Roast Beef or Turkey with Stuffing★
Sweet Pineapple Kugel★
Carrot Kugel★
Green Beans
Baked Apples
Honey Cake★

Mixed Sephardic
Round White Bread
Rodanchos★
Egg Lemon Soup★
Grilled Fish
Stuffed Zucchini with Apricots★
Meat Sambusak★
Green Salad
Fresh Fruit: Grapes, Apples, Plums
Almond Macaroons★

Moroccan
Pain Petri★
Seven Vegetables
Baked White Fish★
Dates Dipped in Anise and Sesame Seeds and Sugar
Apple Dipped in Honey
Lamb Tagine with Prunes and Almonds★
Green Pepper and Tomato Salad★
Carrot Salad★
Meat Pastels★
Fresh Fruit
Cigares★

FOUR-HUNDRED-YEAR-OLD HALLAH

One of the most symbolic foods at Rosh Hashanah has become the round hallah, symbol of life. This bread recalls the image of prayer rising heavenward. Usually the bread is formed in a circle, to signify the desire for a long span of life. But here local traditions take over. Some people insert saffron and raisins to make the bread just a little bit more special than a typical Friday night loaf.

In certain towns of Russia, the round hallah is imprinted with the shape of a ladder on the top. This ladder symbolizes the ascent to God on high. The Midrash states that on Rosh Hashanah, the "Holy One, blessed be He, sits and erects ladders; on them He lowers one person and elevates another...that is to say, God judges those who will descend and those who will ascend."

In the Ukraine, bread for the holidays is baked in the form of a bird. This is a tender image for God's protection of His people, as stated in Isaiah 31:5: "As birds hovering [over their fledglings], so will the Lord of hosts protect Jerusalem." Jews from Lithuania bake hallahs topped with a crown, in accordance with the words of Eleazar Kalir: "And thus let all crown God."

Most typical and easiest to prepare, however, is the sweet round hallah. It can be braided as a long hallah and then twisted into a circle; the dough can be divided into a braided circle topped by a smaller circle, or twisted spiral fashion into a circle with the top of the spiral on top, symbolically ascending to heaven.

This particular recipe comes from Mark Talisman, director of the Washington Action Office of the Council of Jewish Federations and one of our capital's finest cooks. He learned how to make this hallah from Russian-born Esther Becker of Cleveland. Several years ago when Talisman was Administrative Assistant to Ohio Congressman Charles Vanik, he helped Mrs. Becker solve a difficult problem. One day this elderly lady with long braided hair came to see Talisman when he was visiting his family in Cleveland. Like every Jewish mother since antiquity, she came bearing a gift—this time a huge, expertly braided hallah—and asked what she could do to repay him for helping her. "Teach me to make your bread," said Talisman. Now, a woman like Esther Becker "feels" her ingredients rather than measuring them, so Talisman devised a fail-safe system to record the recipe. He placed soft plastic lids over the mixing bowls to rescue and measure the proportions before Mrs. Becker could add each new ingredient.

Talisman has varied the recipe slightly by using a food processor and hard wheat flour. This hallah was made on Friday mornings in Mrs. Becker's family in Russia and has been handed down by word of mouth for generations. From it, two hallahs are made each week, plus three loaves of white sandwich bread and one breakfast raisin bread. The Talismans have continued the Becker tradition and, needless to say, never purchase white bread.

Before eating the round hallah this Rosh Hashanah, don't forget the blessing over the bread, and, instead of dipping it into salt as is done on Friday nights, dip it, for the Days of Awe, in honey. Then say the blessing over a honey-dipped slice of apple: "May it be Thy will to renew unto us a good and sweet year."

3 tablespoons or 3 packages dry yeast	6 extra-large eggs
2 cups very warm (not lukewarm) water	1 cup vegetable oil
Pinch of sugar	½ cup cinnamon and sugar mixture (optional)
15 cups all-purpose flour	1¼ cups raisins (optional)
1½–2 tablespoons salt	Sesame seeds
1 cup honey	Egg and water for glazing

1. In a large glass container, proof the yeast in the water. (It is important that the water not be lukewarm, especially in winter.) Add a pinch of sugar. Stir with a plastic or wooden spoon to mix the yeast. Wait about 5 minutes until the yeast has a head on it, like beer.

2. Place the flour and salt on a floured flat surface and make a well in the center. Using a wooden or plastic spoon, put the yeast mixture in the well and begin to stir flour from the inner edge of the well into it.

3. Add the honey to the well and stir in more flour from the edge of the well. Then, breaking the eggs one by one, stir each into the well. Blend the oil into the yeast mixture in the well. Blend the remaining flour with the ingredients in the well. The dough should be sticky. If it is not, add more water.

4. Either knead by hand for about 10–15 minutes, until the dough is smooth and shiny, or divide the dough into 6 parts and run each part in the food processor, using the steel blade. When the dough forms a ball, it is done. If it is too sticky, add a little flour to the mixture in the food processor; if it is too dry, add a little water. Finished dough should be tacky to touch.

5. Place the dough in a lightly greased bowl. (Use margarine for greasing in winter.)

6. Heat the oven to 140°. Turn the oven off and let the dough rise in it until doubled in bulk. This should take 45–60 minutes.

7. Take 3 of the balls, knead well, shape in oblong balls, and place in greased loaf pans.

8. If desired, you can roll out the fourth roll into a rectangle, sprinkle with cinnamon and sugar, and spread a cup of raisins over it. Roll, starting at the shorter side, jelly-roll fashion and press the dough together into an oblong form. Place in a fourth loaf pan.

9. With the remaining 2 loaves (or all 6 if you prefer), make your Friday night or Rosh Hashanah hallah. Work the remaining ¼ cup raisins into the dough at this point, if desired. Divide each ball into 4 pieces. Make a ball of each piece. Then pat the ball down very hard with your hand. Roll jelly-roll fashion once, press down, and roll again. Then, with your hands, roll out to make a snake about 12″ long. Repeat with all the remaining balls.

10. Place 4 rolls side by side. Press the top ends together and start braiding. Taking the outside braid, place it over the nearest one and then under the next. Then, before braiding the opposite outside rope, pull the braids tight. This is important, because it makes the braids higher during baking, and thus gives a lighter, higher loaf. Continue braiding, and tuck in the ends.

11. For Rosh Hashanah and the first Saturday of each month, gently work the braids into a circle and pinch the ends together. If you want a spiral effect, see the Pain Petri on p. 68.

12. Brush the hallah with egg mixed with water and sprinkle with sesame seeds. Place on a greased cookie sheet. If you prefer, the round hallah may be put in an 8–9″ circular baking pan.

13. Cover all the loaves and let rise again, about 1 hour (or less), until the loaves come above the top of the loaf pans.

14. Preheat oven to 375°.

15. Glaze the hallah with egg mixed with water. Bake in the oven for 30 minutes or until golden. Wrapped tightly, this bread will last through the week—until you run out and it is time to start baking all over again.

Makes 6 loaves. (P)

Note: If you would like to make a saffron hallah for Rosh Hashanah, add ⅛ teaspoon of powdered saffron at the end of Step 1.

PAIN PETRI
(Moroccan Hallah)

In Morocco, as in most Middle Eastern countries, bread for centuries has been bought daily from special bakeries rather than made at home. On the Sabbath and special holidays, however, Jews knead their own sweet bread. With the French colonization of Morocco at the beginning of the twentieth century came an overwhelming desire on the part of Moroccan Jews to adopt everything French—their speech, manners, and cuisine. Today, recipes for Jewish holidays include French, rather than Spanish, names. Moroccan hallah was once called "pan de casa," or " bread of the house," in Hakitia, a mixture of Spanish, Hebrew, and Arabic. In French, the Sabbath bread is called "pain petri," or "kneaded bread," since the women spend a great deal of time kneading it to achieve its perfect smooth, light texture. For the Sabbath and Rosh Hashanah, it is filled with sesame and anise seeds. For Yom Kippur, raisins and blanched almonds are also added. The bread is often braided in intricate, delicate designs for the Sabbath; it is usually a circle, formed in a spiral ascending to heaven, for Rosh Hashanah.

3 pounds (12 cups) unbleached flour	1 teaspoon salt
½ cup sugar	1 tablespoon sesame seeds
3 eggs plus 1 yolk	1 tablespoon anise seeds
½ cup vegetable oil	2 packages fresh yeast
	3 cups warm water

1. Place the flour in a huge bowl. Make a well in the center and add to the well sugar, 3 eggs, vegetable oil, salt, and sesame and anise seeds. Proof the yeast in 1 cup of the warm water. Then add it to the well.

2. Using your hands, gradually work in the flour with the ingredients in the well. Add more water as needed (about 2 cups.) When a medium dough is formed, knead on a wooden board for about 20 minutes.

3. Form the dough into a ball, turn it in a greased bowl to coat the surface, and cover with a towel. Let rise in a warm place for 30–40 minutes or until doubled in bulk. Punch down and knead once more. Divide the dough into 5 pieces. Either shape each into a round ball, or make a long piece of it and twist it into a spiral with the end of the dough at the high point in the center. Cover for about 1 hour and let rise until doubled.

4. Preheat oven to 400°. Cover a cookie sheet with aluminum foil.

5. Remove the dough to the cookie sheet; brush with the remaining egg yolk and a tablespoon of oil and bake for 35 to 45 minutes.

Makes 5 loaves. (P)

BAKED WHITE FISH
(Pescado Blanco)

On Rosh Hashanah, as on Friday nights, fish is served to start the festive meal. Fish represents immortality, fertility, and the special relationship between the Jewish people and the Torah. In Genesis, for example, God blesses both man and fish. There is such a close connection between Jews and the fish in the water that after the afternoon services on the first day of Rosh Hashanah it is customary to perform the Tashlih (throwing-away) ritual near a body of flowing water, preferably containing fish. Observant Jews go to a river or seashore abounding in fish because "man is likened to a fish who may be caught in the net of trouble if he fails to watch his conduct." One custom there is for the religious to throw breadcrumbs from their pockets into the water, symbolically throwing off their sins, to be carried away by the stream. This act, based on an ancient one of throwing bread to the spirits in the water, became popular in Judaism in fourteenth-century Germany. The ceremony is supposed to recall the sacrifice of Isaac by Jacob.

All Jews have their traditional fish recipes. Moroccans serve a whole white baked fish with the head attached. The head is often served first to the head of the table, and the fish is mentioned in the special blessing prior to the commencement of the meal. German Jews eat sweet-and-sour carp or salmon. And of course there is the East European gefilte fish.

1 5-pound whole white fish, trout, or rockfish, gutted and split down the center	4 medium tomatoes, sliced in rings
1 cup chopped fresh parsley	½ green pepper, sliced in rings
1 entire head of garlic, minced	3 lemons, sliced in rings
	½ teaspoon threadlike saffron
	½ cup vegetable oil

1. Place the entire fish in a glass or earthenware baking dish.

2. Stuff the fish with most of the parsley and garlic. Surround the fish with the remaining parsley and garlic, the tomatoes, green pepper, and lemons.

3. Dissolve the saffron in about ¼ cup boiling water and let it sit for a few minutes. Then sprinkle the saffron water over the fish and tomatoes.

4. Preheat oven to 350°.

5. Pour the oil around the fish and tomatoes. Bake uncovered for ½ hour, or until golden and crisp.

Serves 8–10 as a first course. (P)

GEFILTE FISHBALLS

In assimilated America, the prosaic gefilte fish is sometimes disguised. One Jewish resort in Lakewood, New Jersey, dubs it "fresh stuffed deepwater fish en glace." Cracow's renowned Wierzynek Restaurant features on its elegant menu "carp Jewish-style" for its American visitors. A Brookline, Massachusetts, French restaurant serves "poisson farci en glace." Some hostesses change the name to "chilled fishballs."

Delle Sacks of Belmont, Massachusetts, calls her family recipe "gefilte fishballs." She learned how to make gefilte fish from her Austro-Hungarian mother in the Bronx. Besides serving it at family gatherings and on holidays, Delle often uses this hors d'oeuvre at parties she and her husband, Albert Sacks, Dean of the Harvard Law School, give for faculty and students.

1 4–5-pound haddock (fillets, cut and ground), plus the head, skin, and bones—if only smaller fish are available, you can add 1–2 more fillets	6–7 large carrots
	5 tablespoons sugar
	4 teaspoons salt
	Freshly ground pepper to taste
	1 small onion, grated
2 quarts plus ½ cup water	1 egg
1–2 large onions, peeled	2 tablespoons matzah meal or cracker crumbs
Several sprigs parsley	

1. Put the bones, skin, and head of the haddock in a large soup pot. Cover with water to about 2″ over the bones (about 2 quarts). Add the peeled onions and parsley. Cut the carrots on a slant and add them to the pot. Bring to a boil. Add 4 tablespoons of the sugar, 3 teaspoons of the salt, and pepper to taste. Remove scum and simmer.

2. Meanwhile, grind the fillets and place in a bowl. Add the grated onion, egg, matzah meal, 1 teaspoon salt, pepper, 1 tablespoon sugar, and ½ cup water. Mix well.

3. Dip your hands in cold water and form balls 1½″ in diameter (tinier if you want them for appetizers). Drop the balls in the simmering soup and bring to the boil again. Then simmer covered for 1 hour.

4. Remove the balls carefully and extricate the carrots. Pour the liquid stock through a strainer and chill. The bones can be discarded.

Makes about 20 fishballs 1½″ in diameter. (P)

For an hors d'oeuvre, serve the tiny fishballs with a toothpick on a round of carrot, using horseradish as a dip. As a first course or summer luncheon dish, serve with carrots, some fish stock, a sprig of parsley, horseradish, and hallah.

SWEET-AND-SOUR CARP

My father's family, of German-Jewish heritage, has its own symbolic foods for this festival, many of which have been with our ancestral family in Bavaria for centuries. His family served such dishes as sweet-and-sour carp, chicken soup with nockerln (egg drops), and for dessert zwetschgenkuchen (plum cake) and apple strudel, streusel, or kuchen.

In Germany the main course would have been roast goose with cabbage salad, potatoes, and carrots. From this first very young goose of the season, my grandmother would begin saving the schmaltz for cooking oil until Passover.

To authenticate the dishes handed down from Bavaria, I was fortunate to find the well-worn book of favorite recipes my grandmother Lina Bernheim Nathan compiled as a young bride almost a hundred years ago. The following sweet-and-sour carp and nockerln are the first dishes my father recalls relishing. His grandmother Rose Bernheim served them each and every Friday night and on Rosh Hashanah.

1	3½-pound carp, pike, trout, or salmon		1	medium onion, sliced in rings
Salt			1	bay leaf
4	cups water, or enough to cover fish		1	teaspoon whole peppercorns
			½	cup raisins
½	cup red wine vinegar		1	tablespoon salt
1	lemon, sliced and seeded		5	whole cloves
			½	cup brown sugar
			4–5	gingersnaps or lebkuchen

1. Clean, slice, and salt the whole fish, cutting through the bone. Let stand several hours or overnight. (My grandmother preferred using winter or chicken carp, which is a rich or fatter oily fish, with lighter meat, to summer carp for this dish; she always included the head and bones for stock, as they add taste to the sauce.)

2. Boil together the water, vinegar, lemon, onion, bay leaf, peppercorns, raisins, salt, and cloves. Add the fish to the liquid and let simmer uncovered for 10 minutes.

3. Add brown sugar and gingersnaps (the gingersnaps add color to the sauce).

4. Simmer 10–15 minutes more, until the fish is done. The fish should be light and firm to the touch, and the flesh should leave the bones easily.

5. Remove the fish from liquid, skin, and separate the meat from the bones. Arrange on a platter.

6. Boil the liquid 15 minutes longer and let cool. Then strain, removing the onions and raisins from the strainer. Pour the liquid over the fish and garnish with the raisins and onion rings. Refrigerate until the sauce jells. Serve as an appetizer the following day.

Serves 6. (P)

NOCKERLN (EGG DROPS) FOR CHICKEN SOUP

2 tablespoons melted chicken fat or *pareve* margarine	7–8 tablespoons flour Salt to taste
4 eggs	

1. Let melted chicken fat or margarine cool a bit and add eggs, one at a time, beating after each addition.

2. Add the flour slowly while continually beating with a whisk or spoon. Add salt to taste.

3. Drop the nockerln into boiling soup (see recipe, p. 32) by placing a small amount on the tip of a teaspoon, putting the spoon in the soup, and leaving it in for a moment.

4. Boil for 10 minutes and serve.

Makes enough for 2 quarts of soup. (F or P)

TOMATO VEGETABLE SOUP

In 1937 a group of Chicago Jewish housewives decided to write and publish a cookbook to benefit the Jewish Community Center of Chicago. All board members of the Women's Auxiliary of the Center, they thought this would be a preferable way of collecting funds than by direct solicitation. How right they were! The non-kosher book, entitled *Thoughts for Food*, would include the women's best recipes for entertaining. To avoid favoritism, the authors' names would remain anonymous. Forty-one years later, the now famous *Thoughts for Food* series, including *Thoughts for Buffets*, *Thoughts for Festive Foods*, and *Thoughts for Good Entertaining*, has sold over one quarter of a million copies. To this day, very few people know who the authors are and who receives the benefits.

Elaine Frank of Winetka, Illinois, is one of the founding authors of the series. A well-known hostess, she has shared with me her Tomato Vegetable Soup, which appears in *Thoughts for Buffets* and which she serves her family each year on the eve of Rosh Hashanah.

1 beef soup bone with meat, or 1 veal knucklebone	1½ cups diced carrots
5 cups water	2 potatoes, diced (optional)
¼ cup parsley, chopped	3 cups tomatoes, solid pack
1½ cups celery, cut into pieces	2 teaspoons salt
1½ cups sliced onion	½ teaspoon pepper

1. Simmer the soup bone in the water for about 2 hours, covered, over a low flame.

2. Add the parsley, celery, onion, carrots, potatoes, tomatoes, salt, and pepper.

3. Simmer, covered, another hour, or until the vegetables are cooked. Adjust the seasonings.

Serves 6. (F)

RODANCHOS
(Pumpkin Strudel)

Although most Sephardic Jews say the same blessings over dates, pomegranates, gourds, leeks, apple dipped in honey, and the head of a fish or lamb before the commencement of the Rosh Hashanah meal, their manner of preparing these foods differs. For example, Greek symbolic foods include pumpkin in strudel dough and kioftes de prasses (leek patties). The pumpkin strudel recipe follows; a *milchig* variation of the leek patties can be found on p. 194.

1	16-ounce can pumpkin (not pumpkin filling for pies)	½	tablespoon cinnamon
		½	cup vegetable oil
5–6 tablespoons sugar		16	sheets fillo dough

1. Preheat oven to 350°. Grease a cookie sheet.

2. In a saucepan combine the pumpkin, sugar, cinnamon, and 1 tablespoon of the oil. Stirring constantly, heat over a low flame until all liquid evaporates. Then set aside.

3. Taking one sheet of fillo at a time while keeping the rest covered, fold the sheet in half. Brush with oil. Then place 2 tablespoons of the filling along the long side. Close the fillo, rolling jelly-roll fashion.

4. Being very careful, twist the long roll and then roll it up like a snail, with the outside end tucked under. Brush with oil and place on the cookie sheet.

5. Continue until all the filling is used up.

6. Bake in the oven 20–25 minutes, until golden brown. If, at the end of the time, the rodanchos are not yet golden, raise the oven to 375° for a few minutes.

Makes 16. (P)

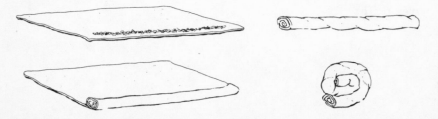

Pumpkin strudel (rodanchos) (drawing: Debbie Insetta)

HONEY ORANGE CHICKEN

Everyone has a favorite holiday chicken recipe. This one, with a happy combination of honey, orange, and fresh ginger, is mine—a perfect beginning for a sweet New Year.

2 eggs	½ cup vegetable oil
2 teaspoons water	1 cup hot water
1 cup breadcrumbs or matzah meal	¼ cup honey
1 teaspoon salt	1 cup orange juice
⅛ teaspoon pepper	2 tablespoons grated fresh ginger
2 3-pound fryers, cut up	or ¾ teaspoon ground ginger, or to taste

1. Beat the eggs with 2 teaspoons of water.

2. In another bowl, mix the breadcrumbs with the salt and pepper.

3. Dip the chicken in the egg mixture and then in the breadcrumbs.

4. Heat the oil in a heavy skillet and brown the chicken on all sides.

5. Preheat oven to 325°.

6. Combine 1 cup hot water with the honey and orange juice. Place the chicken in a casserole and cover with the honey mixture. Add the ginger.

7. Cover and simmer in the oven for 45 minutes, basting occasionally. Serve with rice and a tossed green salad.

Serves 6–8. (F)

COUSCOUS

It is traditional for North African Jews to eat couscous at noon after the morning service of Rosh Hashanah. Couscous is one of the world's famous long-simmering stews. Some of the same legumes blessed in the evening service the night before are included in the couscous itself, as well as in the accompanying sweet vegetable dish. They include carrots, leeks, onions, zucchini, pumpkin, and turnips. The following couscous, unlike that of Algeria, is a sweet stew, perfect for a sweet New Year.

Chick-peas, another traditional vegetable at Rosh Hashanah, are included in the couscous. It was thought that the moonlight caused these beans to grow, and the moon is associated with the flow of water and hence with "merit and favor." *Kara*, the Hebrew word for chick-peas, implies that they are cold (*kar*) on the inside. Therefore, chick-peas are taken to symbolize the cooling down of God's stern judgment. East European Jews also eat chick-peas at Rosh Hashanah, but rather alone, sprinkled with salt and pepper, as on p. 157.

The following couscous recipe and the sweet vegetable dish on p. 80 are those of Ginette Spier, a Moroccan kosher cooking teacher in Chevy Chase, Maryland. Her recipes are from her home in Fez, culinary capital of Morocco.

Read this recipe through carefully before beginning. Use your imagination with the vegetables.

⅓ cup dried chick-peas
1 pound carrots, peeled and halved
1 small cabbage, cored and quartered
1 pound leeks, cleaned and sliced lengthwise in medium pieces
3 large onions, quartered
2 white round turnips, quartered
1 large green pepper, sliced lengthwise with seeds removed (optional)
3 pounds top rib, flanken, breast deckel, or chuck
Meat bones
4 quarts water, or to cover
Salt and pepper to taste

½ teaspoon turmeric (optional)
¼ teaspoon ginger (optional)
½ teaspoon saffron (if using thread type, soak in ½ cup boiling water for 5 minutes and pour in)
4 tomatoes, quartered and peeled (optional)
3 medium zucchini, sliced in thick pieces
1–1½ pounds acorn squash or pumpkin, sliced in 2" pieces
1 pound couscous (never steam more than this at once)
2 cups water with 2 teaspoons salt
¼ cup *pareve* margarine, melted

1. Soak the chick-peas overnight in enough water to cover.

2. Using the bottom part of a large couscoussier (a deep soup kettle) or your own improvisation, put in the soaked chick-peas, carrots, cabbage, leeks, onions, turnips, green pepper, meat, meat bones, salt and pepper to taste, turmeric, ginger, and saffron. Cover with water. Bring to a boil and simmer, covered, for about 2 hours, or until meat is tender.

3. Remove the vegetables and meat to a warm plate.

4. Keep the stock in the bottom part of the couscoussier and add the tomatoes, zucchini, and squash or pumpkin. Let boil and cover with the sieve part of the couscoussier or a sieve. (To retain the steam, tie a cloth or towel between the 2 parts.) Add the couscous. When the steam comes through the couscous, lower the heat, always keeping the stock boiling. Using your hands, continue to stir the couscous for 15–20 minutes, separating the lumps or grains with your hands.

5. Turn off heat and remove the couscous to a deep dish. Sprinkle with some of the salt water and let set until absorbed. Repeat the sprinkling process once or twice. Cover.

6. One half-hour before serving, return all vegetables and meat to the stock and let boil again. Return the couscous to the top half of the steamer and let steam for 10–15 minutes.

7. To serve, use a large dish. In the center, place the sliced meat and the vegetables. Surround with the couscous, which has been moistened with ¼ cup melted margarine. Sprinkle lightly with some stock, and serve the rest of the stock in a gravy bowl.

Serves 10–12. (F)

This can be served as is or with the sweet-potato vegetable dish on p. 80. All beef, all lamb, all chicken, or a combination thereof can be used in this recipe. The same goes with the vegetables listed. Cumin is a common Moroccan spice. A dish of harissa, or hot sauce, can also be included, as well as blanched and sautéed almonds. The couscous can be served in the meat dish or separately, piled like a pyramid and garnished with toasted almonds and raisins.

Algerian couscous would include kofta, or meatballs with green peppers and tomatoes imbedded in the meat and then fried, as in the recipe in *The Flavor of Jerusalem*. The broth would be served separately. The couscous would be hotter, with several spicy salads. This version from Fez is lighter and more delicate.

LAMB TAGINE WITH PRUNES AND ALMONDS

In France and Jerusalem, bitter pickled olives were distributed to the worshippers as they departed from the synagogue on the first night of Rosh Hashanah. This was a reminder to have faith in God, as asserted in the Talmud: "Let my sustenance be as bitter as the olive in the divine charge, rather than sweet as honey in the charge of flesh and blood."

Mercedes Bensimon, formerly of Casablanca, symbolically serves tongue with green (never black) olives for the first night of Rosh Hashanah, because, like most Moroccans, she is superstitious. On the second night she prepares a lamb tagine, or stew, with prunes and almonds. Although the prunes are black, they are sweet, so she can prepare this dish for the second—but never the first—night. Lamb is served to symbolize the ram of Isaac. Moroccan Jews do not avoid nuts at Rosh Hashanah, as is seen from this delicious recipe.

2 pounds onions, chopped	4 pounds lamb, cubed
½ cup plus 2 tablespoons vegetable oil	2 pounds dried prunes, which have been soaked in water
3½ cups water	1 hour
2 tablespoons honey	½ pound (1 cup) blanched almonds
1 teaspoon cinnamon	
2 tablespoons sugar	

1. Cook the onions in ½ cup of oil, stirring occasionally, until they are tender, limp, and almost black (about 1 hour). Combine with the honey, cinnamon, and sugar. Set aside.

2. Using the additional 2 tablespoons of oil, sauté the lamb until golden. Then add ½ cup water, cover, and simmer over a very low flame for 1½ hours, stirring occasionally, until the meat is very tender. Each time you stir, you may need more water, as much as 3 additional cups.

3. Add the onions and the soaked prunes to the meat. Simmer, covered, 20 minutes more.

4. Toast the almonds. Just before serving, sprinkle them over the meat. Serve with rice.

Serves 8–10. (F)

STUFFED ZUCCHINI WITH APRICOTS

As the apple [apricot] tree among the trees of the wood,
So is my beloved among the sons.
Under its shadow I delighted to sit,
And its fruit was sweet to my taste.

Song of Songs 2:3

It is said that in King Solomon's palace there was a room painted with murals showing apricot trees in full bloom. Their fruit was so golden and lifelike that guests could smell their sweet aroma as soon as they entered. Known as "golden apples," apricots were first brought to the Middle East from Armenia at the time of Noah.

Today, in Lebanon and Syria, apricots are still a living treasure, not nearly as expensive as they are in this country. It is only natural, then, for Jews in these countries to celebrate the New Year with apricots in their symbolic dishes. The following zucchini, stuffed with meat and rice and cooked in dried apricots, is a sweet seasonal start to the New Year, both in the Middle East and in the United States, with our often bumper crop of zucchini.

1 cup or about 30 dried apricots, soaked in water overnight	Salt and pepper to taste
	½ teaspoon cinnamon (optional)
6–8 medium zucchini	2 tablespoon pine nuts (optional)
1 cup rice	
1 pound ground meat	Juice of 1 lemon, or to taste

1. Using an apple corer, scoop out the pulp from the zucchini, making sure to keep the outer skin intact and to leave one end closed. Reserve the pulp for another use.

2. Combine the rice, meat, salt and pepper to taste, cinnamon, and pine nuts. Blend well.

3. Stuff the zucchini ¾ full.

4. Open each apricot and place face down in a heavy casserole. Cover with the stuffed zucchini and top with the remaining apricots.

5. Pour 1 cup of the reserved water from the apricots over the zucchini. Cover and simmer over a low heat for 1½–2 hours, until the zucchini are tender. If needed, add more of the reserved apricot water.

Serves 6–8. (F)

SWEET POTATOES AND VEGETABLES

4 large onions, sliced thickly	1–2 sweet potatoes or yams
2 tablespoons oil	¼–⅓ cup dried raisins
⅓ cup dried chick-peas, which have been soaked overnight	¼ cup sugar
1 pound acorn squash, pumpkin, or carrots	2 teaspoons cinnamon

1. Preheat oven to 400°. Prepare the following while the meat and vegetables for the couscous are cooking.

2. Sauté the onions in the oil until golden.

3. Place the chick-peas and onions in the bottom of a greased oblong casserole. Cover with the remaining vegetables. Sprinkle with the sugar and cinnamon, and add a little oil if desired.

4. Bake for 25 minutes or until well browned. Serve with the basic couscous or a simple roast.

Serves 10–12. (P)

FESENJAN
(Pomegranate Walnut Chicken)

Thy lips are like a thread of scarlet,
And thy mouth is comely.

Song of Songs 4:3

Thy temples are like a pomegranate split open
Behind thy veil.

Song of Songs 6:7

The pomegranate (literally: apple with seeds) is one of the oldest and most beloved fruits known to mankind. Israelite secret agents brought these fruits, alongs with grapes and figs, from the "land of milk and honey" to the Jews wandering in the desert.

From antiquity the pomegranate has been a widely cultivated fruit throughout the countries of the Middle East. Since the time of King Solomon, the pulp of the pomegranate has been not only eaten raw, but squeezed to make fresh and cooling summer drinks. The large number of seeds found in each fruit and its bright red color make it a sign of fertility, especially at the time of Rosh Hashanah. In Israel today, Yemenite Jews will have an entire centerpiece of pomegranates at the New Year. My mother-in-law remembers the rare pomegranates in prewar Poland, which voyagers brought from the Middle East. At the New Year they were almost as precious as the etrog.

In Iran, today, Jews and non-Jews alike use pomegranates in their cooking. By halving the pomegranate and placing the cut side in the cup of your hand and smacking the round body with a knife, the seeds will fall into the cup. They can be used in fruit or vegetable salads or sprinkled on the top of dips for coloring and taste! Persian Jews even use pomegranate seeds in haroset at Passover.

One of the prize Iranian dishes is fesenjan, the ancient khoresh or stew made from meat, pomegranates, and walnuts. This delicacy can be made from duck, partridge, chicken, lamb, or veal hind shin, shoulder, or ground meat. It is expensive in this country because of the high price of imported pomegranate juice; it is costly in Iran because of the expense of imported walnuts. A treat reserved for all festival dinners, fesenjan is especially appropriate for Iranian Jews and Jews throughout the world to eat at Rosh Hashanah, when the prayer is said: "In the coming year may we be rich and replete with acts inspired by religion and piety as the pomegranate is rich and replete with seeds."

1 3½-pound chicken	2 cups pomegranate juice or
2 tablespoons vegetable oil	½ cup pomegranate syrup
1 medium onion, chopped	1 tablespoon tomato paste
2 cups ground walnuts	Salt and freshly ground
⅓ cup hot water	pepper to taste
2 tablespoons lemon juice	2 tablespoons sugar

1. Brown the chicken in the vegetable oil and remove to drain on a paper towel.

2. Brown the chopped onion in the same oil.

3. In another pan, brown the walnuts, stirring constantly, without using any shortening. When brown, add the onion. Then slowly add the hot water so that the mixture does not stick. It should not be too liquid—more like a paste. Then add the lemon juice, pomeganate juice, tomato paste, salt, pepper, and sugar, stirring with a spoon. When well mixed, add the chicken.

4. Bring the mixture just to the point of boiling (not a hard boil). Decrease to a simmer and let cook, covered, until the chicken is very tender (about 45 minutes). If the sauce is not thick enough, remove the chicken and boil the liquid down until the desired thickness is reached, stirring as it cooks. When ready to serve, place the chicken on a dish, pour the sauce over, and serve with a chelou.

Serves 4–6. (F)

CHELOU
(Crunchy Persian Rice)

Rice came to the Middle East from the Orient. To Iranian Jews more than any others, a meal is not a meal without some sort of chelou or polou or pilaf. It is not surprising that Americans halve the amount of rice that a Persian calls for in his dish.

Chelou is a simply cooked, oiled rice which is baked in the oven or on top of the stove in such a way as to form a crunchy crust in the bottom of the pan. Chelou is always served with meat dishes having a thick sauce, called khoreshes. A pilaf, on the other hand, consists of cooked, drained rice mixed with a vegetable, fruit, fowl, meat, or nuts. Oil or butter is used to coat the rice; saffron, chopped almonds, pistachios, or spices are the usual flavoring.

Fesenjan is traditionally served with a chelou. This particular recipe, served at Rosh Hashanah, comes from Mohtaran Shirazi, originally from Teheran. When she made the chelou for me, she prepared a khoresh of dried herbs—such as parsley, the greens of leeks, mint, etc.—which were simmered with a small amount of meat and a dried lime. These dried herbs and limes took me back to the time of the ancient Israelites who, with few foods available to them year round, saved every bit they did not eat. Instead of discarding the greens of their leeks and the unused limes, they collected them and dried them in the sun for several days. The dried herbs and fragrant limes provided a base for sauces when fresh foods were not in season.

The difference between Iranian chelou and our rice is that each grain of rice in the chelou comes out feathery, fluffy, and separate. It is essential to cook the rice in a great deal of water. As a general rule, one pound of rice should be covered with hot water to a depth of 8″–10″. Try the following chelou recipe this Rosh Hashanah with the fesenjan or any of the other chicken or stew dishes in this book.

1 pound long-grain rice	½ teaspoon turmeric
3 tablespoons salt	2 potatoes, peeled and sliced
6 tablespoons vegetable oil	about ¼″ thick
¼ cup hot water	

1. Fill a 4-quart saucepan with water and bring to a boil. Add the rice and salt. Boil, uncovered, for 7–10 minutes over high heat. Stir the water occasionally, being careful not to break the rice grains. Taste the rice to see that it is done. Remove immediately and drain in lukewarm water to remove excess starch.

2. Heat a heavy-bottomed saucepan with 4 tablespoons cooking oil mixed with almost ¼ cup hot water. Add the turmeric. Then place the potatoes on the bottom of the saucepan. Pour the rice into the pan; cover with a cloth and a lid. Let simmer over a low flame for about 10 minutes.

3. Mound up the rice in the center of the pan and make a deep hole in the center of the mound. (This hole allows the rice to steam.) Sprinkle about 2 more tablespoons of oil with the remaining hot water all around the rice. Cover and simmer for about 20 more minutes.

4. When ready to serve, uncover the pan and stir the rice gently with a spatula to make it fluffy. Turn the rice out onto a warm serving dish in a mound. Then remove the crust and potatoes from the bottom of the pan and serve separately, or heap the potatoes on the rice on the serving platter.

Serves 3 Iranians or 6–8 Americans. (P)

GERMAN POTATO SALAD

Potatoes have become such an integral part of Jewish cuisine that we forget what a gastronomic newcomer this root vegetable is. Brought to Europe from South America in the sixteenth century, potatoes were introduced into Prussia by Frederick the Great. In 1774 he distributed free seed potatoes to reluctant peasants and ordered the planting of the vegetable to help relieve a famine. Little by little, people began to eat the potato.

My father cannot remember a major meal without potatoes from his youth in Germany. There was potato bread, potato pancakes, potato soup, potato dumplings, roasted, boiled, and fried potatoes, as well as hot and cold potato salad. This is my aunt Lisl's Bavarian cold potato salad, which was always (and still is) a part of the Rosh Hashanah meal.

3	pounds potatoes	½	teaspoon sugar
⅓	cup vegetable oil	1½	tablespoons red wine vinegar
½	cup water	½	medium onion, finely sliced
1	*pareve* bouillon cube		Hard-boiled eggs (optional)
1	teaspoon salt		Mayonnaise (optional)
½	teaspoon black pepper		Parsley (optional)
½	teaspoon garlic powder		Chives (optional)

1. Steam the potatoes in a small amount of water for about 45 minutes. While hot, peel and slice them.

2. Pour oil over them and mix well. Let stand for about 10 minutes.

3. In a small saucepan, bring to a boil the water, bouillon cube, salt, pepper, garlic powder, sugar, and vinegar. Pour the hot liquid over the salad, and add the onion.

4. Mix well, add optional ingredients if desired, and let stand. Serve at room temperature.

Serves 10–12. (P)

Variation: To make an Italian salad, add 4 ounces cut-up party-snack herring in wine sauce; 8 ounces canned cubed red beets; ½ medium apple, sliced; some mayonnaise; and, if you like, some walnuts to the above potato salad.

CARROTS

Today carrots are probably, with apples and honey, the most symbolic food served at Rosh Hashanah. Since carrots were one of the few sweet-tasting vegetables accessible to the poor Jews of Russia and Poland, they became *the* vegetable substitute for the pumpkin and gourd. In some American homes, yams or sweet potatoes seem to have taken the place of carrots for the bright, sweet vegetable served at Rosh Hashanah.

Mohrrüben in German and *mern* in Yiddish mean carrot. The Yiddish word also means "to increase" or "to multiply." Thus, by eating carrots at Rosh Hashanah, the Jew reiterates the hope that the Jewish nation will increase greatly in numbers and merit during the coming year. This hope is based upon the promise stated in the Bible as part of the covenant God made with Abraham: "And He brought him forth abroad, and said, 'Look now toward heaven, and count the stars, if thou be able to count them'; and He said unto him: 'So shall thy seed be'" (Genesis 15:5).

Carrots cooked whole and then sliced into circles resemble coins in color and shape. Carrots, then, signify an increase in numbers and wealth—i.e., a yearning for a prosperous year. Carrots are cooked in kugels, cakes, tsimmes, salads, stews, and even candies for Rosh Hashanah.

CARROT KUGEL

4 eggs, separated
½ cup sugar
1 cup grated raw carrots (tightly packed)
¼ cup shredded apple

¼ cup red wine
2 tablespoons lemon juice
½ teaspoon grated lemon peel
⅓ cup potato flour

1. Preheat oven to 375°.

2. Beat the egg yolks with sugar until light.

3. Add the grated carrot, shredded apple, wine, lemon juice, lemon peel, and potato flour. Blend well.

4. Beat the egg whites until stiff peaks form and fold them into the carrot mixture.

5. Spoon into a well-greased 1½-quart casserole.

6. Bake 35 minutes, or until golden brown. If you serve immediately, the carrot kugel will be very puffy. Served cold, it will fall a bit.

Serves 6. (P)

MOROCCAN CARROT SALAD

2 pounds carrots
3 cloves garlic, minced
2 teaspoons paprika
Hot pepper to taste
1 tablespoon cumin

½ cup lemon juice
Salt to taste
2 tablespoons fresh chopped parsley
3 tablespoons olive oil

1. Peel the carrots and boil in water for about 20 minutes, or until barely tender. Cool and cut into thin rounds.

2. Place the carrots in a mixing bowl and add the remaining ingredients, except the parsley and oil.

3. Cover and refrigerate until thoroughly chilled. Before serving, sprinkle with parsley and oil.

Serves 8–10. (P)

CARROT CAKE

The following carrot cake perfectly illustrates the evolution of baking techniques over the last hundred years. Prior to 1850, in Europe, the leavening of baked goods depended on yeast or sour milk and baking soda. Cream of tartar was another possibility, but was imported from Italy. With the invention of baking powder or monocalcium phosphate in the United States in 1869, immigrant East European women quickly learned new ways to make cakes. Prior to the advent of baking powder, this particular cake was probably denser than it is today. The eggs may have been separated and the whites beaten stiff, with cream of tartar added, to make the cake rise a bit higher. The cream-cheese frosting—and indeed frosting generally—is certainly a twentieth-century addition.

3	cups sifted all-purpose flour	1½	cups vegetable oil
2	teaspoons baking powder	3	cups grated raw carrots
2	teaspoons baking soda		(1 pound)
½	teaspoon salt	4	eggs
2	teaspoons cinnamon	½	cup chopped walnuts
2	cups sugar		

1. Preheat oven to 350°. Grease and flour a 10″ bundt pan.

2. Sift the flour together with the baking powder, baking soda, salt, and cinnamon.

3. In another bowl, combine the sugar and vegetable oil and mix thoroughly. Add the carrots and blend well.

4. Add the eggs, one at a time, to the carrot mixture, beating well after each addition. Fold in the nuts. Then gradually add the flour mixture, blending well.

5. Pour batter into the bundt pan. Bake for 1 hour and then cool.

Frosting:

3	ounces cream cheese	2	cups powdered sugar
¼	cup butter or margarine	1	teaspoon lemon

When cake is cool, blend together the above ingredients and frost.

Serves 8–10. (M)

HONEY CAKE
(Lekakh)

So David and all the house of Israel brought up the ark of the Lord with shouting, and with the sound of the horn....And he dealt among all the people, even among the whole multitude of Israel, both to men and women, to every one a cake of bread, and a cake made in a pan, and a sweet cake.

II Samuel 6:15, 19

Therefore, the Jewish sweet tooth can perhaps be traced as far back as King David! In Hosea 3:1, the "sweet cake" is identified as a raisin cake.

An ancient sweet raisin cake is a logical description since honey, as used in the Bible, referred to the honey and jam extracted from honeycombs, dates, grapes, figs, and raisins. The only bees found in biblical Israel were of the ferocious Syrian variety. They had to be smoked from their hives, so extracting honey from their combs was never an easy task.

During the Roman period, the more docile Italian bees were introduced to the Middle East. Gradually the image of the bee changed to that of a gentler, tame insect, with bee honey becoming a more commonly used food item. The honey and its comb were at that time precious commodities. They were eaten alone, added to drinks, used in cooking, and valued for medicinal properties.

Lekakh, Yiddish for honey cake, is the traditional East European cake served on the first night of Rosh Hashanah and is eaten as a sweet throughout the period between Rosh Hashanah and Simhat Torah. It is also served at the birth of a boy, at weddings, and generally at all happy occasions.

1	cup strong coffee	1	teaspoon cinnamon
1¾	cups honey	¼	teaspoon ground cloves
3	tablespoons cognac (optional)	¼	teaspoon nutmeg
4	eggs	½	teaspoon ginger
4	tablespoons vegetable oil	½	cup chopped toasted almonds
1¼	cups dark brown sugar		or walnuts
3½	cups sifted all-purpose flour	½	cup white raisins
3	teaspoons baking powder	¼	cup chopped candied citron
1	teaspoon baking soda		(optional)

1. Preheat oven to 300°. Generously grease and flour two 9″×5″ loaf pans.

2. In a 2-quart saucepan, combine the coffee and honey and bring to a boil. Let cool, then stir in the cognac.

3. In a large mixing bowl, beat the eggs. Stir in the oil and brown sugar.

4. In another large mixing bowl, sift together the flour, baking powder, baking soda, cinnamon, cloves, nutmeg, and ginger. Stir in the nuts, raisins, and citron.

5. Stir the flour mixture and honey mixture alternately into the egg mixture. Pour the batter into the loaf pans and bake for 70 minutes, or until the cakes are springy to the touch. Do not serve for 24 hours, so that the flavor of the honey has a chance to develop.

Makes 2 loaves. (P)

TEYGLAKH

This honey sweet is eaten by Lithuanian Jews on happy occasions: Rosh Hashanah, Sukkot, Simhat Torah, Hanukkah, Purim, weddings, and *brits*. The honey that is used for cooking the dough is not thrown away but acts as the base for several honey cakes and/or sweet-potato tsimmes.

Dough:		Syrup:	
8	medium eggs	1$\frac{1}{3}$ pounds dark honey	
2	half eggshells full of water	1$\frac{2}{3}$ cups sugar	
3	tablespoons vegetable oil	4$\frac{1}{3}$ cups water	
2	teaspoons sugar	2	teaspoons ginger
2	cups all-purpose flour (about)		
$\frac{1}{2}$	cup walnuts		

1. Starting with the dough, beat the eggs well. Add the water, oil, and sugar. Blend in the flour gradually and knead well, using enough flour to form a soft, manageable dough.

2. Break off some dough, about the size of a large walnut. On a floured board, roll out a coil of dough to $\frac{1}{2}''$ in diameter. Place a quarter of a walnut about $\frac{1}{2}''$ from the end, roll up the dough like a honey bun, and set aside on the floured board. (Another way to make the teyglakh is to take a larger amount of dough in your hands, and roll out a much longer coil and cut it at 4'' intervals. Then proceed as above.)

3. Bring the honey to a boil in a heavy casserole. Add sugar, 3 cups water, and 1 teaspoon ginger. Bring to a boil again. When the sugar has dissolved, drop in the teyglakh, one by one. Bring to a boil again, cover, and boil slowly for 20 minutes without removing the cover. At the end of 20 minutes, start stirring occasionally and cook 40 minutes more. Add 1 more teaspoon ginger (or to taste), cover, and continue cooking for another $\frac{1}{2}$ hour, or until the teyglakh are golden and sound hollow inside when tapped.

4. When the teyglakh are done, add 1⅓ cups cold water to the honey syrup, mix well, and remove with a slotted spoon. Let the teyglakh cool, and serve.

Makes about 50. (P)

Note: The finished teyglakh can be rolled in grated coconut or, instead of forming the dough into coils, bits can be cooked in the honey and then rolled in raisins and ground nuts.

CIGARES

Dainty finger pastries oozing with honey syrup are great delicacies in the Middle East. These cigares, shaped like rolled cigarettes, are served in Moroccan Jewish homes on special occasions. In Casablanca, Mercedes Bensimon made her own paper-thin wrappers. In Washington, she has discovered that Chinese egg-roll wrappers are convenient substitutes.

25 egg-roll wrappers	Grated rind of 1 lemon
3 cups blanched ground almonds	2 cups vegetable oil (or more)
2½ cups sugar	½ cup water
1 egg	2 tablespoons honey
1 tablespoon orange-blossom water	

1. One hour before beginning, remove the egg-roll wrappers from the freezer. Cut each in half. Combine the almonds, 1½ cups of the sugar, and the egg. Mix well and add the orange-blossom water and lemon rind. Combine well. Place 1 heaping teaspoon of the filling in the center of each wrapper and roll up like a jelly roll. Moisten the ends to secure.

2. Fill a heavy frying pan with 4″ of oil. Heat the oil and drop the cigares in, a few at a time. When they are light gold in color, turn and then drain immediately.

3. In a small, heavy saucepan, bring the remaining 1 cup sugar and ½ cup water to a boil over a high heat, stirring until the sugar dissolves. Add the honey. Cook briskly, undisturbed, until a small bit dropped into ice water immediately forms a soft ball. When the syrup cools to lukewarm, dip in the cigares. Drain off the syrup and place on a platter.

Makes 50. (P)

APPLES

At the commencement of the Rosh Hashanah meal, an apple is dipped into honey for a sweet year. Apples, symbol of the Divine Presence, although abundant in autumn, are also considered a new seasonal fruit. The apples of antiquity, however, were originally small and acid, hardly the sweet forbidden fruit associated with the Garden of Eden or of our Rosh Hashanah table today. In fact, the soil and climate of ancient Israel were not suitable to grow them. (Contrary to popular opinion, the apple is not even mentioned in the story of the Garden of Eden.) As apples have been a popular fruit since the Middle Ages, it has become traditional to associate this fruit with the Garden of Eden and, more to the point, with Rosh Hashanah.

Authorities, however, cannot agree on the true apples of antiquity. Some think they may have been oranges, citrons (etrogs), or more likely either apricots or quince. Therefore, an apricot or quince should be dipped into honey.

My father remembers dipping the apple in honey on the first night of Rosh Hashanah and eating figs the second night. On Yom Kippur the children brought with them to synagogue an apple or a lemon stuck with cloves. This was sniffed in case the congregant felt faint. The fruit was saved and later hung in the *sukkah*.

These two apple recipes are typical family favorites at Rosh Hashanah. The apple pie was originally a German kuchen, similar to the dough of the zwetschgenkuchen on p. 92. It became double-crusted when my aunt Lisl watched some of her American neighbors and friends bake.

AUNT LISL'S APPLE PIE

½   pound butter or *pareve* margarine
2   cups all-purpose flour
2   tablespoons sugar
⅛   teaspoon salt
¼   cup cold water
5–6 apples, peeled, cored, and finely sliced

¼   cup raisins
Juice and grated rind of 1 lemon
2   tablespoons grated almonds or walnuts
1   egg yolk

1. Using a food processor or pastry blender, combine the butter or margarine, flour, sugar, and salt. Spin or blend well and slowly add the cold

water. When a soft ball forms, divide in half, wrap in waxed paper, and refrigerate for about 1 hour, or until firm.

2. Preheat oven to 350°.

3. Combine the apples, raisins, and lemon juice and rind.

4. Roll out half the dough and press into a 10″ pie plate. Fill with the apple mixture. Roll out the top crust and, using a rolling pin to lift it, cover the pie. Seal the crust. Make a few air holes with a fork. Sprinkle some grated nuts mixed with egg yolk or lemon rind on top. Bake 40 minutes or until golden.

Serves 6–8. (M or P)

APPLE STREUSEL

6 tart apples, peeled, cored, and sliced	1 teaspoon baking powder
⅓ cup sugar	4 tablespoons *pareve* margarine
½ teaspoon cinnamon	⅔ cup brown sugar
¼ cup orange juice	1 egg
¾ cup all-purpose flour	¼ cup chopped walnuts (optional)

1. Preheat oven to 350°.

2. Add the sugar, cinnamon, and orange juice to the apples. Mix lightly and place in a greased 1½-quart casserole.

3. Sift together the flour and baking powder.

4. Cut the margarine into the flour and rub with your fingertips to a crumbly consistency.

5. Mix the brown sugar and egg. Add the mixture, along with the nuts, to the flour mixture.

6. Sprinkle the streusel over the apple mixture. Bake 45 minutes, or until the apples are tender and the crust golden brown.

Serves 6–8. (P)

PLUM PIE
(Zwetschgenkuchen)

Plums probably existed at the time of the early Israelites, but certainly not in Palestine. They were far away in the cultures of the Far East. Blue, or Italian, plums are fall fruits in the West today, usually in season around the time of Rosh Hashanah. Thus, German Jews traditionally prepare a zwetschgen-kuchen for Rosh Hashanah.

Muerbeteig Crust:

1 cup all-purpose flour	1 egg yolk
1 tablespoon sugar	Salt
½ cup *pareve* margarine	Brandy

1. Mix flour and sugar. Using a food processor or a pastry blender, cut in margarine until the mixture resembles coarse crumbs. Add the egg yolk, a dash of salt, and a dash of brandy to moisten the crust.

2. Turn the dough onto a board and knead briefly. (This step is unnecessary with the food processor.)

3. Place the dough in the center of a 9″ pie plate and with your fingers pat it thinly into the bottom and sides. Refrigerate.

Filling:

⅓ cup plum jam	½ cup sugar
1 tablespoon brandy	1 teaspoon cinnamon
3 pounds Italian plums, washed, quartered, and pitted	Dash of nutmeg
	1 teaspoon grated lemon rind

1. Preheat oven to 375°.

2. Spread plum jam and a little brandy on the crust. Place the plums around in a circle so that each overlaps the other and they eventually form a spiral into the center.

3. Mix the sugar, cinnamon, nutmeg, and lemon rind, and sprinkle over the plums.

4. Bake in oven about 40–50 minutes, or until the crust is golden brown and the plums juicy.

Serves 6–8. (P)

YOM KIPPUR

YOM KIPPUR

Then went up Moses [to Mount Sinai]...and seventy of the elders of Israel; and they saw the God of Israel....And upon the nobles of the children of Israel He laid not His hand; and they beheld God, and did eat and drink.
Exodus 24:9-11

Go your way, eat your bread with joy and drink your wine with a merry heart, for God has already accepted your work.
Ecclesiastes 9:7

We are all familiar with fasting on Yom Kippur. This one day is to be spent humbling the heart in repentance and atoning for sins so that we will be inscribed in the Book of Life for a good year. Yet what is the origin of this fast?

When the early Israelites first beheld the Holy Presence of God at Mount Sinai, they ate and drank. With excessive feasting, they forgot themselves and began to worship the Golden Calf of the heathens. When Moses saw this on his descent with the Ten Commandments, he broke the tablets. Then the Hebrews mourned forty days. When Moses returned to Mount Sinai and descended on the tenth day of Tishri (Yom Kippur), holding the second table of the Ten Commandments in his arms, he found the people fasting and repenting their great sin. The Israelites went forth to him and wept. Moses wept too and told his people that God had accepted their sincere penitence and proclaimed that day as a day of forgiveness throughout all generations.

For thousands of years, on the tenth of Tishri, Jews have fasted and refrained from catering to their physical appetites. It has always been a day when the Jew devotes himself to spiritual requirements in order to be like the angels. For this reason, sexual intercourse, the wearing of leather shoes, the washing of the mouth, entering into money transactions, and anointing oneself with cream are also avoided.

With the stress on fasting, how many of us are aware of the *mitzvah* involved in celebrating two substantial feasts in the afternoon of the day prior to Yom Kippur? The pre-Yom Kippur meals go back to biblical times when Jews living in Galilee and Babylonia held elaborate banquets. Persian Jews at one time prepared seven special meals prior to the great fast. Originally this feast was eaten at noon. In America today, most people eat a substantial but not excessive meal late in the afternoon.

As important as it is to fast, so is it necessary to eat well beforehand. It is easier to fast when accustomed to fasting rather than to eating well. And on Yom Kippur it is so very important to feel hunger pangs, to remind oneself all the more of the difficult task of atonement.

Although most people are supposed to fast, there is an escape clause.

Pregnant and nursing women, the sick, and girls under twelve and boys under thirteen are all exempt.

At the special meal on the eve of Yom Kippur, it is traditional for most Jews to eat chicken. Chicken and rice are pre-fast foods the world over. This is also due in Judaism to the *Kapparot* ceremony, performed that morning, whereby one transfers one's sins to a cock or hen. The chicken is often boiled, but it does not have to be. It merely should not be highly spiced. Rice, carrots, and fresh fruit are also served. All these foods are not seasoned, to discourage thirstiness and indigestion throughout the long fast. For this reason, neither gefilte fish nor spicy foods generally precede the fast. East European Jews eat chicken soup with kreplakh. No nuts are served because of the saliva formed and the throat irritation, making the recital of prayers difficult. At the end of the meal each person eats a small morsel of bread and water as symbolic sustenance throughout the fast.

Unlike the "black fasts"—such as Tisha Be-av, mourning the destruction of the Temple—Yom Kippur is considered a "white fast." White is symbolic of purity in accordance with Isaiah 1:18: "Though your sins be as scarlet, they shall be as white as snow." In the synagogue the rabbi wears a white *kitl*, or robe, the synagogue ark is draped in white, and the Torah scrolls are adorned with white mantles.

After the relatively bland meal before sunset on the eve of the fast, a white cloth is spread over the dining-room table. On it are placed a Bible, a prayer book, and other sacred books, instead of the traditional Sabbath loaves of hallah. The books are covered with a white cloth until the break-the-fast meal the following evening, as symbolic testimony that this holy day is being honored, not with food and drink, but with study and prayer. A lamp in memory of departed members of the family is lit.

According to the Midrash, at the close of the Yom Kippur service a voice calls from heaven telling the faithful that their prayers have been heard. Confident that we have obtained forgiveness, we can rejoice and partake of a post-fast meal. This repast recalls the feast the high priests celebrated after Yom Kippur in gratitude for having been permitted to emerge from the Holy of Holies. Often in the United States today, close friends or family assemble for the post-fast feast. Usually a milk meal is served, beginning with coffee and a sweet—sometimes just an apple dipped in honey—followed by herring or another salty food. From there on, it is up to the imagination of the hostess. Russian Jews often made schnecken; Moroccans, fijuelas, deep-fried pastries oozing with honey; Syrians and Egyptians make a cardamom cake; Yemenites, a ginger cake. Sephardim also serve eggs, the symbol of hope and life. Quinces, pomegranates, watermelon, or other seasonal fruits are also served. It is becoming more and more traditional in this country to serve a glorified brunch with bagels, lox, cream cheese, herring, kugel, etc.

An apple "embalmed" with cloves—to sniff for Havdalah or to keep you from fainting of hunger at Yom Kippur (a southern German custom) (photo: Bruno Stern)

MENUS

For Yom Kippur Eve

Minsk

Hallah★
Chicken Soup with Matzah Balls★
Boiled Chicken or Apricot
Chicken★
Green Salad
Honey-Glazed Carrots★
Baked Apples
Honey Cake★

Greek

Hallah★
Egg Lemon Soup★
Stewed Chicken in Tomato
Sauce★
Fidellos Tostados
(Toasted Pasta)★

Salad
Watermelon

To Break the Fast

Moroccan

Fijuelas★
Meat and Vegetable Soup★
Fruit
Tea with Mint

Russian

Herring in Sour Cream★
Apple Dipped in Honey
Lokshen Kugel★
Salmon with Cream Cheese
Bagels
Schnecken★ or Honey Cake★

MEAT KREPLAKH

Which comes first—kreplakh, pirogi, ravioli, or wonton soup? Each country seems to have its own version of a filled egg-noodle dough, either fried or boiled in water or soup. Most authorities think that this dish originated in China and worked its way via trade routes to the countries of the West. The Jews may have learned about kreplakh from the Chinese or the Italians. Maimonides traces cooked dough to Persia and the Middle East.

The word "kreplakh" itself comes from the French *crêpelle*. Whatever the origin of the food, it requires effort and time to cut, fill, form, and enclose each of these three-cornered bits of dough filled with chopped meat. Thus, they are reserved for special occasions.

The meat of the kreplakh symbolizes inflexible justice; the soft noodle dough denotes compassion. The kreplakh are then a metaphor, a suggestion that the attribute of God's strict justice will be mellowed on the side of mercy.

These pockets of food where the meat is hidden inside the dough also refer to the hidden nature of the three days they are eaten. Although the eve of Yom Kippur, Simhat Torah, and Purim are festivals for eating and drinking, work is not forbidden. The day prior to Yom Kippur is not a full holiday; on Simhat Torah people dance and drink; and on Purim the name of God is never mentioned.

Traditionally served in a soup, these "Jewish wonton" can also be boiled and then fried in chicken fat. My mother-in-law serves them this way, as a starch with meat.

Meat Filling:

1 small onion, chopped	1 egg
¾ pound ground meat (at least half-cooked)	Salt and pepper to taste

1. Sauté the onion with the ground meat. Remove excess fat.

2. Combine with the egg and salt and pepper to taste.

Noodle Dough:

3 eggs	2 tablespoons water
¾ teaspoon salt	2 cups all-purpose flour

1. Using an eggbeater or a food processor, beat the eggs slightly. Add salt, water, and enough flour to make a medium-soft dough. Knead well by hand or in the food processor. Divide the dough into 2 balls. Cover with a moist towel.

2. Working quickly, roll out the dough of 1 ball very thin with a rolling pin and cut into 6 strips, each 1½″ wide. Then cut into pieces 1½″ square.

3. Place ½ teaspoon meat mixture on each square. Fold into a triangle and press edges together firmly, using flour to bind. Leave as is, or press together two of the ends. Repeat with the second ball of dough.

4. Drop into boiling water and cook, uncovered, 15 minutes.

Makes about 60. (F)

Note: After being formed, the kreplakh can be placed on a cookie sheet, frozen, and then transferred to plastic bags for freezer storage.

EGG LEMON SOUP

Greek and other Mediterranean Jews eat egg lemon soup for their pre-fast and major holiday meals. Both kreplakh and the traditional matzah balls in chicken soup are foreign to them.

6 cups rich chicken broth	Salt to taste
½ cup uncooked rice or dry alphabet soup	2 eggs
	Juice of 1 lemon, or to taste

1. In a medium saucepan bring the broth to a boil. Add the rice or alphabet soup and simmer, uncovered, until the rice or noodles are tender. Add salt to taste.

2. In a separate bowl, beat the eggs well; add the lemon juice and mix well. Add a little of the stock, beating constantly with a wire whisk. Slowly add the remainder of the soup, always stirring.

3. Return the soup to the saucepan, bring to a boil, and remove from the heat immediately. Adjust seasoning and serve.

Serves 6. (F)

Note: At Passover the same soup is served with broken pieces of matzah or farfel replacing the rice.

STEWED CHICKEN IN TOMATO SAUCE
(Pollo en Salsa de Tomat)

The most superstitious custom associated with food in Judaism is that of the *Kapparot*, the expiation of sins or "scapegoat" offering. On the morning of the day prior to Yom Kippur, each member of the family would swing a live fowl around his head three times. These words were then recited: "This fowl is my substitute, this is my surrogate, this is my atonement." Some old texts even add, "May it be designated for death and I for life." In essence, this *Kapparot* ceremony is the transferral of our sins to the fowl, an ancient custom rife in sorcery. In ancient days the scapegoat was sent out into the desert, carrying the sins of the community. Babylonians employed their abundant rams, lambs, or goats, instead of the chickens used later in East Europe. According to one account, after the fowl was slaughtered, the dead and dried entrails were thrown onto the roof.

Although this custom still prevails in some very observant communities, in the first edition of the *Shulhan Arukh*, around 1565, Joseph Karo wrote, "This is a silly custom and its observance should be checked." His opinion did not prevail, however, and his comment was never included in any other edition of the Code of Jewish Law.

My mother-in-law remembers the *Kapparot* tradition in Zamosc, Poland. Early in the morning of the day prior to Yom Kippur, the fowl was whirled about the head of the penitent. Her father would whirl a rooster, her mother a hen, and she and her siblings a pullet or a cockerel. As a child, she was always frightened by the fluttering feathers. After the whirling, her mother would race to the *shohet* and have the fowls ritually slaughtered to make food for the meal prior to the fast. All the fowls would be cooked and any extras given to bachelor relatives or to the poor. Chicken soup would be made for the kreplakh and the boiled chicken eaten as a mild main dish.

In some homes a fish might be used if a fowl was not available. Since there were five children in my mother-in-law's family, seven fowls were whirled, but in larger families a donation to charity of about eighteen cents, or *hi*, might be substituted for each child. Today this custom of using a live fowl for the ceremony is not as common as it used to be. Most people who observe this rite substitute money wrapped in a handkerchief and swing it around the head.

To this day, chicken and rice are pre-fast foods the world over. Even the poorest Jew tries to serve a chicken at least once a year, for the meal prior to the Yom Kippur fast. The following is a mild, typically Greek chicken dish served on the eve of Yom Kippur.

1 3-pound frying chicken, cut up	1 35-ounce can Italian tomatoes
Salt to taste	1 onion, chopped (optional)
¼ cup olive oil	½ teaspoon dry oregano
Water	(optional)

1. Salt the chicken and sauté in oil in a large skillet or pot. As the chicken begins to brown, add small amounts of water, letting the chicken cook until the water is absorbed. Remove all except 2 tablespoons of the oil.

2. Strain the tomatoes to remove the seeds, and pour over the chicken. Add the onion and oregano, if desired. Cover and cook slowly for about 45 minutes or until done. This dish is usually served with fidellos and leeks.

Serves 4–6. (F)

TASTY APRICOT CHICKEN

This easy-to-make chicken is an American convenience recipe which a Russian Jewish caterer shared with me. I tasted a similar one, with quince jam, at the home of Vivian and Simha Dinitz, former Israeli Ambassador to the United States.

2 3½-pound broiling chickens,	½ pound apricot preserves
cut up	6 ounces Russian dressing
Salt and pepper to taste	1 package dry onion soup
Garlic salt to taste	

1. Preheat oven to 350°.

2. Season the chicken well with salt, pepper, and garlic salt to taste.

3. Mix together the apricot preserves, Russian dressing, and dry onion soup. Pour over the chicken and bake in the oven about 50 minutes, or until golden brown.

Serves 6–8. (F)

FIDELLOS TOSTADOS
(Toasted Pasta)

Contrary to popular opinion, pasta was probably introduced to the seaports of Spain from China via the Middle East as early as the eleventh century and even possibly much earlier. By the early thirteenth century, fifty years before

Marco Polo's journey to the East, the Jews of Spain were eating a threadlike noodle called fidellos, meaning "angels' hair."

Fidellos tostados is a typically Jewish dish found in Greece and other countries to which the Spanish Jews fled. It is basically a tomato noodle kugel, with the coils fried until golden brown before being softened in boiling water. Curiously, fidellos is now eaten throughout Latin America and is slowly being introduced into the American pasta-manufacturers' market to meet the demand of the great influx of Latin Americans. The following is an old Spanish Jewish recipe.

1 12-ounce package fidellos or fideos (a vermicelli-like pasta) ½ cup olive oil	2 cups strained stewed tomatoes 3 cups water 1 teaspoon salt, or to taste

1. Pan-fry the fidellos coils in oil until golden brown. Set aside in another pan.

2. Add the tomatoes, water, and salt to the original pan, and boil. Add the fidellos. Simmer, semi-covered, for about 10 minutes, stirring occasionally with a long fork to separate coils and keep noodles from sticking. Cook until fidellos are tender and liquid is absorbed.

3. Remove from heat and let sit, covered, about 10 minutes before serving. Stir again. This dish goes well with stewed chicken in tomato sauce.

Serves 6. (P)

Note: Preparing this dish in advance only improves the taste. Cover to reheat.

HONEY-GLAZED CARROTS

A simple dish of honeyed carrots is a light vegetable for the pre-fast meal.

2 pounds carrots 1¼ cups water 2 tablespoons cornstarch	½ cup honey Salt to taste Ginger to taste

1. Peel and cut the carrots into 1″ rounds. Combine with 1 cup of water. Cover and simmer until barely done (about 20 minutes).

2. Dissolve the cornstarch in the remaining ¼ cup water. Add to the carrots, along with the honey, salt, and ginger. Stir over low heat until mixture thickens.

Serves 6–8. (P)

HERRING IN SOUR CREAM

First she chopped the milk roe with onion—this the appetizer. The herring brine was the base for a potato soup. The second onion was sliced and flavored with vinegar—the salad, to be sure. The herring itself was the roast, which she wrapped in a wet newspaper and then placed on the red coals in the range.

Sholem Asch, THE MOTHER

Small fish in brine are good to eat after fasting.

Avodah Zarah 29A

In the poor East European *shtetl*, a four-course meal could be made from a milk roe, herring, a potato, two onions, and a piece of day-old bread, as novelist Sholem Asch shows. This raw salt herring, often chopped with onion, an apple, a slice of bread, and a little vinegar, was distinctly the Polish-Russian-Lithuanian gift to Jewish cookery. Once a major part of the diet during the week, it has become for us a coveted hors d'oeuvre or Sunday breakfast dish.

After eating a sweet and tea to break the fast of Yom Kippur, it is traditional to eat herring to help restock the body with salt. In my family, herring with sour cream and red onions is served. I have added a bit of dill to this originally Polish dish. Another variation might include apples and nuts.

1 13-ounce jar herring in wine sauce	2 tablespoons fresh lemon juice
1 red onion, sliced in rings	1 tablespoon sugar
¼ cup sour cream	Sprig of dill (optional)

1. Drain herring and remove onions.

2. Replace the original onion rings with about 5 red-onion rings. Mix in the sour cream, lemon juice, and sugar. (The amount of sour cream and onion rings can vary according to taste and the number of guests.)

3. Place in a larger, covered glass container and chill in the refrigerator for a few hours, or overnight. Sprinkle with dill and serve with crackers. This will last for weeks in the refrigerator.

Makes about 3 cups. (M)

Variation: Omit the dill and add 1 chopped apple and ½ cup coarsely chopped, blanched almonds.

FIJUELAS

This recipe came to McLean, Virginia, from Morocco, via four generations of Sultan Levy Rosenblatt's family who lived in Brazil. It is a crisp pastry which is eaten with Moroccan mint tea to break the fast of Yom Kippur.

1 cup warm water	Vegetable oil for frying
2 egg yolks	2 cups sugar
2 tablespoons vegetable shortening	1 cup water
or *pareve* margarine	1 teaspoon orange-blossom water
1 teaspoon salt	Cinnamon
4 cups all-purpose unbleached	
flour	

1. Combine the warm water, egg yolks, shortening or margarine, and salt. Gradually add the flour, kneading gently as you go. Knead about 10 minutes, until you reach a firm dough. Cover with a towel and let rise for 1 hour.

2. When the dough has risen (it will not rise very much), break off a piece the size of a plum and flatten it out with the palm of your hand. Shape into a rectangle and roll it out in strips approximately 3″ × 9″. It is easiest to use a spaghetti-making machine for this. Otherwise, use a rolling pin. It should be almost as thin as fillo dough. When it is as thin as possible, stretch it out gently. Place each piece of dough on a floured cookie sheet. Cover with a towel while making more. Continue until all the dough is used up.

3. In a heavy casserole, prepare oil for deep frying, to about 375°. With a slotted spoon, place one end of the thin strip in the oil. As it cooks, it will roll up like a jelly roll. When it is golden brown, let it drain tilted on the edge of the pan. Drain again on paper towel. You must work very quickly to cook and then to drain it, so that it does not retain too much fat. Continue until all pieces are completed.

4. Combine the sugar and water and boil until syrup is formed. Add the orange-blossom water. Let cool somewhat.

5. Pour the syrup over the fijuelas and sprinkle with cinnamon. The fijuelas will last several weeks if covered.

Makes 24. (P)

ALMOND MILK

From being forbidden by their usages to mingle butter, or other preparation of milk or cream with meat at any meal, the Jews have oil much used in their cookery of fish, meat, and vegetables. Pounded almonds and rich syrups of sugar and water agreeably flavoured, assist in compounding their sweet dishes, many of which are excellent, and preserve much of their oriental character; but we are credibly informed that the restrictions of which we have spoken are not at the present day very rigidly observed by the main body of Jews in this country, though they are so by those who are denominated strict.

As a substitute for milk, in the composition of soufflés, puddings, and sweet dishes, almond-cream as it is called, will be found to answer excellently. To prepare it, blanch and pound the almonds, and then pour very gradually to them boiling water in the proportion directed below; turn them into a strong cloth or tammy, and wring it from them with powerful pressure, to extract as much as possible of it from them again.

Almond-cream: (for puddings, etc.) almonds, 4 oz.; water, 1 pint. For blancmanges, and rich soufflés, creams and custards; almonds, ½ pound to whole pound; water, 1 to 1½ pints.

Obs. As every cook may not be quite aware of the articles of food strictly prohibited by the Mosaic law, it may be well to specify them here. Pork in every form; all varieties of shell-fish, without exception; hares, rabbits, and swans.

The above quotation comes from Eliza Acton's *Modern Cookery for Private Families*, published in London in 1845. Not only did this book include recipes for Roman Catholic fast days, it also provided a chapter with kosher recipes for Jewish households.

Almond milk is one of the first drinks known to mankind. It was, and still is, recommended for nursing mothers.

Before the advent of commercial bottled drinks, more naturally flavored beverages were prepared, especially in warm lands. To this day, Jews from the Middle East drink a variety of sweet fruit and nut beverages to break the fast of Yom Kippur. Persian Jews prepare afshoreh seeb, an apple drink with rosewater; Lebanese prefer an apricot drink with nuts, similar to amardin, with which the Moslems break the daily fast of Ramadan. Iraqi Jews drink hariri, or almond milk, because its white color symbolizes purity and it acts as a good lining to an empty stomach.

In a thickened state, it was used by Jews instead of cream sauce over fruit desserts with a meat meal. Although wealthy Russian Jews from Riga ate it over kichel or cranberry or rice pudding, it most probably originated with Sephardic Jews. The following is a Moroccan variation still used to this day.

4 cups water	1 cup sugar
1 pound blanched almonds	¼ cup orange-blossom water

1. Place 1 cup water in a blender or food processor. Add ½ cup almonds, ¼ cup sugar, and 1 tablespoon orange-blossom water. Whirl until pulverized.

2. Press the mixture through a cheesecloth. Then blend once more. Repeat the process 3 more times with the remaining ingredients. Combine the 4 batches.

3. Serve with ice and dilute with water until the desired consistency is reached.

Makes about 4½ cups. (P)

MEAT AND VEGETABLE SOUP
(Harira)

A meal without soup is no meal.

Berakhot 44

This rich soup is eaten by some Moroccan Jews for the meal after the fast of Yom Kippur. Basically an Arab dish to break the fast of Ramadan, Jews of southern Morocco have adapted it to their diet. Except for the tomatoes in this recipe, the other ingredients are extremely old and could date back to the biblical period.

1 cup dried lentils	2 tablespoons fresh coriander or
1 cup dried fava or lima beans	parsley
1 pound stewing meat, cubed	Salt and pepper to taste
2 medium onions, chopped	4 cups water
4 tablespoons oil	2 tablespoons flour
1 pound tomatoes, chopped and	Juice of 2 lemons
peeled	Lemon slices
1 bunch celery with leaves, diced	

1. Soak the lentils and fava or lima beans overnight.

2. In a heavy saucepan, sauté the meat and chopped onions in oil. When the meat is brown, add the lentils, beans, tomatoes, celery, coriander or parsley, salt, and pepper. Add the water and simmer, covered, for about 2 hours.

3. When the meat is tender and the beans soft, adjust the seasonings. Bring to a boil.

4. Mix the flour into about 2 more tablespoons cold water and stir into the boiling soup. Keep stirring to avoid lumps.

5. After 1–2 minutes, turn off the heat and add the lemon juice. Serve very hot with lemon slices.

Serves 4–6. (F)

SCHNECKEN

If the benevolent eighteenth-century Russian hasidic rabbi Levi Itzhak ben Meir of Berditchev, who judged his people with compassion-colored spectacles, were to look down on the Washington food scene today, he would not be surprised to see his descendant, Marian Fox Burros, defending the American consumer. As food editor of the Washington *Post*, television consumer advisor, and author of six cookbooks, Marian is involved in all aspects of cooking.

Throughout Marian's books she includes old Russian family favorites such as schnecken. Schnecken is a German word for snails, and indeed the pastry—rolled up with nuts, cinnamon, and raisins—resembles snails. Rabbi Levi Itzhak's wife might well have made her schnecken from leftover strudel dough, however. Marian's recipe, a traditional break-the-fast treat, is one she watched her mother prepare. A variation of the original appears in her second book, *Freeze With Ease*, and is reprinted here.

3 cups all-purpose flour	1 cup chopped walnuts or
½ pound unsalted butter	pecans
3 egg yolks	1½ cups sugar
1 cup light cream	2¼ teaspoons cinnamon
1 tablespoon (1 package) dry yeast	

1. Mix the flour and butter until well blended.

2. Combine the egg yolks and the cream.

3. Add the egg mixture to the flour and blend well. Sprinkle the dry yeast over the top of the dough and mix it in with your hands.

4. Divide the dough into 6 parts and wrap each in tin foil. Refrigerate overnight.

5. Roll each piece of dough into a circle on a floured board.

6. Preheat oven to 325°.

7. Combine nuts, sugar, and cinnamon and then divide into 6 portions. Place one circle of dough on top of each of these portions. Press down, turn over, and repeat, so both sides are covered with the mixture. Cut each circle into 8 wedges, like a pie. Roll up each wedge, starting at the wide end.

8. Bake on a greased cookie sheet for 25 minutes, or until golden.

Makes 48. (M)

LOKSHEN KUGEL

Since no cooking is permitted during the fast of Yom Kippur, foods must be prepared ahead of time. A sweet noodle kugel is a perfect beginning to a new year.

½ pound broad noodles
4 eggs, separated
½ cup margarine
½ pound cottage cheese

½ pint sour cream
½ cup sugar
¼ cup graham-cracker crumbs

1. Cook noodles according to directions on package. Drain.

2. Preheat oven to 350°.

3. Beat the egg whites until stiff peaks form. Combine the remaining ingredients, except the crumbs, and fold in the egg whites.

4. Transfer to a greased 1-quart soufflé dish and sprinkle with graham-cracker crumbs.

5. Bake 45 minutes, or until golden brown.

Serves 4–6. (M)

HUNGARIAN KUGELHOPF
(Coffee Cake)

This yeast kugelhopf is served to break the fast of Yom Kippur in Hungary. The recipe, originally Alsatian, came from Alex Lichtman, one of the original owners of Mrs. Herbst's famous bakery in New York.

4½ packages dry yeast
2 cups warm milk
3 medium eggs
2¾ cups sugar
1 teaspoon salt
1 teaspoon vanilla
6 cups sifted all-purpose flour

1¼ cups unsalted butter
2 tablespoons unsalted butter, melted
2 tablespoons cinnamon
½ cup raisins
Warm water

1. Dissolve the yeast in ½ cup warm milk and proof. Set aside.

2. In a large mixing bowl, combine the eggs, ¾ cup sugar, salt, vanilla, and

the rest of the milk. Add the yeast mixture and gradually stir in the flour. Use the first speed of an electric mixer for 3 minutes, then turn to the fast speed until the dough separates from the sides of the bowl.

3. Place the dough in a pan dusted with flour and refrigerate for 15 minutes.

4. On a floured board, roll out the dough to a rectangle 12″ × 8″.

5. Place the unmelted butter on half the dough. Turn the other half over the butter, sprinkling the table and the top of the dough with flour. Roll out and fold over again.

6. Refrigerate the dough for 15 minutes and roll the dough out twice. Each time, roll in all four directions.

7. Brush the top of the dough lightly with melted butter. Cover with freezer paper.

8. Divide the dough in 3 parts and roll out each to a size about 8″ × 10″. Sprinkle a mixture of the remaining 2 cups sugar and 2 tablespoons cinnamon on top. Then cover with raisins. Roll up tight, jelly-roll fashion, and place one end against the other end to form a circle. If using cookie sheets, either mold into a freeform circle or leave long.

9. Grease 3 kugelhopf or bundt pans well. If you don't have these, use cookie sheets.

10. Place the filled dough, seam side up, in the mold and let rise at least 1 hour, until the mold is filled (about double in bulk).

11. Preheat oven to 375°.

12. Brush the top of the dough with water and bake 50–55 minutes.

Makes 3. (M)

SUKKOT

SUKKOT

Three times thou shalt keep a feast unto Me in the year. The feast of unleavened bread shalt thou keep; seven days thou shalt eat unleavened bread, as I commanded thee, at the time appointed in the month Abib—for in it thou camest out from Egypt; and none shall appear before Me empty; and the feast of harvest, the first-fruits of thy labours, which thou sowest in the field; and the feast of ingathering, at the end of the year, when thou gatherest in thy labours out of the field.

Exodus 23:14-16

Sukkot, the Feast of the Ingathering, marked the successful harvest of the preceding year and the time of the first rains, a clean start for the following year. The principal features of the original celebration were the actual reaping of crops and fruits and the bringing in of grapes and olives, for which Palestine was famous. Special ceremonies were performed to induce the first rainfall of the year. One was the waving of the four species.

To this day, the four species decorate the *sukkah* and are held in the hands during the blessing each evening. They are the etrog (citron), the palm, the myrtle, and the willow branches. There are many explanations for the four species. One is the following: The feminine etrog, shaped like a heart and symbolizing the hope of divine forgiveness for the murmuring and desires of our heart, is held in the left hand. In the right is the masculine *lulav*, or palm branch, symbolizing Israel's singlehearted loyalty to God, intertwined with the *hadas* or myrtle, shaped like an eye and symbolizing the hope of divine forgiveness for greed and envy, and the *arava*, the willow, shaped like a mouth and symbolizing the hope of divine forgiveness for idle talk and falsehoods. In ancient times a combination of one feminine and three masculine symbols would bring rainfall. In the same way that these four plants cannot exist without water, the world must have rain.

People lived in trellis-roofed cabins throughout the period of harvesting. The booths were later reinterpreted as a reminder of those in which the ancestors of Israel had dwelled when they wandered through the wilderness on their journey from Egypt to the promised land. This holiday then became a logical sequel to Passover and Shavuot, which commemorated the escape from bondage and the conclusion of the Covenant at Sinai. Of course, the Jews wandering in the desert probably never lived in wooden booths with green roofs. They dwelled in portable tents.

To this day, many Jews build a *sukkah* with wood or canvas and use branches of trees for the roof, as the sky must show through. In fact, the popular *Jewish Catalogue*, with instructions for building your own *sukkah*, has interested more and more young families in preparing their own and even organizing *sukkah*-making parties. Only men above the age of thirteen are

Sukkot in New York, circa 1908 (photo: The Bettmann Archive)

required to eat every meal for seven days in the *sukkah*. Today, in most families, the entire family eats its meals there, especially on the first night and day. In case of a drizzle, the meal in the *sukkah* can continue, but if rain is falling in the food, the participants can retire to the house.

Seasonal fruits and vegetables—all symbols of plenty—decorate the branches and are prepared in daily dishes for the eight days of the festival. When the harvest festival first began, the foods included figs, dates, pomegranates, apricots, squash, romaine lettuce, onions, barley and wheat bread, as well as freshly killed lamb.

The eighth day of Sukkot is Shemini Atzeret, when memorial services are held. On the next day, Simhat Torah, the Torah is carried around the synagogue and everyone dances. Drinking and eating are part and parcel of this joyous occasion when the annual cycle of the reading of the Torah is concluded. If you are not Orthodox, seek out the most religious synagogue in your area to watch this colorful procession.

Throughout history Jews have built *sukkot* and celebrated Sukkot in many lands. In East Europe seasonal fruits and vegetables included cabbage, cucumbers, sweet potatoes, and apples. Thus, dishes such as stuffed cabbage, pickles, tsimmes, and apple strudel are traditional at Sukkot there; kreplakh traditionally begin the Simhat Torah meal. In this country, vegetables such as zucchini, eggplant, and tomatoes are abundant in the fall. We have added our own dishes to the seasonal foods of our forebears. Since our American Thanksgiving festival was originally the English harvest festival, also observed in October, at the time of Sukkot, it is understandable that many dishes Americans serve for Thanksgiving can also be prepared for Sukkot.

There is a midrashic saying that in Sodom seven kinds of trees interlaced and grew one on top of the other: vine trees and fig, pomegranate, date, peach, almond, and other nut trees. With the destruction of Sodom these trees were laid waste and the land became the Dead Sea, salty and desolate. It was believed that, with the coming of the Messiah, Sodom would be rebuilt and its trees would bloom once more. It was also thought that those celebrating the Feast of the Tabernacles would then be given a place in the fruitful *sukkah* of Sodom redeemed.

MENUS

Yaprak (Stuffed Grape Leaves
with Apricots)★
Turkish Stuffed Zucchini★
Carrot Salad★
Baklava★
Fresh Fruit

Eggplant and Pepper Salad★
Sukkot Tsimmes★
Kosher Dill Pickles★
Hot Fruit Compote★
Aunt Eva's Cookies★

Mushroom and Barley Soup★
Sweet-and-Sour Stuffed Cabbage★
Cucumber Salad★
Apple Strudel★

Chicken Soup with Matzah Balls★
Turkey with Bread Stuffing★
Sweet-Potato Tsimmes with
Pineapple★
Chestnuts and Prunes★
Green Salad
Plum Pie★

CABBAGE STRUDEL

Cabbage, one of the oldest known vegetables, was highly regarded by Jews for both nutritive and medicinal purposes.

Because the grapevine and the cabbage plant loathed one another, cabbage came to be thought of as a prevention against intoxication. If a man ate cabbage while drinking, he would not become inebriated. It was also a cure for hangovers.

It is no wonder, then, that Hungarians traditionally prepare cabbage strudel for Simhat Torah and Purim, the two holidays when drinking and revelry take place. This scrumptious dish can be served as an elegant hors d'oeuvre, a vegetable accompaniment to goose, chicken, or pot roast, or, sprinkled with confectioners' sugar, as a dessert. I first tasted it with caraway seeds in Jerusalem at the enchanting home of Josef Tal, the famous Israeli composer, whose wife Paula is one of the most creative cooks I have ever met.

1 head (2 pounds) cabbage	1 tablespoon sugar
2 teaspoons salt	1 teaspoon cinnamon
4 tablespoons vegetable oil	8 fillo leaves
1 medium onion, coarsely chopped	6 tablespoons butter or *pareve* margarine, melted
Freshly ground black pepper	½ cup fine breadcrumbs
1 teaspoon caraway seeds (optional)	1 egg white

1. Remove the core from the cabbage and shred, using a food processor or grater.

2. Sprinkle with salt and let stand about 15 minutes. Squeeze out the excess water.

3. Place about 4 tablespoons oil in a heavy frying pan. Brown the onion until golden. Remove, and begin sautéing the cabbage (you will probably have to do this in two batches), cooking carefully until wilted.

4. Combine the cabbage and the onions. Sprinkle with pepper, caraway seeds, sugar, and cinnamon. Adjust seasoning to taste.

5. Preheat oven to 350°.

6. Cover a pastry board with a cloth. Taking 1 fillo leaf at a time, lay it on the board and brush with melted butter or margarine, 1 tablespoon breadcrumbs, and pepper. Lay the next fillo leaf on top and brush with the identical combination. Continue until you have 4 layers of fillo leaves and topping. Along the longer side of the fillo, spoon out half the cabbage filling about 4″ from the edge of the dough. Fold the edge over the cabbage. Then, using both hands, lift the cloth and let the cabbage roll fall over and over itself, jelly-roll fashion, until the filling is completely enclosed in the pastry sheet. Place, seam side down, in a greased jelly-roll pan. If the roll is too long, cut with a serrated knife to fit your pan.

7. Repeat the above process with the remaining 4 fillo leaves, breadcrumbs, cabbage, and pepper.

8. Brush the crust with additional melted butter or margarine. Then brush with egg white, which has been lightly mixed.

9. Bake 45 minutes, or until golden. Slice thin and serve immediately. Or serve lukewarm, sprinkled with confectioners' sugar, as a dessert.

Serves 8–12 as an hors d'oeuvre or vegetable accompaniment. (M or P)

Note: After the rolls have been formed, you can freeze them on cookie sheets and then remove them to plastic containers for freezer storage.

MARINATED EGGPLANT SALAD

Superstitions surround eggplant, the purply-black fruit in season at Sukkot. Because of its dark color, some Moroccan Jews will not serve it for Rosh Hashanah. Other Europeans believe that the eggplant must be salted to get rid of the bitter and sometimes evil juices. If you select smooth, dark-skinned fruits that are light to the touch, the eggplant will not be bitter. I never salt eggplants before using them.

Vegetable oil for frying	1 28-ounce can tomatoes
3 green peppers	5 tablespoons cider vinegar
1 medium eggplant	1 large garlic clove, minced
1 medium onion, sliced in thin rings	Salt and pepper to taste

1. Pour about 2″ of oil in a heavy frying pan and heat to 375°.

2. Quarter the green peppers, remove seeds, and cut each quarter in 3 pieces. Deep-fry in the oil. Drain, and place in a ceramic or glass bowl.

3. Quarter the eggplant lengthwise and slice thinly across the width. Deep-fry half the slices at a time. Drain. Add to the green peppers.

4. Add the onion rings to the eggplant mixture.

5. Cube the tomatoes and add to the eggplant, along with 2 tablespoons of the juice from the can.

6. Add vinegar, garlic, and salt and pepper to taste, and blend well.

7. Adjust seasoning, cover, and serve several days later. The longer the marination period, the tastier the salad.

Makes 8 cups. (P)

RUMANIAN EGGPLANT AND PEPPER SALAD

Bulgarians use mostly green peppers in their salads; Russians use all eggplant. Serbians use more eggplant than green pepper, and Rumanians more green pepper than eggplant. Whatever your choice, just remember to prick the eggplant before putting it in the oven—otherwise, it will explode!

1 large eggplant	¼ cup vegetable oil
4 green peppers	3 tablespoons white vinegar
2 medium onions, chopped fine	2 teaspoons salt
1 clove garlic, crushed	1 tablespoon sugar

1. Preheat oven to 450°.

2. Prick eggplant with a fork and bake with peppers on a cookie sheet in the oven until charred (about 20 minutes). Alternatively, they can be rotated over a gas grill until charred on the outside. When cool, peel the eggplant and the peppers.

3. Chop the eggplant and peppers with the onions and garlic. Add the oil, vinegar, salt, and sugar. Adjust seasoning, and let marinate at least one day. Serve alone or as a dip with crackers. This will last about 1 week covered in the refrigerator.

Makes about 2 cups. (P)

SWEET-AND-SOUR STUFFED CABBAGE

Call it holishkes, praches, or just plain stuffed cabbage. Symbol of plenty, it is traditional to Sukkot. It is just as tasty the second day, especially on a cold winter evening! There are probably as many different stuffed-cabbage recipes as there are towns in Central and East Europe.

While many stuffed vegetables filled with meat and rice come from the Middle East, stuffed cabbage was known in Hungary prior to the Turkish occupation of the seventeenth century. It can be assumed that it was even then an ancient Hungarian dish.

However, Hungarian stuffed cabbage is not sweet-and-sour, contrary to that of Poland and Russia. Ada Baum Lipsitz, originally from Russia, has been experimenting with her sweet-and-sour version for more than sixty years. Doctored up for American tastes, it is delicious!

1 large cabbage, frozen	**Sauce:**
2 pounds ground beef	1 28-ounce can tomatoes
½ tablespoon salt	1 16-ounce can tomato sauce
½ teaspoon pepper	Salt and pepper to taste
½ teaspoon garlic powder	2 large onions, sliced
¼ cup catsup	½ teaspoon garlic powder
3 eggs	½ cup catsup
1 handful uncooked rice	2 6-ounce cans concentrated
1 medium onion, grated	lemonade
	1 tablespoon brown sugar

1. Freeze the cabbage for 2 days. Defrost it the night before cooking. This insures soft, tender leaves and saves the step of boiling the cabbage.

2. Combine the ground beef, salt, pepper, garlic powder, catsup, eggs, rice, and grated onion; set aside.

3. In a saucepan, combine the tomatoes, tomato sauce, salt and pepper, onions, garlic powder, catsup, lemonade, and brown sugar. Bring to a boil and let simmer until the cabbage rolls are ready.

4. Preheat oven to 300°.

5. Remove the core from the head of cabbage. Separate the leaves. Place 1 heaping tablespoon of the meat mixture on each leaf. Tuck the ends in and roll up. Place in a 6-quart casserole.

6. Pour the sauce over the cabbage. Bake, covered, for 4 hours and then uncovered for 1 hour. This is even more delicious the second day.

Serves 6–8. (F)

TURKISH STUFFED ZUCCHINI

With the continually escalating price of meat and poultry, and with frequent medical findings demonstrating that the American diet is unhealthily meat-oriented, more and more people are inserting additional vegetables into their diet. Sephardic Jews have been combining meats, vegetables, and grains for centuries. Originally courtly food at the time of the Ottoman Empire, stuffed grape leaves, zucchini, eggplant, onions, and tomatoes have become everyday cuisine throughout the Middle East.

This Turkish zucchini stuffed with rice and meat is based on a recipe from *Cooking the Sephardic Way*, put out by Temple Tifereth Israel in Los Angeles, with my own variations.

7 medium fresh ripe tomatoes, peeled, seeded, and finely chopped, or 2½ cups canned tomatoes, drained and chopped

1 cup finely chopped onions

2 teaspoons salt

Freshly ground black pepper to taste

6 medium zucchini or other summer squash, about 7"–8" long

1 pound lean ground lamb or beef

⅔ cup uncooked long-grain white rice

2 teaspoons fresh or 1 teaspoon dried mint

2 tablespoons fresh parsley, sliced

¼ teaspoon ground nutmeg

½ teaspoon ground allspice

2 tablespoons currants or raisins

2 tablespoons pine nuts or chopped almonds

1. Combine the tomatoes, onions, 1 teaspoon of the salt, and pepper in a heavy casserole large enough to hold the zucchini in 1 or 2 layers. Stirring frequently, bring to a boil over high heat. Reduce the heat to low, cover, and simmer for 20 minutes.

2. Scrub the zucchini under cold water. Pat dry and cut about 1" off the stem end. With an apple corer, carefully tunnel out the center of each zucchini, leaving a shell ⅛" thick all around.

3. Combine the meat, rice, mint, parsley, remaining 1 teaspoon salt, nutmeg, allspice, currants, pine nuts, and freshly ground pepper to taste. Spoon the stuffing into the squash, tapping the bottom end lightly on the table to shake the stuffing down. Fill the squash completely.

4. Lay the zucchini flat in the tomato sauce. Bring to a boil over high heat. Reduce heat, cover tightly, and simmer for 30 minutes, or until the squash shows only the slightest resistance when pierced with the point of a sharp knife.

Serves 6. (F)

This can also be served with an egg-lemon sauce. Eggplant, green peppers, or onions can replace the zucchini.

SUKKOT TSIMMES

A tsimmes is a fruit-and-vegetable stew eaten on the Sabbath and at Sukkot. My husband's family, from Poland, eats a carrot tsimmes without meat. The following recipe includes meat, fruit, and vegetables, and I think it is a happy combination of many traditions in East Europe. In Yiddish, to make a "tsimmes" means to make a big fuss over someone.

2	pounds flanken or chuck		2	white potatoes, peeled and quartered
1	tablespoon salt		½	pound large prunes
3	medium onions, sliced		½	pound dried apricots
2	tablespoons chicken fat or *pareve* margarine		¼	cup corn syrup
	Water or beef bouillon to cover		¼	cup brown sugar
2	large sweet potatoes, peeled and quartered			Dash of nutmeg
5-6	large carrots, or up to 6 pounds carrots, peeled and thickly sliced		½	teaspoon cinnamon
				Rind and juice of 1 orange
				Salt and pepper to taste

1. Sprinkle the meat with salt and brown, with the onions, in chicken fat or margarine.

2. Add water to cover, and simmer, uncovered, 1 hour.

3. Preheat oven to 350°.

4. Place meat, onions, and juices in a 4-quart casserole, surrounded by the sweet potatoes, carrots, white potatoes, prunes, apricots, corn syrup, brown sugar, nutmeg, cinnamon, and orange juice and rind. Cover with water or beef bouillon. Cover and bake 1 hour.

5. Uncover, season with salt and pepper, and cook an additional 2 hours, or until the liquid disappears and the top turns crusty.

Serves 6. (F)

A recipe from Vilna includes dumplings made from 2 cups flour, 2 eggs, 1 large grated white potato, 1 tablespoon chicken fat, salt and pepper to taste, and ½ cup water. These are cooked in the middle of the tsimmes.

SWEET-POTATO TSIMMES WITH PINEAPPLES

This typical Thanksgiving dish, which my mother serves, is perfect for Sukkot. The marshmallows are obviously a very American addition to an essentially East European recipe.

4 sweet potatoes	½ teaspoon salt
2 tablespoons butter or *pareve* margarine	1 tablespoon brown sugar
1 8-ounce can crushed pineapple, undrained	Paprika or marshmallows

1. Boil sweet potatoes in their jackets until cooked. When done, cool, peel, and mash. Stir in the butter or margarine. Fold in the pineapple, salt, and brown sugar.

2. Preheat oven 400°.

3. Grease a medium casserole and spoon in mixture. Either sprinkle with paprika or, for a sweeter taste, place marshmallows on top, pressing gently into the sweet potatoes, and cook 10 minutes or until the marshmallows are golden brown.

Serves 6–8. (M or P)

TURKEY STUFFING

Just as the first pilgrims to America probably did not eat the tough, wild, dark-meated, forty-pound turkey covered with ticks available at the time of the first Thanksgiving, but rather lobster, clams, and venison, so the Jews in the desert ate whatever wild game they could find, perhaps venison or quail. There was no poultry as we know it in the Middle East until the fifth century B.C.E.

Brought to Europe in 1523–24 from Mexico by Turkish merchants (very possibly Sephardic Jews) going to the eastern Mediterranean, the turkey was dubbed the "Turkish bird" by the English. The French in turn called the bird the *"coq d'Inde,"* meaning Indian cock (the West and East Indies being one and the same in most people's minds in those days), which shortened to *dinde* or *dindon*. In Hebrew, too, turkey is called *hodu,* meaning India. In India they called turkey "Peru," which at least is geographically closer to the truth, although the turkey originated in North, not South, America.

The following stuffing recipe is a standard American Jewish variety made from day-old hallah. It comes from Fran Monus, a nutritionist and fine cook from Youngstown, Ohio.

½ cup *pareve* margarine or chicken fat	1 teaspoon poultry seasoning (optional)
1 cup sliced onions	¼ cup chopped parsley
1 cup diced celery with leaves	2 teaspoons salt
½ loaf hallah, toasted golden brown, cubed, and dried	¼ teaspoon black pepper
Sautéed turkey livers	2 eggs
Sautéed turkey hearts, cut in small pieces (optional)	

1. Melt shortening. Add onions and celery and cook until tender.

2. Soften the dried bread with water and press water out.

3. Add the bread, livers (and hearts, if desired), and seasonings to the vegetables. Add eggs and lightly mix.

4. When filling cavity of bird, do not pack stuffing tightly—leave room for expansion during cooking.

Stuffs a 14-pound turkey. (F)

PERSIAN RICE AND FRUIT STUFFING

While East European Jews use bread and potatoes as fillers for most foods, Persian Jews use rice. The following rice stuffing with dried fruits is from Teheran. (Baghdad Jews would use almonds, rose petals, nutmeg, and cloves.) It is served on many festive occasions (including Passover, when rice is permissible for Persians) and is perfect for a large gathering inside a *sukkah*.

1 cup uncooked long-grain rice	¼ cup chopped parsley
1 tablespoon vegetable oil	Salt and pepper to taste
3 spring onions, chopped	½ teaspoon cinnamon
¼ cup sliced dried prunes	½ teaspoon turmeric
¼ cup sliced dried apricots	1 cup water

1. Rinse and soak the rice in hot water for ½ hour.

2. Drain the rice and sauté with the onions in the vegetable oil for a few minutes, until the onions are golden.

3. Add the prunes and apricots, parsley, salt and pepper, cinnamon, turmeric, and water. Simmer for about 5 minutes.

4. Meanwhile, prepare the turkey for stuffing. Stuff the turkey and cook as you normally do.

Stuffs a 12–14 pound turkey. (P)

SWEET-AND-SOUR PICKLED TONGUE

And Abraham hastened into the tent unto Sarah, and said: "Make ready quickly three measures of fine meal, knead it, and make cakes." And Abraham ran unto the herd, and fetched a calf tender and good, and gave it unto the servant; and he hastened to dress it.

Genesis 18:6–7

When the ministering angels visited Abraham, he prepared a feast for them. The "calf tender and good" refers to three oxen. Why three? According to Rashi, Abraham wanted to give each angel a great delicacy—a tongue with mustard. So it is that tongue has been a special treat for the Jews from Banquet Number One.

In Germany, Jewish cooks learned how to make sweet-and-sour sauces (with mustard, of course!). This recipe, traditional at Sukkot, comes from the German side of my family.

1 4-pound pickled beef tongue	1 tablespoon mustard
2 tablespoons *pareve* margarine,	3 tablespoons red wine vinegar
melted	⅓ cup brown sugar
5 tablespoons catsup	

1. Parboil a beef tongue 4 times, changing the water each time, to make it taste less salty.

2. Then boil in water, uncovered, about 3 hours. If the tongue is small, it may fit in a pressure cooker and will take only 45 minutes to cook. Test with a fork; when it is tender, take it out of the water and peel while hot.

3. Mix the margarine, catsup, mustard, vinegar, and brown sugar. Simmer in a saucepan, uncovered, for 10 minutes. Slice the tongue and pour the sauce over it.

Serves 6–8. (F)

MOUSSAKA
(Eggplant and Meat Casserole)

This recipe is from my good friend Liliane Sivan, the wife of the Israeli Ambassador to Denmark. It is a kosher rendition of the famous Greek moussaka, which includes cheese with the meat. Eggplant casseroles like this are traditional in Israel today and have their roots in Rumania, Greece, and Turkey.

1½ medium onions, finely chopped	Pinch of sugar
	1 pound ground lamb
2 cloves garlic, finely chopped	½ pound ground beef
4 tablespoons vegetable oil	½ teaspoon nutmeg
6 large tomatoes, peeled and chopped	2 tablespoons parsley
	Salt and pepper to taste
1 teaspoon dried basil	3 medium eggplants
1 teaspoon dried oregano	

1. Sauté the onion and garlic in oil until golden. Divide into 2 parts and place half in a large heavy saucepan. Add the tomatoes, ½ teaspoon basil, and ½ teaspoon oregano. Cover and simmer over a low heat for 1 hour. Add a pinch of sugar.

2. To the other part of the onion mixture, add the ground meat and the remaining ½ teaspoon basil and oregano. Brown the meat, but do not overcook. Add the nutmeg, parsley, salt, and pepper. Set aside.

3. In a heavy frying pan, using an additional ¼ cup oil, fry the unpeeled eggplants which have been thinly sliced lengthwise and wiped dry. As they become golden brown on each side, remove them onto a paper towel to drain off the oil. (An alternative method which I have discovered is to oil a cookie sheet, then brush each eggplant with oil and broil until golden on each side. This method takes half the time and uses much less oil.)

4. Preheat oven to 350°.

5. Place 1 layer of eggplant in a 2-quart casserole. Add some of the cooked tomatoes, then some of the meat mixture, and continue in layers until the ingredients are used up, ending with a layer of tomatoes.

6. Bake uncovered until brown on top. It can take up to 1½ hours. It is best to cook the casserole for 45 minutes the night before serving and then another 45 minutes the next day. Recooking improves the flavor.

Serves 6–8. (F)

SAKAU
(Eggplant and Meat Casserole)

Similar to the preceding recipe for moussaka, this sakau dish comes originally from the island of Marmora, via the Sephardic community of Seattle. The rolled eggplants look quite festive in the casserole.

2 medium eggplants	1 teaspoon pepper
3 eggs, beaten	2 tablespoons uncooked rice
½ cup oil (for frying the eggplant)	½ teaspoon sugar
1 small onion, chopped	¼ cup water
2 tablespoons chopped parsley	¾ cup tomato sauce
1 pound ground beef	1 tablespoon chicken fat or
1 teaspoon salt	*pareve* margarine (optional)

1. Peel and cut eggplants lengthwise into slices about ½″ thick. Dip slices into 2 of the beaten eggs, and fry in heated oil on both sides until brown. Set aside.

2. Brown onion in the same oil. Add parsley. Remove from heat.

3. Combine the remaining egg with ground beef, salt, pepper, and rice. Add to onion pan and brown.

4. Preheat oven to 350°.

5. Place a teaspoon or so of meat mixture at one end of each slice of fried eggplant. Roll up the slices jelly-roll fashion. Arrange them in a baking dish, sprinkling sugar over them.

6. Add water, tomato sauce, and chicken fat. Bake for about 35 minutes.

Serves 6–8. (F)

KOSHER DILL PICKLES

[Merrymakers] invade the homes of the well-to-do householders and treat them to an elaborate Simchas Torah kiddush. . . . *The unwilling hosts have no choice but to bring out the best brandy and wine and set the table with food. If they don't, the revelers will get it themselves. They know where everything is kept. They can find their way to the oven, they can drag the preserves out of the cupboard, they can go down to the cellar and bring up the cherry wines, the pickled melons and the cucumbers that the wealthy housewives have prepared for the winter.*

Sholom Aleichem, TEVYE'S DAUGHTERS

For those pickle enthusiasts who want to pickle in small quantities, try this Ukrainian recipe. Ukrainian Jews serve the pickles all year long—except at Rosh Hashanah, for fear that their sour taste might lead to a "sour" year.

4 quarts water	12 cloves garlic
½ cup kosher salt	2 tablespoons pickling spice
4 tablespoons white vinegar	Dill
40–50 small pickling cucumbers, depending on size	

1. In a large pot, boil the water. Add the salt and boil 2 minutes. Let cool for about 5 minutes. Then add the vinegar and let the mixture cool for 3–5 hours.

2. Wash the cucumbers twice in cold water. Dry with paper towels.

3. Fill 6 sterilized 1-quart jars with the pickles.

4. To each jar, add 2 cloves garlic, halved, and 1 teaspoon pickling spice.

5. Fill each jar with the water mixture. Place a large twig of dill in each jar and keep semi-covered for 2–3 days. When the jar starts to bubble, let it bubble a day or two. Then cover and put it in a cool place.

Makes 6 quarts. (P)

AUNT EVA'S COOKIES

The following cookie recipe comes from my great-aunt Eva, whose parents came from Cracow. It is basically a thin pastry dough spread with jam or cocoa and cinnamon and rolled up jelly-roll or strudel fashion. After it is cooked, finger-size cookies are cut. This cookie has its origins in the German strudel of the following recipe. Other fillings for this and similar doughs might include apples or cheese.

6 tablespoons butter or *pareve* margarine	3 teaspoons baking powder
½ cup plus 1 tablespoon sugar	Pinch of salt
2 eggs	1 cup apricot marmalade, or 4
1 teaspoon vanilla	tablespoons cocoa and 1
2½ cups unbleached all-purpose flour	teaspoon cinnamon

1. Using a food processor, electric mixer, or wooden spoon, cream the butter. Add ½ cup sugar and mix well. Add the eggs and vanilla. Slowly add the flour, baking powder, and salt. Knead the dough well.

2. Form the dough into 4 balls and place in the refrigerator overnight.

3. Preheat oven to 350°.

4. Roll each ball of dough into a flat rectangle about ⅛″ thick. Spread with apricot preserves or a mixture of cocoa, cinnamon, and the remaining 1 tablespoon sugar. Roll jelly-roll fashion. (The easiest method is to flatten the dough on a pastry cloth, then lift the edge of the cloth so that the dough rolls into a long cylinder.)

5. Place 2 of the rolls on a large greased cookie sheet, leaving room between them, as they will spread and flatten out. Bake about 20–30 minutes, until golden brown. When cool, slice at an angle at about 1½″ intervals, making finger-length slices.

Makes 4 loaves or 48 slices. (M or P)

EASY APPLE STRUDEL

Strudel dough has one of the most interesting culinary histories. First made in Bavaria or Austria, it was later perfected in Hungary, where East met West.

In the late Middle Ages, German peasant women prepared a dough made of flour, water, and perhaps oil or butter. They filled it with fish or cabbage and ate it as a main dish on meatless Fridays or when meat was not available. Later, they made a sweet by filling the dough with apples, cottage cheese, plums, poppy seeds, or cherries. Jewish women followed suit.

The dough was prepared in two ways. Either two pieces of dough sandwiched a filling; or it was rolled out paper-thin, spread on one side with filling, and rolled—jelly-roll fashion—secured, and baked. As the Jews moved eastward from Germany into Poland and Russia in the late Middle Ages, they took this dough with them and used the sweet version as a basic dessert.

When this strudel reached Hungary, sometime in the sixteenth or seventeenth century, it met with a still thinner, finer dough, brought with the Turkish invasion. Hungarian bakers then learned how to make this fillo dough, which they called rêtes. They soon became the world's masters at stretching and pulling the dough gently over a table. They filled the retês with the sweets of the Germans and rolled it up, jelly-roll fashion, rather than layering it and filling it with the nuts and honey and the spinach and sour cheeses of the Easterners. Unlike the Germans, the Hungarians also filled theirs with ground nuts and, even better, apricot preserves, long known throughout the Middle East. When the filled rêtes reached the coffeehouses of Vienna and Budapest, they became known as strudel.

The following recipes for apple (symbol of plenty at Sukkot) strudels include two doughs: the Bavarian dough handed down in my family, and ready-made fillo dough, which is found at most twentieth-century supermarkets.

2 cooking apples	4 sheets fillo dough
¼ cup sugar	½ cup butter or *pareve* margarine,
¼ cup raisins	melted
2 tablespoons chopped nuts	¼ cup fine dry breadcrumbs
½ teaspoon cinnamon	Confectioners' sugar
Rind of 1 lemon	

1. Preheat oven to 375°.

2. Peel and core the apples. Then combine with the sugar, raisins, nuts, cinnamon, and lemon rind.

3. Take one sheet of fillo and spread out on a dry board. Brush with the melted butter and sprinkle with 1 tablespoon of the breadcrumbs. Place a second fillo leaf on top. Brush with butter and sprinkle with breadcrumbs.

4. Place half the apple mixture at one end of the fillo sheets, leaving a 1″ border. Starting with that end, carefully roll, jelly-roll fashion, ending with the seam on the bottom. Brush the top with more butter and place in a greased jelly-roll pan.

5. Repeat with the remaining filling and the remaining fillo dough.

6. Bake 35 minutes, or until golden. Just before serving, sprinkle with confectioners' sugar. Serve warm. It is delicious with rum raisin ice cream.

Serves 4–6. (M or P)

APFELBUWELE
(German Apple Boy)

Apfelbuwele ("little apple boy" in German), sometimes called schalet, was the favorite Sabbath eve and Sabbath noon dessert in southern Germany. According to some, it was to remind the Jews of the manna eaten in the desert. Manna had many tastes and consisted of many layers. The buwele was basically a yeast strudel or stollen dough filled with apples, rolled jelly-roll fashion and then twisted into a circle before it was baked in a heavy black pot. Like manna, the buwele had many layers and sometimes had many tastes during the fall harvest festival, with other fruits such as pears, peaches, and plums in abundance. Most of the time, however, it was filled with the apples stored in the fall and usually available until February or March. This is my father's family recipe.

Dough:	Filling:
8 cups flour	6 medium apples, peeled, sliced,
2 yeast cakes	and diced
1 teaspoon salt	½ cup raisins
1 cup warm milk or water	¾ cup sugar
1 cup sugar	½ teaspoon cinnamon
½ cup butter or vegetable	1 tablespoon butter or vegetable
shortening	shortening
1 teaspoon vanilla	Handful of raisins
Grated rind of 1 lemon	
3 eggs plus 2 yolks	

1. The day before cooking, put the flour in the bowl to be used for mixing and place in a warm but unlit oven.

2. Place 7 cups flour in a large bowl. Make a well in the center and add the yeast, salt, and about 1 tablespoon warm milk. Stir. Sprinkle with sugar.

3. Melt the butter or vegetable shortening in 1 cup warm milk or water.

4. Add the vanilla, lemon rind, eggs, and egg yolks to the well.

5. When the shortening is melted, add to the flour mixture.

6. Knead the dough by hand until shiny and smooth, adding the remaining 1 cup flour as needed. Or divide the dough into thirds and whirl, using the steel blade, in a food processor, until the dough is shiny and a ball is formed. Cover and let rise in a warm place for 2 hours, or until doubled in size.

7. Preheat oven to 350°.

8. Divide the dough in half and roll out into a rectangle about 24" × 18" on a floured board. The dough should be about ⅛" thick. Then gently pull the corners with your hands to make the dough still thinner.

9. Mix the apples, raisins, sugar, and cinnamon and spread over the dough, leaving a 1" border around the edges.

10. Dot with 1 tablespoon butter.

11. Carefully roll the dough, jelly-roll fashion, tucking the ends under. When the roll is completed, either leave as is and transfer to a greased jelly-roll pan, or carefully form the apfelbuwele into a circle and place, seam side up, in a greased 10" circular pan with high sides.

12. Bake for 30 minutes or until golden. As the apfelbuwele starts to cook, the juice from the apples will accumulate. Occasionally brush the crust with a cooking brush to form a glaze.

13. When finished, let sit a few minutes and then carefully, using a spatula, loosen the crust from the pan. Cover with a plate and then turn over. Tap the pan, and the apfelbuwele should fall out. Turn once again, and *voilà!* Serve warm with ice cream or whipped cream.

14. With the remaining dough, you can do a variety of things. Of course, you can make another apfelbuwele. Or you can make a stollen by filling the dough with ½ cup raisins and ½ cup candied fruits before the rising and working into the dough; you twist the stollen like a hallah. Or you can roll out 2 rectangles and fill with raisins, cinnamon, sugar, and nuts or your favorite fruits. For this last variety, just cook a shorter time and make a confectioners' sugar glaze on top.

Makes 2 apfelbuwele or 1 apfelbuwele and 1 stollen. (M or P)

Aunt Lisl filling the apfelbuwele (photo: Allan Gerson)

"EMBALMING" AN ETROG

The Jewish ladies, it would seem, are in some particulars quite as fanciful as Christians; and they particularly covet the possession of a citron that has been offered at the Feast of the Tabernacles as an emblem of fertility and plenty. Therefore, the husbands, brothers, fathers and sons are eager to purchase; and hence the price paid for these consecrated citrons is often more than double the original cost.

1842 Scripture Herbal, London

The etrog, known as Adam's apple and the apple of paradise, is the bitter citron fruit carried in the left hand as one of the four species at Sukkot. Oval in form, it is symbolically the female egg wrapped in the long masculine *lulav*. Shaped like a heart, it represents the hope of divine forgiveness for the murmurings and desires of our hearts.

Known in ancient Egypt and possibly brought to Palestine from India at the time of Alexander the Great, the etrog has always been regarded for its beautiful color, perfect shape, and fragrant aroma, rather than for its fruit, which is extremely bitter. During the period of the Second Temple, it was an ornamental motif on coins, the walls of synagogues, and mosaics. Although etrogs in general were abundant from the biblical period, an especially beautiful one was always hard to come by and therefore expensive.

A perfect etrog must conform to certain rules. If the larger part is covered with scars, if its nipple is removed, if it is peeled, split, or perforated so that any part is missing, it is invalid. Potential purchasers scrutinize the fruit very carefully for defects.

Throughout the centuries and the great dispersals, Palestinian Jews have sold etrogs to those living in Spain, Russia, Germany, and elsewhere to fulfill the *mitzvah* of Sukkot. Until the end of the nineteenth century, a center for etrog cultivation was also the island of Corfu, whose Jewish population, under Venetian and later French rule, acted as the broker of goods between Venice and the Levant.

After the holiday of Sukkot was over, the etrog's thick skin was eaten pickled in vinegar or boiled to a pulp. A perfume was extracted from its peel, which was also highly valued as an antidote for snakebite. If you have a leftover etrog, add it to grapefruit and orange peel for citrus preserves (in ancient times, this confection was made from etrog and citron, but it is rather bitter). A folk custom relates that a woman who bites into an etrog will become pregnant within a year. So beware!

You can "embalm" your etrog and use it throughout the year at the Havdalah ceremony, as Dov Rosen of Jerusalem does. Here is his method. Use the embalmed etrog as our ancestors did: not only for Havdalah, but to relieve hunger pangs at Yom Kippur and as a good-luck charm during childbirth.

Rules for
"EMBALMING" AN ETROG

1. The etrog should be firm, not soft; smooth, not rough. One of small or medium size is recommended. Special care should be taken not to cut the upper protuberance, i.e., the nipple narrowing toward the pistil.

2. The cloves should be of the type normally used for cooking, hard and dry, with their tops intact. Only after they have been inserted all the way up to (but not including) their heads should the buds be detached by a finger or tool.

3. Each clove must be inserted in a separate perforation. No perforation should touch another, for otherwise a hole will form. Each clove must touch the next; this will prevent shrinkage. Here is the rule: The nearer the perforations to one another, the closer will the cloves be to one another, and the better for the etrog.

4. Any one of a variety of instruments may be used for making the perforations, as long as it is pointed and narrow.

5. The perforations should not be deep. This will prevent juice from seeping out, keep the cloves from moving, and force them to remain rigid.

6. After the "embalming" operation is completed—i.e., the entire etrog is covered completely with cloves—it should be left exposed to the air, preferably in the sun, for several days. When the fruit begins to harden, it should be placed in an etrog box, which should be kept closed. To preserve the etrog even better, it is advisable to line the bottom of the box with the remains of the cloves.

Sam the Argentine Baker with the author (photo: Judith Shepard Rosenfeld)

HANUKKAH

HANUKKAH

Can you guess, children, which is the best of all holidays? Hanukkah, *of course....You eat pancakes every day....Mother [is] in the kitchen (rendering goose fat, mixing batter for pancakes).*

Sholom Aleichem, "Hanukkah Money"

On Kislev 25 in the Jewish calendar, Jews throughout the world light the first Hanukkah candle. The holiday commemorates the Maccabean victory over Antiochus of Syria some twenty-one centuries ago. Going to cleanse and rededicate the Temple, the Maccabees found only enough sacred oil to light the menorah for one day. But a miracle occurred, and one day's supply lasted eight. For each of the eight nights of Hanukkah, therefore, an additional candle is inserted, from right to left, and lit by the *shammas* (or helper), from left to right, until an eight-candled menorah is aglow. After the candle ceremony, it is traditional to sing songs, play with the dreidel (spinning top), open presents, and eat latkes (fried pancakes) and fried foods generally.

The East European origin of latkes becomes apparent in contemporary distinctions between the Ashkenazic and Sephardic communities' celebration of Hanukkah. Edgar Nathan, III, president of the Spanish and Portuguese Synagogue of New York and a descendant of one of the first American Sephardic families, cannot remember a latke tradition in his family. It was, after all, not until the sixteenth century that potatoes were discovered and brought from Bolivia and Peru to western Europe. By that time, the Nathans, because of the Inquisition, had left Spain.

Sephardim have their own Hanukkah traditions, however. Their culinary customs, like those of the Jews in the Ukraine, were probably taken from the surrounding peoples. Greek women claim their loukomades—deep-fried puffs dipped in honey or sprinkled with powdered sugar—are more like the cakes the Maccabees ate, while Persian Jews prefer zelebi, a snail-shaped, deep-fried sweet. Israeli sufganiyot are basically raised jelly doughnuts, and probably adapted from these same traditions.

The symbolism behind the pancakes is threefold. Made initially of flour and water, they served as a reminder of the food hurriedly prepared for the Maccabees as they went to battle before their military victory. The oil in which the pancakes are prepared symbolized the cleansing and rededication of the Temple after it was defiled by the Assyrians. The third meaning, added in medieval times, was one I was never told as a child: the latkes symbolize the cheesecakes the widow Judith served the Assyrian general Holofernes before she cut off his head, thus delivering her people from the Assyrians. The latkes signify the victory of her chastity and humility over the lust and pride of Holofernes, who would have had the Jews slaughtered had Judith not fed him so well and given him so much wine that he fell asleep.

Originally, Hanukkah was a solstice festival and commemorated the Maccabean saga. It was in the Middle Ages that it evolved from a distinctly minor Temple festival to a major family one, during which the *Shulhan Arukh* forbids fasting and mourning and encourages singing and rejoicing. It was about that time that the deep-fried sweet emerged, which later, in East Europe, became the famous latke that we know and love today.

MENUS

Russian Vegetable Soup★
Sauerbraten★
Potato Latkes★
Applesauce★
Green Salad
Nut Horns★

Consommé
Roast Goose with Chestnut and Apple Stuffing★
Rumanian Fried Noodle Pudding★
Endive, Grapefruit, and Avocado Salad
Apple Streusel★

Mushroom and Barley Soup★
Zucchini Potato Latkes★
Applesauce★ and Sour Cream
Sufganiyot (Jelly Doughnuts)★
Rugelach (Cream Cheese Cookies)★

POTATO LATKES

What exactly is the Hanukkah-latke connection? *Latke* is the Yiddish word for pancake. According to Webster's, it probably goes back to the Greek *elaion* (olive oil). "Kartoflani platske" is still the term used to describe a potato pancake eaten in the Ukraine. It is the same food that the Jews, living in the Pale of Settlement in the seventeenth century, probably adapted for Hanukkah. Because their daily diet consisted of potatoes and bread, they wanted to include a special dish cooked in oil to symbolize the main miracle of Hanukkah. This potato pancake, already used by Ukrainians with goose for Christmas, seemed a good and relatively inexpensive choice. Because Hanukkah falls at the season when geese are plentiful, goose fat was an obvious and inexpensive substitute for the original olive oil.

For American Jews intrigued with the gastronomic side of Judaism, Hanukkah appears to be the preferred holiday. It is difficult to equal the taste of brown, crisp potato latkes. Can gefilte fish, matzah balls, haroset, or even hamantashen compare with them? Certainly not. Moreover, every latke lover seems to know how to make these potato pancakes—admirers of, say, gefilte fish may be forced to an outside source—and has strong opinions about them. One will swear by a medium grater, another by the larger variety, and modernists by the grater on the food processor. Some prefer pepper; others, salt. Some add apples; others, grated zucchini, carrots, or parsley. Some insist on grated and others on sautéed onions. And then, of course, there are the purists who contend that only old potatoes and bruised knuckles will do.

Latkes have become a versatile delicacy. They can be made from buckwheat or potatoes with a touch of flour. They can be served for breakfast, brunch, lunch, dinner, or as cocktail-party fare. They can be eaten plain or fancy, with sugar, applesauce, sour cream, or even with chicken soup.

10 medium potatoes	Salt and white pepper to taste
2 medium onions	Vegetable oil
2 large or 3 medium eggs	
¼ cup unbleached all-purpose flour, breadcrumbs, or matzah meal	

1. Peel the potatoes if the skin is coarse; otherwise, just clean them well. Keep them in cold water until ready to prepare the latkes.

2. Starting with the onions, alternately grate some of the onions on the large holes of the grater and some of the potatoes on the smallest holes. This will keep the potato mixture from blackening. Press out as much liquid as possible and reserve the starchy sediment at the bottom of the bowl. Return the sediment to the mixture.*

3. Blend potatoes with the eggs, flour, salt, and white pepper.

4. Heat 1″ of oil in a frying pan. Drop about 1 tablespoon of mixture for each latke into the skillet and fry, turning once. When golden and crisp on each side, drain on paper towels. Serve with yoghurt, sour cream, sugar, or applesauce.

Serves 8–10. (P)

Note: People are always asking me about freezing potato latkes. You can! After making them, place them on a cookie sheet, freeze, and remove to a plastic bag. When ready to serve, place in a 450° oven for several minutes.

RUMANIAN ZUCCHINI POTATO LATKES

2 pounds zucchini	1 teaspoon vegetable oil
2 large potatoes	¾ cup matzah meal
1 medium onion	Salt and pepper to taste
3 eggs	Vegetable oil for frying

1. Peel the zucchini and grate down to the seeds (discard the seeds). Squeeze out the liquid.

2. Peel the potatoes and grate into the zucchini. Once more, remove the liquid. This is important!

3. Grate the onion and add to the zucchini mixture. Add the eggs, oil, and matzah meal, starting with ½ cup of matzah meal and continuing to add more if necessary, until there is body to the mixture. Season with salt and pepper to taste and blend well.

4. In a large, heavy frying pan, heat some vegetable oil until almost smoking. Using a large tablespoon, spoon a round portion of zucchini mixture into the pan and brown on both sides. Serve hot with sour cream or applesauce.

Makes 18 large pancakes and serves 6–8. (P)

*The steel blade of a food processor or the grating blade are less painful ways of grating the potatoes and the onions. The blade makes a smooth consistency and the grater a crunchy one.

RUSSIAN PASHTIDA
(Pan-fried Potato Latkes)

Leftover potato latke batter from the preceding recipe (p. 136)
Handful of raisins (less or more depending on amount of leftover batter)
Dash of cinnamon
Vegetable oil

1. Squeeze the water from the leftover potato mixture, which will probably have turned black overnight. Discard the water.

2. Add raisins and cinnamon.

3. Heat oil in a medium frying pan and cover with potato mixture. Cook until golden. Then cut across the middle and gently turn each half to brown on the other side. Pashtida can be eaten as a starch with the meal or as a dessert.

The amount this recipe feeds depends on the number of latkes eaten the night before! (P)

APPLESAUCE

What would potato latkes be without applesauce? This is my own recipe, which I especially like because the apples are cooked in their skin, there is very little sugar, and it is easy!

4 pounds apples
1 lemon
2 cinnamon sticks
½ cup apple juice, cider, or water
Honey, brown sugar, or maple sugar to taste

1. Quarter the apples and the lemon. Place in a heavy pot with the cinnamon sticks. Add ½ cup apple juice, cider, or water.

2. Cover, bring to a boil, and then simmer over a low heat, stirring occasionally to turn the apples and making sure they do not stick. You may want to add some liquid. Cook about 20 minutes, or until the apples are soft.

3. Put the sauce through a food mill and adjust seasoning by adding honey, brown sugar, or maple syrup to taste.

Makes about 1 quart. (P)

RUMANIAN FRIED NOODLE PUDDING

Potato latkes may not be essential to Hanukkah, but cooking with oil is. If you want a change from potato pancakes, try this Rumanian fried noodle pudding, which goes well with sauerbraten or roast goose.

½ pound fine egg noodles	6 tablespoons vegetable oil
2 tablespoons *pareve* margarine	2 eggs, beaten
1 large onion, diced	Salt and pepper to taste

1. Cook the noodles according to the directions on the package and drain. Transfer to a large bowl and add margarine, blending well. Set aside.

2. Sauté the onion in 2 tablespoons vegetable oil, until golden. Add the onion to the noodles. Add the eggs and salt and pepper to taste. Mix all ingredients well.

3. Heat the remaining 4 tablespoons oil in a large, heavy frying pan. Add the noodle mixture and let brown on the bottom and sides, taking care not to burn.

4. When browned on one side, place a large plate over the pan. Turn over onto the plate and then slide back into the pan to brown the other side.

Serves 4-6. (P)

SAUERBRATEN À LA NATHAN

Before the middle of the nineteenth century, beef was not a widespread food. Most Jews ate chicken, goose, or, in the Middle East, lamb. Potting what beef was available was a good way to preserve it. It is no wonder, then, every Jewish mother has her special pot roast recipe, something that can be prepared in advance of Jewish holidays. Here is my mother's, a perfect accompaniment to potato latkes and applesauce.

2	teaspoons salt	1	5-pound brisket of beef,
3	tablespoons brown sugar		shoulder roast of beef, chuck
1	cup chili sauce		roast, or end of steak
1½	cups white vinegar	1	cup chopped celery leaves
2	teaspoons seasoning salt	2	onions, sliced

1. Mix salt, brown sugar, chili sauce, vinegar, and seasoning salt together. Pour over meat and let stand overnight in the refrigerator.

2. Preheat oven to 325°. Place the meat in an ovenproof casserole, pouring marinade over meat. Cover with the celery leaves and onions.

3. Cover and bake for about 3 hours, basting often with marinade. Remove cover for 1 more hour. (Allow approximately 1 hour per pound for roasting.)

4. This dish is best prepared in advance so that fat can be easily skimmed from the surface. When ready to serve, slice and reheat in the strained pan marinade.

Serves 8. (F)

ROAST GOOSE WITH CHESTNUT AND APPLE STUFFING

Geese is my business. . . .but you think it's as easy as all that? The first thing you got to do is this: you start buying geese right after Sukkoth, in the autumn. You throw them into a coop and keep them there all winter, until December. You feed them and take good care of them. Comes Hanukah, you start killing them, and you turn geese into cash. If you think it's so easy to buy them, feed them, kill them, and turn them into cash, you're wrong. First of all, I fry the skin and the fat and make goose fat out of it. I make Passover fat every year, for my Passover fat is considered the best and most kosher fat in the village. When I make kosher for Passover goose fat, Passover steps into the house smack in the middle of Hanukah. . . .Goose meat. You'd be in some pickle if you only depended on the goose meat. Besides that there were fried scraps and livers and gizzards and heads and feet. Then there were the gullets and wings and tongues and hearts and kidneys. Not to mention necks.

Sholom Aleichem, "Geese"

As the above tale relates, the goose became the most cost-effective meat within the Jewish economy of Europe. Although one goose required four-to-five times as much feed per pound of meat as a chicken and used the same small plot of land, its yield to its owner was greater. First, there was the meat. Then there was all the rendered fat used for cooking. The neck could be stuffed and the skin and fat fried into grieben. The feathers could be sold as quills and the down stuffed into pillows. The fattened liver could be sold for pâté de foie gras.

It is no surprise that the area surrounding Strasbourg in Alsace-Lorraine, long a Jewish area of settlement, is one of the centers of the goose-liver industry. There is even a factory selling kosher pâté de foie gras. Moreover, a large percentage of the goose livers used today in that delicacy are exported from Israel to France. A side effect is that Israeli newspapers have advertisements encouraging people to eat geese.

In sixteenth-century Germany, geese were known as "the Jews' fowl." Beef and pork were the everyday meat of the poor. Wild game was that of the rich. Since Jews are not traditionally hunters, they sought out meat which conformed to their religious beliefs. Chicken and geese were the most appropriate, within easy reach of a *shohet*.

In northern countries, no *pareve* margarine or vegetable oil existed until the turn of this century. Olive oil, produced in the Middle East, was prohibitively expensive. For Jews, who did not use pork fat in their cooking, geese were all the more essential. The rendered goose fat was used in cooking throughout the winter. It is therefore understandable that geese would be known as the Jews' fowl.

My father still remembers eating geese as a boy in Germany. Young geese were eaten from May to September and the older ones throughout the winter. His father had his own jar of grieben, skin which had been deep-fried. German Christians traditionally eat goose for Christmas; Jews eat it at Hanukkah. The following is a recipe which my grandmother, Lina Nathan, made for goose stuffed with chestnuts and apples. The recipe appears in the cookbook she gave my aunt Lisl on her wedding day in 1921.

Note: Instead of this stuffing, you can use whole apples.

1 8–10-pound goose	½ cup raisins
2 cups cooked, peeled chestnuts, quartered	1 cup prunes
	Salt to taste
6 cups peeled, cored, and quartered apples	

1. Remove excess fat from the cavity and giblets. Render the fat and use in cooking.

2. Combine the chestnuts, apples, raisins, and prunes, and stuff the cavity about ¾ full. (Figure 1 cup of stuffing per person. Vary ingredients to suit the size of your goose. Any leftover stuffing can be cooked in tin foil alongside the goose for the last hour.) After stuffing the goose, truss it, and place the bird, breast side up, on a rack in a roasting pan. Rub with salt.

3. Preheat oven to 400°.

4. Roast for 1 hour. Prick the skin with a fork at ½" intervals to let the fat escape. Reduce the temperature to 350° and roast for another hour. As the fat accumulates, remove it with a bulb baster. To see if the goose is done, prick the thigh with a fork. It is done if the juices are yellowish. If not, reduce the oven to 325° and continue cooking.

5. Let sit 15 minutes while you make a gravy, and serve. This goes well with potato latkes (p. 136) or cabbage strudel (p. 113) and a light salad.

Serves 8. (F)

GRANDMOTHER'S NOTES ON ROAST GOOSE

1. A young goose can be roasted in 1 hour. It has to be covered with salt, pepper, and onion.

2. To render as much fat as possible from a goose, use an older one. Remove the skin completely and cut into small squares. Place in an iron casserole, add salt and some water, and bring quickly to a boil. Then turn down the heat. The crispy grieben should be light brown when they are done, with all the fat removed from the skin. The grieben should be removed from the fat, pressed to extrude remaining fat. Fresh, they taste delicious, but are of course fattening!

3. Leave the fat from the grieben standing until it is clear; then pour it into a stone pot, where it will keep all winter.

4. *Geschundenes* [hurt goose] is the goose without the skin. Roast it in the oven like any other roast. It takes 2–3 hours.

5. Ganef [see the Hungarian version on p. 49]—stuffed goose neck or even back of the goose. You can cut around the skin where the neck starts and pull the skin off whole. This can be stuffed in various ways. Soak 3 slices of white bread in water; press as much water out as possible. Add slices of onion and parsley and fry everything together in some goose fat or margarine. Add ¼ pound ground beef, salt, pepper, and other spices to taste, and 1 egg. Mix everything and stuff the skin of the neck, which you sew closed. Roast the neck in bouillon in the oven for 1 hour.

6. Goose Liver: Put salt and pepper on the liver and fry it in goose fat, turning it frequently. Takes 8–10 minutes. Cool in the fat and leave fat around the liver. Serve on slices of toast.

RUSSIAN VEGETABLE SOUP

Substance and authority are words to describe Jewish soups. Why else would chicken soup be called Jewish medicine? No insipid bouillons or consommés for us hearty eaters! Try this Russian-style vegetable soup at Hanukkah. Soak up the gravy with the Russian rye bread which follows.

3 carrots	½ cup lima beans
2 medium white potatoes	½ cup green split peas
1 sweet potato	½ cup large whole barley
4 quarts water	½ pound fresh string beans, diced
2 pounds top rib, cut in stewing pieces	4 ribs celery, diced
1 package dry mushrooms or 1 cup fresh sliced mushrooms	Salt and pepper to taste

1. Grate the carrots, potatoes, and sweet potato on the large holes of a grater, or use the grating or steel blade of a food processor.

2. Bring 4 quarts of water to the boil and add all ingredients. Cover and simmer about 2 hours, stirring occasionally. If, when finished, you prefer a thinner soup, add more water.

Serves 8–10. (F)

SAM THE ARGENTINE BAKER'S MEDIUM RYE BREAD

"You don't have to be Jewish to love Levy's rye"—or any rye bread, for that matter. That you don't have to be Russian or Polish is more to the point. Rye flour was never grown in ancient Israel and needs a cold climate. Rye originated as a weed in parts of Asia where wheat was cultivated thousands of years ago. From here it was probably brought to northern Europe. Although rye 'n injun, made from rye and corn, was the staple bread of the early American colonists, it was Russian Jewish bakers at the turn of the century and later advertising techniques that made it so popular.

The earliest bread prepared by the Jews was made of flat cakes baked between layers of slow-burning camel dung, as in the Book of Ezra. They also parched the grain, like the reapers in the Book of Ruth. If they had a hearth, they roasted the dough in the ashes.

When the Jews settled down and began baking bread, they baked well. Their best bread was of wheat "kemach solet," "essence of flour," from which they made Temple sacrifices to God and bread for the rich. Barley was used by the poor and for horse feed. To make barley palatable, ground lentils, beans, and millet were added.

At first, Jewish housewives and their daughters tended the ovens; later, maidservants helped. Later still, when Jews became city dwellers, men became bakers. In Jerusalem there is still a bakers' street in the Old City. The first breads were small round loaves slightly raised in the center and about as thick as a finger. Three breads per person were eaten at each meal. Thus, at the meal Abigail prepared for David and his men, she served two huge jugs of wine and two hundred loaves of bread.

Rye bread, often considered inferior to wheat, is sometimes not eaten on holidays. But during the week of Hanukkah it is perfectly acceptable with a hearty vegetable soup.

Black bread—rye bread made from dark, coarsely ground flour—is what poor Russian Jews ate during the week, with hallah or white bread for the Sabbath. American rye is lighter, so we need coffee, cocoa, and/or blackstrap molasses to achieve the desired dark effect.

It takes an expert to prepare excellent rye bread. Rye flour is harder to handle than wheat. The dough is stickier, more difficult, and must be kneaded longer.

The finest bread baker I have ever met is seventy-six–year–old Sam the Argentine Baker, a Washington legend. Born in Russia and raised in Argentina, he came to Washington and opened the city's finest bread bakery until he retired to Israel in 1974. On a recent visit to Washington, Sam spent several days making empanadas, knishes, hallah, pizza, and rye bread at my home. He probably has the strongest fingers I have ever seen, for he took only a few moments to knead the following rye bread. His movements appeared effortless. It was only when I tried to repeat his recipe that I learned how very talented he is.

1 square (0.6 ounces) fresh yeast	¾ pound (2¾–3 cups) rye flour
1½ teaspoons sugar	¼ pound rye bran*
2½ cups water	1¾ teaspoons salt
1¼ pounds (5 cups) all-purpose flour	3 tablespoons vegetable oil

1. Proof the yeast with the sugar in about 1 cup lukewarm water. Set aside. In winter, make sure the temperature in your kitchen is at least 65 degrees.

*If you cannot find rye bran, whole wheat will do.

2. On a marble or pastry board, place 4 cups white flour, 2 cups rye flour, and the bran. Make a well and put in the yeast mixture. Work the wet ingredients into the dry, using your hands and a pastry scraper. Add 1½ cups more water, salt, and vegetable oil. Slowly work in the remaining cup of white flour and ¾ cup rye flour. (Dividing the dough in 3 and using a food processor is by far the easiest way.) When you have added the flour, the dough will be sticky, heavy, and difficult to manage. Scrape under the dough, folding it over. Using your hands, continue to lift and fold, adding more flour as needed, and scraping the board. Knead for about 5 minutes, until the dough is soft, velvety, and elastic.

3. Shape the dough into a ball, dust with flour, and place in a bowl. Cover and let rise in a draft-free place. This will take ¾–1½ hours.

4. Punch down the dough, knead, and make 2 balls from it. Shape into oblong forms and place on a greased cookie sheet. Cover and let rise about ½ hour more, or until the loaves rise.

5. Preheat oven to 400°.

6. Using your hands, spread a little oil on the dough. With a razor make 4 flat slits in each loaf.

7. Place the loaves on a cookie sheet on the next-to-lowest rack of the oven. Bake for 10–12 minutes. Then lower the oven to 350° and bake about 45 minutes more, until the loaves sound hollow when tapped. If your oven does not seem too hot at 400°, keep it that high. Sam checked the loaves periodically and kept turning them around for even baking. Sam believes that rye bread should be eaten the next day. "When it's too fresh it's like a stone in the stomach."

Makes 2 loaves. (P)

RUGELACH
(Cream-Cheese Cookies)

In the Middle Ages it was traditional to eat cheesecakes at Hanukkah in commemoration of the cheesecakes or pancakes Judith gave to General Holofernes. After eating these cakes, the general became thirsty for wine, which Judith also served him. Soon he swooned, Judith slew him, and the Jews were saved. Today many people serve sour-cream pancakes at Hanukkah in memory of Judith. Others serve rugelach, a half-moon cream-cheese cookie, which may be a far cry from the original cheesecake but is nevertheless a melt-in-the-mouth delicacy perfect for the fanciest party.

Dough:
½ pound unsalted butter, softened
8 ounces cream cheese, softened
2 cups all-purpose flour

Raisin Nut Filling:
½ cup sugar
½ cup seedless raisins

1 teaspoon cinnamon
1 cup finely chopped nuts
¼ cup sugar (for topping)

Strawberry Jam Filling:
½ cup ground almonds
½ cup strawberry jam
¼ cup sugar (for topping)

1. In a mixing bowl or food processor, cream the butter and cream cheese together.

2. Beat in the flour, little by little. Knead the dough lightly until all the flour is incorporated.

3. Refrigerate at least 1 hour. Divide the dough into 2 portions.

4. Prepare one of the fillings by combining the ingredients (except the ¼ cup sugar for the topping), and set aside.

5. Preheat oven to 350°.

6. Roll out one of the portions of dough in a circle about 1/16″ thick. With a knife or pastry wheel, cut the pastry into 16 pie-shaped wedges. If the dough is sticky, dust it with a little flour.

7. Sprinkle or spread the filling of your choice on the little wedge. Beginning at the wide edge, roll the dough up toward the point.

8. Place on an ungreased cookie sheet and carefully sprinkle with a tiny bit of the reserved sugar. Repeat with the rest of the dough and filling.

9. Bake for 15–18 minutes, or until golden.

Makes 32. (M)

NUT HORNS

Most countries have a recipe for half-moon butter cookies with ground nuts and sugar. The Greeks have kourambiedes and the Viennese kupferlin. Crescent-shaped rolls and cookies in Budapest date from the year 1686, during the Turkish siege of the city. Bakers working at night heard the Turks digging an underground passage into the city and were able to warn the authorities. To reward the bakers who saved the city, they were permitted to make a special crescent pastry in the emblem that decorates the Ottoman flag. The following nut horn or crescent recipe—originating in Austro-Hungary, continuing to the Bronx and Belmont, Massachusetts—requires less sugar than many Hungarian and Austrian versions of kupferlin.

¼ cup sifted confectioners' sugar
2 cups sifted all-purpose flour
½ pound unsalted butter or *pareve* margarine

3 ounces ground pecans or unblanched almonds

1. Preheat oven to 350°.

2. Combine the sugar, flour, and butter by cutting the butter into the dry ingredients. (This is done very simply with a food processor.)

3. Add nuts, mixing with your hands or a food processor, until the dough is smooth and no longer sticky.

4. Taking a handful of dough at a time, roll it into long 1″-wide cylinders. Slice into ½″ long pieces and shape into small crescents. Place on ungreased cookie sheets.

5. Bake 10–15 minutes. Remove to a plate and sprinkle with confectioners' sugar.

Makes about 30. (M or P)

GINGERBREAD COOKIES

Jewish parents often find themselves in a quandary at Christmas. Neighbors are busily baking cookies to give as gifts and to have on hand for guests. Although more of a traditional Jewish custom at Purim, there is no reason to feel left out. A satisfying way for your children to share in the Hanukkah preparations is to spend a "cookie day" making free-form designs of menorahs. Just watch their eyes light up as their hands get into the dough. Forget the cookie-cutters. Four-to-six–year–olds might need some assistance but the six-and-above set quickly create their own cookie world of plumed birds, alligators, and, of course, Judah Maccabees.

From a light honey and a dark molasses dough, you can create two-tone fantasy figures in your own style or in the grand tradition of Matisse cutouts. A garlic press will do nicely to make curly hair or just curlicues.

LIGHT HONEY GINGERBREAD

⅓ cup vegetable shortening	1 teaspoon lemon flavoring
⅓ cup sugar	3 cups sifted flour
1 egg	1 teaspoon baking soda
⅔ cup honey	1 teaspoon salt

1. Combine the shortening, sugar, egg, honey, and lemon flavoring in a large bowl. Blend thoroughly with a wooden spoon or mixer.

2. Sift together the flour, baking soda, and salt onto wax paper. Add the dry ingredients to the wet, about a cup of flour at a time, mixing well after each addition. Add more flour if necessary, and pat into a large ball. Keep in a plastic bag in the refrigerator at least 1 hour before using.

3. Preheat oven to 350°. (A toaster oven will do nicely if the cookies are being made in a school or playroom.)

4. Before working the dough, dip your hands in flour. For each cookie, take about a handful of dough. Roll it out on aluminum foil with a rolling pin or press it with your hands, until the cookie is about ¼″ thick.

There are a number of ways to use this basic dough:

Free form: Cut into shapes with a dull knife, popsicle stick, pastry wheel, or any blunt instrument. Do not try to draw with the knife as this will produce fuzzy edges, but actually cut the contours of basic shapes with small, swift strokes. You can cut out abstract designs, animals or human shapes of your choice. Don't add detail, as shapes spread in baking. Leave sufficient space between the cookies to allow for spreading.

Two tone: Use this dough with the following dark one to make two-tone, free-form designs, animals and people. Use one dough for the body and another for the head, tail, or feet. The light and dark doughs will merge when placed next to each other.

Cutouts: To make cutouts, first make a design on drawing paper; cut out with scissors. Then use a knife or other sharp instrument to outline the design in the cookie dough.

5. After the cookies are cut out, decorate with sunflower seeds, blanched almonds, pignolia, pecans or walnuts, currants, yellow or black raisins. Use a garlic press to make hair from the dough, and the tines of a fork for lines.

6. Bake 8–10 minutes or longer, according to the thickness of the cookie. Test for doneness by pressing the dough with your finger. If it springs back, the cookie is ready. Leave the cookies as they are, or decorate with icing and place candies, sprinkles, nuts, candied fruit, etc., on top. Icing alone can make decorative mustaches, feathers, and designs. Press long strands of licorice or soft ribbons of icing into the dough for legs and arms.

Makes 24 5" cookies. (P)

DARK MOLASSES COOKIES

⅓	cup vegetable shortening	2	teaspoons baking soda
1	cup light brown sugar	1	teaspoon salt
1½	cups molasses	½	teaspoon cinnamon
⅔	cup water	¼	teaspoon nutmeg
6	cups sifted flour	¼	teaspoon ginger

1. Combine the shortening, sugar, molasses, and water in a large bowl. Blend thoroughly with a wooden spoon or mixer.

2. Sift together the flour, baking soda, salt, cinnamon, nutmeg, and ginger onto wax paper. Add the dry ingredients to the wet, a cup of flour at a time, mixing well after each addition. Add more flour if necessary, and pat into a large ball. Keep in a plastic bag in the refrigerator at least 1 hour, or until ready to use.

3. Preheat oven to 350°.

4. Shape and decorate as you would the light honey cookies. Bake for 15 minutes or longer, according to the thickness of the dough.

Makes 24 5" cookies. (P)

BROWNIES

If memory serves me, [my mother] carried mostly chalk and carob—two items with a big turnover in Kasrilevke. Chalk was needed for whitewashing the houses, and carob provided sweet snacks that were cheap and plentiful. The kheder boys spent all their breakfast and lunch money on carob, and the groceries did a thriving business.

Sholom Aleichem, "The Dreydl"

In Sholom Aleichem's world, children nibbled on carob chips while playing with dreidels at Hanukkah. The evergreen carob tree is indigenous to ancient Israel. Its 6"–8" dark pods have a dark, chewy substance with the flavor of chocolate. The ground powder was used in cakes. The tougher pods were food for the poor or fodder for the cattle. In traditional Jewish lore, the carob symbolizes humility.

In affluent America, carob powder has become a health-food substitute for chocolate. The following is my favorite chocolate brownie recipe—a good accompaniment to dreidel-spinning!

¼ pound butter or *pareve* margarine	3 squares bitter chocolate, melted and cooled, or 3 tablespoons carob powder
1 cup sugar	1 cup sifted all-purpose flour
2 eggs	½–1 cup broken walnuts or pecans
1 teaspoon vanilla	

1. Preheat oven to 350°. Grease a shallow 8" × 8" pan.

2. Cream the butter or margarine and gradually add the sugar. Add the eggs, one at a time. Add vanilla and melted chocolate.

3. To the wet ingredients, add the flour gradually. Fold in the nuts.

4. Pour into the pan and bake 18 minutes (30 minutes if using carob powder). Test. If too moist, leave in the turned-off oven a few minutes longer. Cut into squares.

Makes 16. (M or P)

SUFGANIYOT
(Jelly Doughnuts)

Modern Israel's legacy to Hanukkah is sufganiyot, jelly doughnuts rolled in sugar. Sufganiyot are descended from one of the oldest sweets known to mankind—the Greek loukomades, a sweet fritter dipped in honey-and-sugar syrup. Loukomades were originally wheatcakes fried on an iron grill, then covered with grape-derived molasses. The honey syrup used today as a coating was borrowed from the Turks; the cooking method has changed to deep-frying. This Israeli holiday fare reflects the melding of East and West. The fritter is of Sephardic origin, and the jelly filling and granulated-sugar coating replacing the honey syrup come from Western immigrants, most probably Germans, who ate an apricot-filled glazed doughnut on Hanukkah.

2 tablespoons dry yeast	Pinch of cinnamon
3½ tablespoons sugar	1½ tablespoons softened
¾ cup lukewarm milk	margarine
2½ cups all-purpose flour	Plum or strawberry preserves
2 egg yolks	Vegetable oil for deep-frying
Pinch of salt	Granulated sugar

1. Dissolve the yeast and 2 tablespoons sugar in the milk.

2. Sift the flour. Place it on a board and make a well in the center. Add the yeast mixture, the egg yolks, salt, cinnamon, and the remaining sugar. Knead well. Add the margarine and knead until the dough is elastic.

3. Cover and let rise 2 hours.

4. Sprinkle flour on the board. Roll the dough out thin. Cut out with a glass into rounds about 2″ in diameter. Cover and let rise 15 minutes more.

5. In a heavy pot, heat the oil to 375°.

6. Drop the doughnuts in the oil, 4–5 at a time, turning when brown. Drain on paper towels.

7. With a tiny spoon, take some jam and fill the sufganiyot. Insert the spoon in the top of the doughnut, revolve it inside the doughnut, and remove it from the same hole made on entering.

8. Roll in granulated sugar and serve. You can make larger sufganiyot if you like. Whatever you decide, eat them immediately!

Makes 30–35. (M)

Mozelle Sofaer rolls out the dough for sambusak (photo: Dan Scheuer)

PURIM

PURIM

The Shalachmones *that* Black Nechama *carried consisted of a fine slice of strudel, two big sugar cookies, a large honey* teigl, *two cushion cakes stamped with a fish on both sides and filled with tiny sweet* farfel, *and two large slabs of a poppyseed confection, black and glistening, mixed with ground nuts and glazed with honey. Besides all this, there lay on the plate, smiling up at them, a round, golden sweet-smelling orange that wafted its delicious odor right into their nostrils.*

Sholom Aleichem, "Two Shalachmones"

Purim places a greater emphasis on physical delights than does any other Jewish holiday. When Purim approaches, troubles are forgotten and festivities begin. It is a holiday of letting go, of celebrating a festival meal, and of joy.

Celebrated on Adar 14, which falls in February or March, Purim is a reminder of the Jewish people's deliverance from serious danger in the remote past. Wicked Haman, the favorite and minister of the Persian King Ahasuerus, wished to exterminate all the Jews of the Persian Empire because he thought the Jew Mordecai had failed to show him proper respect. Mordecai, helped by his cousin and foster daughter Esther, who was also the second queen of King Ahasuerus, foiled his plot. On Adar 13, the Jews were to be destroyed. Instead, on this day the Jewish population overcame those who wanted to wipe them out and then celebrated the victory the next day.

In their ecstasy, Mordecai and Esther proclaimed that the festival of Purim should be celebrated for all time, by two annual recountings of the story of the Megillah (the Book of Esther) in the synagogue (on the evening prior to and on the day of Purim), a *seudat Purim*, or festival meal in the late afternoon of Purim, charity to the poor—usually in the form of money to at least two people—and the sending of gifts (*mishloah manot*). Gifts and charity are given because the Jews were rescued from the wicked Haman through repentance. Repentance requires prayer, fasting, and charity. On Purim all three are to be fulfilled. To remind us of the three-day fast which Esther made before her dangerous approach to the king, one fast day on Adar 13—the Taanit Esther—was introduced in the ninth century.

The origins of Purim lie shrouded in mystery. Most authorities doubt the historic validity of the Megillah, and consider it an allegorical story. Throughout history, however, stories similar to that of Purim have repeated themselves, with the Jews being saved in the nick of time.

Wine plays a vital role in Purim, because the downfall of Haman was attributed to the wine and other drinks Esther served liberally at the banquet. In addition, the first queen, Vashti, was killed because the king was drunk; her death paved the way for Esther. The Talmud recommends drinking until it is impossible to distinguish (*ad lo yada*) between Haman and Mordecai. Wine is also a sign of happiness and "wine makes the heart of man happy." It also inaugurates all Jewish religious ceremonies.

At the Purim feast, kreplakh, sambusak, chick-peas, and turkey are typical foods. Turkey (see p. 120), considered to be a stupid animal, is often served in remembrance of Ahasuerus, who was a foolish king and who "reigned from India unto Ethiopia." A turkey in Hebrew is called an Indian cock.

In the seasonal cycle of Jewish holidays, Purim's gastronomic position is quite important. As the last festival prior to Passover, it is an occasion to use up all the year's flour, so many delicacies with risen flour are prepared. All kinds of deep-fried and baked pastries are prepared the Jewish world over.

In the Russia of Sholom Aleichem, for example, women baked strudels, teyglakh, sugar cookies, and of course hamantashen. In Morocco, women bake small breads filled with hard-boiled eggs. In Iraq, they make all kinds of sambusak, or turnovers filled with chicken or cheese. In Tunisia, Lebanon, and Egypt, deep-fried pastries filled with nuts and oozing with honey are prepared.

The many varieties of baked goods were made into *shalah manot*, or portions sent through a messenger, often a young child. The sending of *shalah manot* goes this way: At least two different kinds of food are placed on a tray. One should be of flour and one of a fruit that does not have to be cooked. Two blessings are recited, one over grain and one over fruit. Through the years it became traditional to fill sweet trays with honey cakes, gingerbread Haman's ears, pockets, or whatever the national representation of a cookie Haman might be, and dried figs, pomegranates, or oranges. One woman would send a portion to a friend. Not to be outdone, the friend would repay the gift, with at least one additional sweet added to it. A third would fill her tray with still more delicacies, and so on.

Last year, while testing hamantashen recipes for this book, I invited in several neighborhood children to help. After explaining to them the concept of *shalah manot*, the girls went to various neighbors bearing portions of cookies and fruit. Both the recipients and the donors were delighted—and molding the cookies was a perfect afternoon's entertainment.

Try making the cookie recipes in this section or those listed under Hanukkah and the Sabbath for your own *shalah manot*. And don't forget the fruit!

MENUS

Meat Sambusak★
Turkey with Persian Rice and
Fruit Stuffing★
Fagots de Légumes★
Ma'amoul (Nut-filled Cookies)★
Figs Stuffed with Walnuts★

Chicken Soup with Matzah Balls★
Sauerbraten★
Kasha Varnishkes★
Chick-peas★
Green Pepper and Tomato Salad★
Sliced Oranges and Strawberries
with Liqueur
Beigli★

Mushroom and Barley Soup★
Roast Chicken★
Chestnuts and Prunes★
Rice
Salade à ma Façon★
Fresh Fruit Cup
Hamantashen★

Baked White Fish★
Cheese Sambusak★
Zucchini Fritada★
Hamantashen★

CHICK-PEAS FOR PURIM

*The table was more richly prepared than for any other meal in the year—
foods and drinks of all kinds; twisted loaves that shone yellow, a huge baked
fish touched up with saffron, golden colors that harmonized with the light of
the candles stuck in the big Menorahs, or seven-branched candlesticks, that
burned brilliantly, one at each end of the table. But in the center of the
table, and near each Menorah, had been placed three piles of plain boiled
chick-peas. I asked my mother why these plebeian dishes had been permitted
in the midst of this glorious company. And she explained that they were
commemorative of the extreme piety of Esther the Queen. For Esther was a
good Jewish daughter and, though she lived in the luxurious and profligate
palace of the great king, she would touch none of the food. Haman the wicked,
knowing of the laws of the Jews, had forbidden the presence of a Shohet, or
ritual slaughterer, in the palace. And Esther therefore contented herself, at all
the feasts, with plain peas and beans; yet, on this diet she was as well fed, and
as beautiful, as those that gorged themselves on the most tempting dishes.*
Schmaryahu Levin, CHILDHOOD IN EXILE

Esther was not the only one in Jewish history to restrict herself to a vegetarian
diet lest she disobey the dietary laws. Daniel would eat only porridge or the
edible seed of peas and beans in the court of Nebuchadnezzar.

Nahit, or chick-peas, are traditional at Purim. I first tasted this easily
prepared vegetable or hors d'oeuvre at the Jerusalem home of my co-author
for *The Flavor of Jerusalem*, Judy Stacey Goldman.

1 20-ounce can chick-peas or garbanzo beans	Salt to taste Freshly ground pepper to taste

1. Place the chick-peas with the liquid from the can in a saucepan. Simmer a
few minutes, until heated through.

2. Drain the water. Sprinkle with salt and freshly ground pepper to taste.
Serve in a dish with toothpicks, or eat the chick-peas as you would sunflower
seeds or peanuts.

Makes about 2 cups. (P)

MUSHROOM AND BARLEY SOUP

When I was an aide to New York City's former Mayor Abe Beame, we had dinner one evening at Ratner's Dairy Restaurant on Manhattan's Lower East Side. The mayor, not known for his gourmet tendencies, whispered excitedly to his press secretary that he was going to order a favorite dish—mushroom and barley soup. Intrigued by what had caught the mayor's fancy, I followed suit. It was a heavenly combination of dried and fresh mushrooms, dill, and barley—thick, but not so heavy as many other varieties.

At home I have tried to duplicate the soup. Although the result was satisfactory, I could not of course duplicate the flavor of a Ratner specialty without the presence of one essential Ratner ingredient: Old World gentleman waiters.

1 1-pound can tomatoes, chopped, with the juice	½ cup whole barley
2 quarts water	½ cup small dried lima beans
1 onion, thinly sliced	1 carrot, sliced
2 ribs celery with leaves, diced	1 pound mushrooms, sliced*
2 tablespoons chopped parsley	2 tablespoons salt
½ green pepper, chopped	2 tablespoons snipped fresh dill

1. In a large saucepan, combine the tomatoes, juice, water, onion, celery, parsley, green pepper, barley, and lima beans. Bring to a boil. Simmer, covered, 1½ hours.

2. Add the carrot, mushrooms, salt, and dill. Continue simmering until the carrot is tender (about 20 minutes).

3. Correct seasonings and sprinkle on additional dill, if desired.

Serves 8-10. (P)

*In East Europe, dried mushrooms are used instead of fresh. People were often afraid that fresh mushrooms were poisonous; and the dried are tastier. This soup can also be made with a meat base.

MADELLINE KAMMAN'S JAFFA SALAD

In 1977, around Purim, Boston's Quincy Market became a Jerusalem souk. To honor this Jerusalem Month, Madelline Kamman, owner of Newton's Modern Gourmet Restaurant, teacher, and author of several French cookbooks, created a salad which she demonstrated for the public in the rotunda of Boston's original marketplace.

4 endives	½ cup homemade mayonnaise
1 bunch watercress, with the stems removed	2 tablespoons Dijon mustard
	½ cup heavy cream
3 large navel oranges, peeled and sliced in rounds	Salt and pepper to taste

1. In your salad bowl, layer the endives, watercress, and oranges, ending with oranges on top.

2. Just before serving, combine the mayonnaise and mustard, beating well with a whisk. Slowly add the cream, beating constantly. Season with salt and pepper.

3. Add to the salad. Toss at the table.

Serves 6–8. (M)

ROAST CHICKEN

My grandmother, Martha Kops Gluck, had a millinery store in New York City. Because she was busy during the day, it was my great-grandmother or a maid who did the cooking in their home. Each Friday, however, my grandmother made one dish—roast chicken. Hers is low in calories, delicious, and easy to prepare. Serve it with rice and chestnuts and prunes (p. 162), perfect for a Purim dinner.

2 3½-pound broiler chickens, quartered	Seasoning salt to taste
Salt to taste	Paprika to taste
Pepper to taste	2 small onions
Garlic salt to taste	½ cup water
	½ cup white wine

1. Preheat oven to 350°.

2. Season the chicken with salt, pepper, garlic salt, seasoning salt, and paprika. Lay each piece, skin side up, in a roasting pan.

3. Slice the onions and lay them over and around the chicken.

4. Roast 20 minutes. Turn the chicken over and roast 20 minutes more. Add a little water if the pan becomes dry. Then turn the chicken over once more and roast 20 minutes with the skin side up. Baste with the wine.

5. If you like the skin crisp, place the chicken under the broiler before serving. Otherwise, mere basting from the drippings will add to the flavor.

Serves 6–8. (F)

SAMBUSAK
(Sephardic Stuffed Pastries)

When Abe Sofaer, judge of the Southern District Court of New York, was a young boy in Bombay and later in New York City, he did not take sandwiches to school for lunch. His mother filled his lunchbox with sambusak. These pastries stuffed with cheese or meat are traditional for Iraqi, Indian, or Persian Jews. Eaten at any time, sambusak filled with dates or chicken are especially prepared for Purim. Who knows? Perhaps Queen Esther ate cheese-filled sambusak in Ahasuerus' palace. The following is the recipe of Mozelle Sofaer, Abe's mother.

2 tablespoons (2 packages) active dry yeast	2 pounds (about 8 cups) all-purpose sifted flour
2 cups lukewarm water	1 tablespoon ground anise
Pinch of sugar	Vegetable oil for deep-frying meat
1 teaspoon salt	sambusak
½ pound *pareve* margarine	

1. Proof the yeast in about ½ cup warm water. Add a pinch of sugar.

2. Add the salt, remaining water, margarine, and some of the flour. Gradually add the remaining flour and the anise. Blend with your hands and knead well. If the dough is too soft or sticky, add more flour. (Abe Sofaer's mother insists that hands are best—and good therapy. "Don't use a machine," she insists. If you do succumb to a food processor, however, divide the dough in half and work in the remaining flour.)

3. Place in a greased bowl and let rise, covered, until doubled in bulk (about 1 hour or more.)

4. Punch down, knead again, and let rise again until doubled.

5. Take a piece of dough the size of a plum and roll it into a ball. Press it down on a floured board until it flattens into a circle. Place 1 tablespoon of filling in the center. Fold over and pinch down into a half-moon shape.

6. For meat sambusak, heat the oil to 375°. Deep-fry until golden on each side. Drain and serve.

7. For cheese sambusak, preheat oven to 400°. Place on a greased cookie sheet and bake about 15 minutes, or until golden.

Makes about 36. (F and M)

Meat Filling:

1 tablespoon vegetable oil	Dash of ginger
1 bunch (about 5) scallions, diced	Dash of turmeric
1 pound very lean ground meat	1 teaspoon cinnamon
(the Sofaers use top sirloin)	Salt to taste
Dash of garlic powder	

1. Heat the oil. Add the scallions, meat, and spices. Keep turning the meat as it browns.

2. When cooked, turn the heat up so all the water evaporates. Let cool.

Cheese Filling:

2 cups feta cheese	2 eggs, separated

1. Combine the feta cheese with the yolks of the eggs.

2. Beat the egg whites until stiff peaks form. Then fold into the cheese.

Note: The Sofaers serve the sambusak with chutney, grated coconut, and parsley. Mrs. Sofaer suggests making sambusak when the kitchen is warm, and when you have a great deal of time and patience. She uses the formula of 2-2-2-2, up to 10-10-10-10—meaning that 2 pounds of flour go with 2 packages of yeast, 2 cups of water, and 2 sticks of margarine. She often makes 10 times everything and, after forming the pastries, freezes packages of them. She always has some sambusak in her home.

CHESTNUTS AND PRUNES

Ever since I can remember, my mother has craved chestnuts. Whenever we visited museums in New York City or watched the Macy's Thanksgiving Day parade, she would buy a bag of hot roasted chestnuts and tell us about growing up in New York. So it was no surprise to me that she recalled a dish prepared by her grandmother for special occasions—chestnuts and prunes. Together we reconstructed the recipe, which has again become a family favorite at holiday festivals. It is perfect with chicken or turkey at Purim or Sukkot.

1 pound chestnuts	1 pound prunes
Water	Juice of ½ lemon
5 tablespoons sugar	½ teaspoon cinnamon
1 tablespoon *pareve* margarine	

1. Freeze chestnuts for 24 hours. Defrost in a baking pan for 2 hours. Pour boiling water over the chestnuts and let sit for 5 minutes. Then pick the nuts out of the water. Using a sharp knife, shell and skin.

2. Place in a saucepan and add water to cover, 1 tablespoon of the sugar, and margarine. Cook until just tender (about 5 minutes). Cool, drain, and halve.

3. In another saucepan, place the prunes in water to cover. Cook 20 minutes. Add the 4 remaining tablespoons sugar, lemon juice, and cinnamon. Add the chestnuts and cook 5 minutes more. Serve hot or cold.

Serves 6–8. (P)

KASHA VARNISHKES

Just as marmaliga or polenta was the daily fare of the poorer Jews in Rumania, kasha was that of the poor in Russia. Usually made from buckwheat groats or grains, it could also be made from wheat, oats, barley, millet, or any other grain. Buckwheat is the grain most indigenous to Russia. Cooked with water, milk, or broth, whole buckwheat groats make a hearty and nourishing porridge. Kasha was also a thick soup made of barley and lima beans. Grains are often browned first to produce a crunchy, nutty flavor.

Kasha and bread-and-potato or cabbage soup were the basic foods of the poor Jews in Russia and Poland. Kasha varnishkes was a dish for special occasions. Eaten on Purim, it is made from sautéed onions, kasha, and noodles made in squares or in the shape of bowties or shells.

2 cups kasha	Salt and pepper to taste
4 tablespoons chicken fat or vegetable oil	2 cups varnishkes (shell- or bowtie-shaped noodles)
4 cups water	2 large onions

1. Place the kasha in a pan with 2 tablespoons chicken fat or vegetable oil. Sauté until the grains become dry and crunchy. Then add the water and salt and pepper to taste, and bring to a boil. Cover and simmer for about 20 minutes.

2. Cook the varnishkes according to the directions on the package. Drain.

3. Sauté the onions in the remaining chicken fat or oil until golden.

4. When the kasha is ready, combine with the onions and noodles. Adjust seasoning and serve, alone or with a pot roast.

Serves 6–8. (F or P)

FIGS STUFFED WITH WALNUTS

And the eyes of them both were opened, and they knew that they were naked; and they sewed fig-leaves together, and made themselves girdles.

Genesis 3:7

The Talmud asserts that Adam and Eve sinned and ate of the same fig tree, the tree of knowledge. First they ate of the forbidden fruit, and then the leaves covered Adam and hid him after the fall.

Riding through the hillsides of the West Bank, my husband and I never fail to buy a bag of fresh figs, a rare delicacy in this country and such a refreshing snack in Israel.

12 dried figs	Grated coconut (optional)
12 walnut halves	

1. Open the center of each fig.

2. Place a walnut half in the center of each fig and roll the stuffed fruit in grated coconut. Place on a dish with other fruit and serve.

Serves 6. (P)

BEIGLI, OR KINDLI

These yeast-dough cookies, served by Hungarian and German Jews at Purim, resemble little children wrapped in blankets—thus the name kindli. They can also be shaped like three-cornered hats or hamantashen. The poppy-seed filling includes jam, lemon, orange, rum, and sugar, rather than the traditional Polish and Russian honey. Ingredients of wine and rum at Purim are especially appropriate, since this is the one holiday where drinking to excess is encouraged.

Dough:

2	pounds all-purpose unbleached flour	1¾	cups potatoes, peeled and boiled (still warm)
2	whole eggs	1	cup sugar
3	egg yolks		Dash of salt
1	cup unsalted butter or *pareve* margarine	1	teaspoon vanilla
2	tablespoons dry yeast		Rind of 1 lemon
4	tablespoons water	2–3	tablespoons white wine

1. Place the flour in a large bowl and make a well in the center.

2. Put the whole eggs plus 1 egg yolk into the center and blend with your fingers.

3. Add the softened butter or margarine and knead together.

4. Dissolve the yeast in the warm water and then add to the potatoes. The warm potatoes will help to activate the yeast. Purée the potatoes and add to the flour mixture.

5. Add the sugar, salt, vanilla, lemon rind, and enough wine to bind the ingredients together. Knead well until a hard, smooth dough. is achieved. (You can divide dough and work in the food processor.)

6. Divide into 6 round balls and let stand, covered, while you make the filling, about 45 minutes. Preheat oven to 325°.

7. When the filling (see below) is ready, punch the dough and divide each ball of dough again into 6 or 7 round balls. Or proceed, if you prefer, with the large rolls, which can be sliced into small individual pieces.

8. If you are making small cookies, roll the dough out and cut circles 3″ in

diameter. Then put 1½ tablespoons filling in a line down the center, leaving a ½" border.

9. Fold the top and bottom of the circle over to cover the ends of the filling. Then take the left side and fold over ⅔ of the dough to cover the line of filling. Fold the right side over to the left edge. Press the sides together at the center and edges, as if you were tucking a baby into his blanket. Place on an ungreased cookie sheet. Brush with the remaining 2 egg yolks.

10. To make a large kindli, take one of the original 6 balls and roll out the dough into a circle about 7" in diameter. Smear with the filling. Fold the top and bottom over into 1" flaps. Then roll from one side like a jelly roll. Pinch down the edges. Brush with the egg yolks and place on an ungreased cookie sheet.

11. Bake about 30–45 minutes, until golden brown. Halfway through cooking, it is a good idea to brush more egg yolk on the kindli to achieve a lovely glazed effect.

Makes 6 large or 36 small kindli. (M or P)

The following 2 fillings will each make enough for the entire dough recipe. A quarter of each will fill the hamantash dough (p. 166).

Poppy-seed Filling:

1	pound sugar	2	tablespoons rum
½	cup water	4	ounces raisins
1	pound poppy seeds	2	ounces figs, chopped
2	egg whites		Cinnamon to taste
1	teaspoon vanilla	2	cups apricot or raspberry jam
	Rind and juice of 1 lemon	½	cup unsalted butter or *pareve*
	Rind and juice of 1 orange		margarine

1. Combine the sugar and water and simmer while stirring over a low heat.

2. Grind the poppy seeds in a food processor or blender. Add to sugar mixture.

3. Add the egg whites, vanilla, lemon rind and juice, orange rind and juice, rum, raisins, figs, and cinnamon. Simmer over a low heat for about 5 minutes. Add the jam and butter, and continue simmering until the butter is melted and all the ingredients are combined. Use as is, or put in the refrigerator for a few minutes until the filling becomes a bit firmer.

(M or P)

Nut Filling:

2	cups walnuts, ground	1	teaspoon cinnamon, or to
1¾	cups sugar		taste
1	teaspoon vanilla	1	cup orange marmalade or
	Rind and juice of 1 lemon		apricot jam
	Rind and juice of 1 orange	½	cup unsalted butter or *pareve*
2	tablespoons rum		margarine, creamed or melted
½	cup raisins	2	large egg whites
4	figs, chopped		

Combine all the above ingredients and mix well.

(M or P)

HAMANTASHEN

Hamantashen have through the centuries become known as *the* Purim sweet. As in so many questions Jewish, there are disputes as to the origin of the word "hamantash." Some say it comes from *tash kocho*, meaning, "May Haman's strength become weak." Others say it was merely Haman's hat. And then there is the theory that *mun-tasche* [bag of poppy seeds] is the correct name, and "hamantash" merely an error. A Midrash attributes the three corners of the cookie to represent Abraham, Isaac, and Jacob, whose merit saved the Jews.

Not everyone eats hamantashen at Purim. German Jews make gingerbread men and eat smoked meat. Egyptians eat ozne Haman, or deep-fried sweets shaped like Haman's ears. In fact, everyone has some part of Haman to be eaten at Purim.

Just as there is great controversy over light versus heavy matzah balls, there seems to be discussion about which are better—yeast- or cookie-dough hamantashen. This is the tastiest cookie-dough base I have ever tried. Use one-quarter of either of the fillings on pp. 165–66.

⅔ cup *pareve* margarine or butter	½ teaspoon vanilla
½ cup sugar	2½–3 cups sifted all-purpose
1 egg	unbleached flour
3 tablespoons milk or water	

1. Cream the shortening with sugar. Add egg and continue creaming until smooth.

2. Add the milk and vanilla. Stir in the sifted flour until a ball of dough is formed (a food processor is excellent for this).

3. Chill for 2–3 hours, or overnight.

4. Preheat oven to 375°.

5. Taking one-fourth of the dough, roll out on a lightly floured board to a thickness of ⅛". Cut into 2" circles. Fill with 1 teaspoon of poppy-seed or nut filling and fold into three-cornered cookies. (Press two sides together; and then fold the third side over and press the ends together.)

6. Bake on a well-greased cookie sheet 10–15 minutes, until the tops are golden.

Makes about 36. (M or P)

Feasting on hamantashen (photo: Allan Gerson)

MA'AMOUL
(Nut-filled Cookies)

Have you ever visited the marketplace of Jerusalem and noticed small wooden imprinted molds with handles? To be sure, the merchant is hard put to explain their significance. They are ma'amoul molds. Ma'amoul means "filled" in Arabic, and these molds make filled cookies eaten by Jews and Arabs throughout the Middle East, especially in Syria, Lebanon, and Egypt.

A piece of short-pastry dough the size of a walnut is pressed into the crevices of the ma'amoul mold. A tablespoon of date or nut filling is inserted, and you close the pastry with your fingers. Holding the handle of the wooden mold, you slam it on the table, letting the enclosed dough fall out. On the top is a lovely designed cookie. After baking and rolling in confectioners' sugar, the design stands out even more. Of course, the ma'amoul mold is not necessary to the preparation of these sweets, but it certainly adds to the beauty. The tines of a fork, tweezers with a serrated edge, or a tool of your own devising will do quite well.

The following ma'amoul recipe came from Aleppo to the Syrian Jewish community in Ocean Parkway, Brooklyn. These cookies are served at Purim. A similar cookie, called karabij here (nataife in Syria), topped with marshmallow fluff, is also served at Purim. Arasibajweh—rolled cookies from the same dough and stuffed with dates—are served at the New Year or Hanukkah.

Dough:	Filling:
2½ cups unbleached all-purpose flour	1½ cups roughly ground walnuts
½ cup semolina	1 teaspoon cinnamon
2½ sticks *pareve* margarine or 2 sticks butter	½ cup sugar
2 teaspoons vegetable oil	
¼–½ cup water	

1. Combine the flour, semolina, margarine, and vegetable oil. Add the water gradually. Blend well. (A food processor is splendid for this.) Cover and set aside for 10–15 minutes.

2. Combine the walnuts with the cinnamon and sugar.

3. Preheat oven to 350°.

4. Either use the ma'amoul mold described above or take a piece of dough about the size of a walnut. Roll it into a ball and hollow out the center. Inside, place a heaping teaspoon of walnut filling. With your hands, mold the dough closed.

5. Place each cookie on an ungreased cookie sheet. With the tines of a fork or tweezers with a serrated edge, make designs on the top of the cookie, being sure not to penetrate the skin.

6. Bake in the oven for about 30 minutes. Do not brown; the cookies should look white. Cool. When hard, roll in confectioners' sugar.

Makes 35–40. (P or M)

GHOURIBI
(Moroccan Sugar Cookies)

On the morning of Purim, Moroccan Jews decorate the table with flowers and sweets. Marzipan-stuffed prunes with walnuts and such cookies as ghouribi are a few of the delicacies. Ghouribi are easily prepared walnut cookies which children enjoy rolling with their hands.

1 cup vegetable oil or butter	⅓ cup finely ground walnuts or
1 cup sugar	almonds
3 cups unbleached all-purpose flour	Cinnamon

1. Preheat oven to 350°. Lightly flour an ungreased cookie sheet.

2. Place oil and sugar in a large bowl and mix well. Gradually add the flour, a cup at a time, and knead well. Blend in the nuts.

3. When the dough feels smooth, use the palm of your hand to roll it into balls the size of an egg. Pat into a round cookie about 2″ in diameter. The cookie should not be flat.

4. Place on the cookie sheet and sprinkle the center of each cookie with cinnamon. Bake for 45 minutes. Do not let the cookies become even slightly brown; they must remain off-white.

Makes about 30. (P or M)

A Turkish variation uses cocoa instead of cinnamon and is sprinkled with powdered sugar. These cookies can also be shaped into crescents. Made with butter, they are similar to the Austro-Hungarian nut horns (p. 147).

PURIM PUFFS

Gershom Mendes Seixas was a famous Jewish American revolutionary figure. The minister of the Shearith Israel Synagogue in New York, he led his co-congregants out of the city when the British invaded, carrying the Torah scrolls in his arms. He later resettled in Philadelphia, the seat of the revolution, and headed another synagogue.

A religious man, Seixas described Purim in a letter of 1813, three years before his death. "With all the merriment and festivity usually practiced in my family, the children seated at our large Table, in the Parlour, with two lighted Candles, and a great display of fiar Tea (no water and milk for a mockery), a sweet loaf, gingerbread, and some few nic-nacs from our friend L in Broad St.—sent in the morning for Shalah Monot."

The sweets mentioned show how, early on, Jews became assimilated in the United States. A loaf and gingerbread sound vastly more American than they do Sephardic. The Seixas family may well have also eaten Purim Puffs which I found in *The Twentieth Century Cookbook* of 1897. The clue to the Jewishness of the doughnuts is in the title and in the fact that here goose grease or butter is used as opposed to the lard of other recipes.

½ tablespoon dry or ½ cake yeast	½ cup unsalted butter
1 cup lukewarm milk	2 eggs, beaten
6½ cups sifted all-purpose flour	Confectioners' sugar
1 cup plus 1 teaspoon sugar	Unsalted butter or oil for frying
1 teaspoon plus a pinch of salt	

1. Dissolve the yeast in the warm milk. Gradually add 1½ cups sifted flour, 1 teaspoon sugar, and a pinch of salt to form a soft dough. Knead well, cover, and set aside to rise in a warm, draft-free spot.

2. When the dough has risen, cream together the butter and the remaining 1 cup sugar. Gradually add the eggs, the dough, and 1 teaspoon salt. Work in 5 cups flour, kneading until the dough leaves the sides of the bowl. Set aside to rise again.

3. When the dough is well risen, roll out on a floured board to a thickness of ½". Cut in triangles and lay on a floured board to rise.

4. When well risen, drop the puffs into a deep kettle of boiling butter or oil. Use a spoon to baste with the butter until brown. Remove with a perforated skimmer and sprinkle with powdered sugar. Serve immediately.

Serves 6. (M)

PASSOVER

PASSOVER

*I peeked into our own courtyard and saw all the neighbors washing and
scrubbing, scraping and rubbing, making the tables and benches kosher-for-
Passover. They carried huge pots of boiling water, heated irons and red-hot
bricks, all of which gave off a white vapor.... We had bought our matzohs a
long time ago and had them locked in the cupboard over which a white sheet
had been hung. In addition, we had a basketful of eggs, a jar of Passover
chicken-fat, two ropes of onions on the wall, and many other delicacies for the
holiday.*

Sholom Aleichem, "The Passover Eve Vagabonds"

Passover is probably the Jewish holiday that occasions more joyful
anticipation than any other. It is one of the world's oldest continually
observed festivals and still, despite intrusions of modernity, retains its ancient
charm.

It is celebrated in commemoration of the Exodus of the Jews from
Egypt. For eight days we do not partake of any leavening agent in our food.
A reading of the Haggadah—a narration of the Exodus—is a central part of
the first (and second) night of Passover.

For weeks prior to the festival, houses are thoroughly cleaned to remove
any trace of leavening, and the day before the Seder feast, the head of the
household searches for leavening (*hametz*). Before the search (*bedikat
hametz*), someone, usually the mother, places breadcrumbs on napkins and
hides them in various rooms of the house. The head of the household then
recites a blessing on the *hametz* (which is actually burned the following
morning) and proceeds to search the house for any crumbs overlooked during
the cleaning. One hopes no *hametz* is found, except the crumbs left by the
mother. The crumbs serve the purpose of not allowing the head of the
household to make the blessing on the burning of the *hametz* in vain.

No products made from regular flour and no leavening agents can be
eaten at Passover. Although the Sephardim eat all vegetables and some even
eat rice, Ashkenazim eschew such vegetables as corn, string beans, and
peas. They also refrain from lentils, chick-peas, and other dried beans.

Conservative and Orthodox families who can afford it have separate
sets of dishes, cutlery, and cooking utensils for Passover, which are kept
carefully packed away the rest of the year. Less well-to-do have certain
utensils made kosher for Passover. Dishes, pots, and silverware can be
converted for Passover use by being scalded in boiling water. Metal pans can
be passed through fire and broilers heated red hot.

The observance was originally a nature festival celebrated by nomadic
desert Jews, with roasted sheep or goat as the central food. Centuries later,

the peasants of Israel had a spring grain observance, the Festival of Unleavened Bread.

Later still, the seasonal aspect of the festival was transformed into a freedom holiday representing more closely the history and social and spiritual strivings of the Jewish people.

The meal of the first two nights has been formalized into a Seder (order), imbuing the original lamb, bitter herbs, and matzah with new symbolism. Additional foods were to recall the historical trials of the Jewish people. The Seder is a family meal, and those sitting at it are reminded, both by narration and by the foods to be eaten, of the rich heritage of thousands of years and the suffering through those millennia.

Pesah means "passing by" or "passing over," and the holiday was called Passover because God passed over the Jewish houses when He slew the firstborn of Egypt. Matzah, unleavened and quickly baked, now recalls that the Jews fleeing Egypt had no time to leaven their bread and to bake it properly. Usually two hallahs are served at ceremonial meals; but on Passover, three matzot are placed on the table instead.

Maror, bitter herbs, are served as reminders of the bitterness of enslavement in Egypt. Haroset, a blend of sweet fruits and nuts, represents the mortar used by Jewish slaves in building for their masters. A roasted egg (*betzah*) represents the festival sacrifice brought to the Temple and is thus a symbol of mourning for the destroyed Temple. *Karpas*—parsley or other available greens such as celery or romaine—recalls the "sixty myriads" of Israelites oppressed with difficult labor.

Four cups of wine are poured during the service; a fifth cup is left for the Prophet Elijah, harbinger of freedom and the Messiah. The wine symbolizes the four divine promises of redemption found in the Scripture in connection with Israel's liberation from Egypt: "I will bring you out...I will deliver you...I will redeem you...I will take you to Me" (Exodus 6:6–7).

Since the destruction of the Second Temple in 70 C.E., there have been no sacrifices at Passover. Therefore, for some it is forbidden to eat roast lamb at the Seder meal until the Temple is rebuilt. Jews usually substitute turkey or chicken as a main Seder dish and lift *zeroa*, a roasted lamb shank bone, as a reminder of the pascal sacrifice at the Temple.

Each civilization has left its mark on the customs and foods of the Seder. Wine and soft sofas upon which to recline were added in Graeco-Roman times, as these were part of a feast. East European Jews may eat parsley, while Sephardic Jews choose romaine lettuce. The haroset varies, too, depending on the availability of ingredients.

Today, despite the dispersal of Jews throughout the world, the eight-day festival maintains its family character and begins with the traditional Seder meal. The central object of every table is the Seder plate arranged with the symbolic foods. There is no rule for menus for the meal, although there are traditions, as shown in several of the menus which follow. Some families repeat the same menu both nights; others have two different ones. From what I have ascertained, what once had to do with the wealth of the family became a nostalgic custom. Some families with no servants repeated the menu, making it easier for the housewife. Wealthier families had no problem in varying the food for large gatherings.

Besides the traditional Seder dish with symbolic foods, Passover recipes themselves have evolved throughout the years, according to the country to which Jews immigrated.

FLOUR MEASUREMENTS FOR PASSOVER

1 cup regular flour = ¼ cup matzah cake meal
= ¾ cup potato starch

½ cup regular flour = 2 tablespoons matzah cake meal
= 6 tablespoons potato starch

The Seder plate with the haroset in the center. Clockwise from top: parsley, water with salt, lamb bone, parsley, bitter herbs, parsley, roasted egg, and more parsley (photo: Providence-Journal Bulletin)

SEDER MENUS

Traditional American (based on *The Settlement Cook Book*)

Chicken Soup with Matzah Balls★
Apricot Chicken★
New Potatoes with Chopped Parsley
Fresh Asparagus
Honey-Glazed Carrots★
Salade à ma Façon★
Almond Lemon Torte★
Stuffed Prunes★

Russian

Gefilte Fish★
Chicken Soup with Matzah Balls★
Passover Tsimmes★
Potatoes
Green Salad
Passover Popovers★
Apple Blintzes★
Lemon Sponge Cake★

Mixed Sephardic

Egg Lemon Soup★
Veal with Artichokes★
Asparagus
Stuffed Prunes★
Rice
Fresh Fruit
Almond Macaroons★

Mixed Ashkenazic

Gefilte Fishballs★
Chicken Soup with Matzah Balls★
Roast Turkey with Matzah Stuffing★
Vegetable Kugel★
Tossed Green Salad
Krimsel★ with Stewed Prunes

HAROSET

Haroset, the blend of fruits and nuts symbolizing the mortar which our forefathers used to build pyramids in Egypt, is one of the most popular and discussed ritual foods served at the Seder. The fruit and nuts found in almost all haroset recipes refer to two verses in the Song of Songs closely linked with the spring season: "Under the apple-tree I awakened thee" (8:5) and "I went down into the garden of nuts" (6:11). The red wine recalls the Red Sea, which parted its waters for the Jews.

The real purpose of the haroset is to allay the bitterness of the *maror* (bitter herbs) required at the Seder. And from this combination of haroset and *maror* between two matzot, the sandwich may have been invented by Rabbi Hillel, the great Jewish teacher who lived between 90 B.C.E. and 70 C.E.. Haroset also shows how Jewish cookery was developed by the emigration from Mediterranean countries to East Europe and by local ingredients supplemented or discarded depending on their availability.

Although most American Jews are familiar with the mixture of apples, almonds, cinnamon, wine, and ginger, this is by no means the only combination possible. Walnuts, pine nuts, peanuts, or chestnuts can be mixed with apricots, coconuts, raisins, dates, figs, and even bananas.

Whereas Ashkenazic haroset is quite universal, differing only texturally, that of the Sephardic Jews changes according to the country and sometimes even the city of origin. On the island of Rhodes, for example, dates, walnuts, ginger, and sweet wine are used. The Greek city of Salonika adds raisins to this basic recipe; Turkish Jews, not far away, include an orange. Egyptians eat dates, nuts, raisins, and sugar, without the ginger and wine. Yemenites use chopped dates and figs, coriander, and chili pepper. An interesting haroset from Venice has chestnut paste and apricots, while one from Surinam, Dutch Guiana, calls for seven fruits including coconut. Each Israeli uses the Diaspora haroset recipe of his ancestors or an Israeli version that might include pignolia, peanuts, bananas, apples, dates, sesame seeds, matzah meal, and red wine.

Most people like their haroset recipe so well that it is not only spread on matzah and dipped in horseradish at the Seder table. Some families make large quantities to be eaten for breakfast, lunch, and snacks throughout Passover.

EGYPTIAN HAROSET

1 pound dried raisins	¼ cup sugar
8 ounces pitted dates	¼ cup chopped walnuts or pecans
2 cups water	

1. Place the raisins and dates in a bowl with enough water to cover. Let stand for 1 hour.

2. Add the sugar and whirl the mixture in a blender, a few spoonsful at a time. Or divide the mixture in thirds and place in a food processor.

3. Transfer the chopped fruits to a heavy saucepan and let simmer over a low heat until the fruits are cooked and the liquid absorbed. It should take about 20 minutes.

4. Remove from the heat and place in a jar. When cool, sprinkle with chopped nuts.

Makes 4 cups. (P)

VENETIAN HAROSET

This delicious haroset recipe comes from the famous Luzzatto family of Venice. Members of the family have lived in Italy since 1541 and probably before. Names like Benedetto Luzzatto, Simone Luzzatto, Moses Haim Luzzatto, and Samuel David Luzzatto were well known to Italians from the Renaissance to the Enlightenment as authors, professors, and rabbis. Francis Luzzatto of Washington, D.C., works for the Peace Corps and is a keeper of family traditions; the following is his family's recipe.

1½ cups chestnut paste	½ cup pine nuts
10 ounces dates, chopped	Grated rind of 1 orange
12 ounces figs, chopped	½ cup white raisins
2 tablespoons poppy seeds	¼ cup chopped dried apricots
½ cup chopped walnuts	½ cup brandy
½ cup chopped almonds	Honey to bind

Combine all the ingredients, gradually adding just enough brandy and honey to make the mixture bind.

Makes about 4 cups. (P)

Other Italian haroset recipes include mashed-up bananas, apples, hard-boiled eggs, crushed matzah, pears, and lemon.

SEVEN-FRUIT HAROSET FROM SURINAM

Many Sephardic Jews went to Holland at the time of the Inquisition. From there some went to Dutch colonies, often engaging in the sugar and spice trade. Mrs. Abraham Lopes Cardozo (née Robles) is a fine cook who makes an effort to preserve for her family and friends her Surinam culinary heritage. She is the wife of the hazan of Shearith Israel Synagogue in New York City, the former minister of the Sephardic Congregation in Surinam.

At Passover, Surinam customs are quite unusual. Mrs. Cardozo explained to me, for example, that matzot were a rarity in Surinam. Because they had to be imported from Holland and later on from the United States, cassava (a kind of potato) meal was often used instead to bake sweet breads for Passover. The potato was first grated and washed, then dried in the sun for weeks. Once dried, it was ready to be mixed with other ingredients, as we use matzah flour for sweet desserts.

Easier for us to make is Mrs. Cardozo's haroset recipe, which I tasted for breakfast one morning at the Cardozo home.

8 ounces unsweetened coconut	8 ounces dried apples
8 ounces walnuts, chopped, or almonds, grated	8 ounces dried prunes
¼ cup sugar	8 ounces dried apricots
1 tablespoon cinnamon	8 ounces dried pears
8 ounces raisins	4 ounces cherry jam
	Sweet red wine

1. Combine everything except the jam and wine in a large, heavy pot. Add water to cover. Simmer over a low fire, stirring occasionally with a wooden spoon. Add small amounts of water periodically, so that the mixture does not stick to the pot. Continue stirring.

2. Cook for at least 90 minutes. When the mixture is cohesive, stir in the cherry jam. Let stand until cool.

3. Add enough sweet wine to be absorbed by the haroset mixture. Refrigerate.

Makes about 5 cups. (P)

ASHKENAZIC APPLE-NUT HAROSET

6 apples, peeled and coarsely
   chopped
⅓ cup chopped almonds
2 tablespoons sugar

½ teaspoon cinnamon
Grated rind of 1 lemon
1 tablespoon sweet red wine

1. Combine all ingredients, mixing together thoroughly. Add a little more wine as needed.

2. Blend (you can use a food processor) until you reach the desired consistency (I like my haroset in large pieces, with a crunchy texture, but my husband's Polish family prefer theirs ground to a paste). Chill.

Makes about 3 cups. (P)

PERSIAN HAROSET

Herbs for Passover must be separated from those used during the year. So, two months prior to the holiday, Persian-born Mohtaran Shirazi buys whole spices and herbs such as turmeric, rock salt, cinnamon, and cardamom and methodically washes and sun-dries them before pounding them with a mortar and pestle. The same procedure is used for watermelon and sunflower seeds, as well as pistachio nuts; after being washed and dried, they are baked in the oven. Some of these spices are used in her tempting haroset with pistachio nuts and pomegranate.

25 dates, pitted and diced
½ cup unsalted pistachio nuts
½ cups almonds
½ cup yellow raisins
1½ apples, peeled, cored, and
   diced
1 pomegranate
1 orange, peeled and diced

1 banana, sliced
½–1 cup sweet red wine
¼ cup cider vinegar
½ tablespoon cayenne
1 tablespoon ground cloves
1 tablespoon ground cardamom
1 teaspoon cinnamon
1 tablespoon black pepper

1. Combine all the fruits and nuts.

2. Add the wine and vinegar until a pasty consistency is reached.

3. Add the spices and blend well. Adjust seasonings.

Makes about 5 cups. (P)

MATZAH

This is the bread of affliction, the poor bread which our ancestors ate in the land of Egypt. Let all who are hungry come and eat. Let all who are in want share the hope of Passover. This year we celebrate here. Next year in the land of Israel. Now we are all still servants. Next year may all be free.

The Passover Haggadah

Seven days shall ye eat unleavened bread; howbeit the first day ye shall put away leaven out of your houses; for whosoever eateth leavened bread from the first day until the seventh day, that soul shall be cut off from Israel.

Exodus 12:15

Despite the commercialism now attached to matzah, it still remains the ancient unleavened bread of affliction. Matzah, without yeast and quickly baked, represents the bread of slavery eaten under the pharaohs and recalls that the Jews fleeing Egypt had no time to leaven their bread and bake it properly. The original matzah, manually molded in circles and roughly hewn, was thicker than the crispy machine-made brands available today.

Matzah must be prepared without any yeast. The unbleached flour is watched from the time the wheat is reaped (for *shmurah*, or hand-made, watched matzah allowing no water to brush the stalks of wheat) or from when it is brought to the mill (for regular Passover matzah). Even today the water used in baking must sit for twenty-four hours, with no foreign elements allowed to contaminate it.

Mills are reserved to grind the Passover flour. The factories are carefully cleaned. Workers, versed in the traditional rules, watch over the machines reciting "for the sake of the *mitzvah*" (religious obligation) of making matzah. The flour is then set aside until the time comes to make Passover products.

According to Jewish law, the mixing of the flour and water, the kneading on one side lest rising take place, the piercing of holes, and the baking must take no more than eighteen minutes from start to the emergence of the finished product from the oven. Otherwise, the waiting period will cause the bread to rise and it will no longer be fit for Passover.

The matzah of the Seder table consists of three sheets placed one above the other to symbolize the three classes of Jews: Kohanim (priests), Levites, and Israelites. At the beginning of the Seder, the central matzah is divided. The larger part, or *afikomen* (meaning "dessert" in Greek), is put aside and hidden. It should be the last item of food eaten at the Seder.

At the beginning of the reading of the Haggadah, the leader holds up the remaining half of the *afikomen* and recites the passage given above. Today, many American Jews hold up a fourth matzah, which they call the Matzah of

Hope, to remind them of the Jews of the Soviet Union who often cannot obtain Passover matzah and cannot practice Judaism freely.

Although the great majority of people use commercial matzah throughout the Seder, it is considered a *mitzvah* to use *shmurah* matzah at least for the three central matzot. If you cannot find them easily in your community, ask at your synagogue.

The first food eaten at the Seder is a piece of matzah. Later, one eats a symbolic sandwich of matzah and the bitter herbs which have been dipped in the haroset and shaken dry. Rabbi Hillel insisted that such a combination be eaten in order to fulfill the commandment to eat bitter herbs and unleavened bread together: "And they shall eat the flesh in that night, roast with fire, and unleavened bread; with bitter herbs they shall eat it" (Exodus 12:8).

The *afikomen*—that hidden piece of matzah which keeps the children's attention throughout the long Seder meal—was once a good-luck omen. Even today the lucky person who finds the *afikomen* wins a prize. In ancient times, a woman in childbirth would often bite into this matzah for good luck. By the Middle Ages, Jews used it as an amulet, hanging in the house throughout the year or carried in the pouch or wallet. Venetian Jews do so even today. Some Jews save the remains to use for the *bedikat hametz* the following year.

Matzah is not only central to the Seder meal, it is central to all Passover cuisine. As a substitute for bread, it is best spread with whipped butter and salt or honey; the haroset from the Seder also makes an excellent topping.

Due to the stringent laws concerning the baking of matzah, one should not try to make it at home for Passover. The specially processed flour required is not available commercially. But this recipe is good for use at other times, and to show how it is done.

2 pounds unbleached all-purpose flour	1½ cups water

1. Preheat oven to 500°.

2. Place the flour on a board and slowly add the water, kneading the dough with your hands until it is firm. Take a handful of dough and roll out into a circle, using a long rolling pin. Prick on one side with a fork.

3. Place in the oven on a cookie sheet for about 10–15 minutes, or until light brown.

Makes 8 8" matzot. (P)

MATZAH-MEAL PANCAKES

1 cup matzah meal	1½ cups club soda
1 teaspoon salt	4 tablespoons *pareve* margarine
6 eggs, separated	

1. In a mixing bowl, mix the matzah meal and salt. In another bowl beat the egg yolks with club soda (which makes lighter pancakes than does water). Pour the egg yolks into the matzah meal and let rest for ½ hour.

2. Beat the egg whites until they are stiff and stand in peaks. Fold into the matzah meal, blending well.

3. Melt margarine in a pan. When it is hot, drop the mixture in by spoonfuls. Brown on both sides.

Serves 4–6. (P)

PASSOVER POPOVERS

½ cup vegetable oil	1 cup matzah meal
1 cup water	1 tablespoon sugar, or to taste
½ teaspoon salt	4 eggs

1. Preheat oven to 375°. Grease a cookie sheet.

2. Bring the oil, water, and salt to a boil. Add the matzah meal and stir with a spoon. When the mixture becomes sticky, let it cool.

3. Add the sugar and eggs, beating well after each addition.

4. Dipping your hands in cold water first, take dough about the size of a tennis ball and mold into a ball. Place on the cookie sheet. Repeat until all dough is used up, dipping your hands in water before forming each popover.

5. Bake in the oven 15–20 minutes, until the popovers are puffy. Then turn down the oven to 325° and bake another 30 minutes, until golden brown.

Makes about 12. (P)

MATZAH BALLS
(Kneydlakh)

Pesakh essen mir
Matzo kneydlakh
Vayl arum dem tish
Zitsn file meydlakh

While doing research for this book, I visited the Hebrew Home for the Aged in Rockville, Maryland. There I conducted a culinary exchange session with the elderly. Each food I mentioned triggered off a memory, which these people—mostly Russian immigrants—shared with me. All of a sudden, a woman in her eighties who did not seem to be listening chanted the above verse from her childhood in Vilna.

Others had their own opinions of kneydlakh, or matzah balls. To some, the eggs should be separated; others added a speck of ginger or a few ground almonds. Some attributed success to sufficient chicken fat to make the matzah balls firm and tender at the same time.

When I speak before groups about my first book, *The Flavor of Jerusalem,* no food causes so much discussion as the late Golda Meir's matzah ball recipe. Hers—the heavy variety—invites women to give me their own opinion about separating eggs, not separating eggs, adding onion, etc. Even Haim Shapiro of the Jerusalem *Post* contrasted Golda's recipe to that of his mother, whose matzah balls are "the lightest and fluffiest imaginable." According to Shapiro, they are the only ones that "quiver" when breathed upon.

My friend Heidi Wortzel of Newton, Massachusetts, is a master French chef and a marvelous maker of matzah balls. In her recipe for the light variety, she adds soda water, separates the eggs, and attributes success to not opening the pot for 20 minutes, until the matzah balls are done.

4 eggs, slightly beaten
4 tablespoons chicken fat
1 cup matzah meal
2 teaspoons salt

4 tablespoons chicken soup or
  water
4 quarts salted water

1. In a medium bowl, beat the eggs and the fat together. Stir in the matzah meal and salt. Add the chicken soup or water. Refrigerate for 1 hour or more, to permit the meal to absorb the liquids.

2. In a 6-quart pot with a lid, bring the salted water to a boil. Reduce the water to a simmer and drop in balls of the matzah mixture about 1½" in

diameter. Cover the pot and cook just at a simmer for 20 minutes. When they are ready, they may be placed in chicken soup to serve.

Makes 20. (F)

Note: There is a light-and-fluffy school of matzah balls and a cannonball school. These belong to the former and are achieved by a simple trick. *Never* take the lid off the pot while they are cooking, or you will boil instead of steaming the dumplings.

If you have extras, they can be served the next day. Although they will be a little denser in texture, they will still be tasty. They are also very good as a starch when browned in margarine. They must be refrigerated thoroughly before frying or they will fall apart.

MATZAH BREI

My husband considers matzah brei a real treat. It is one of those holiday recipes that has nothing whatsoever to do with religion—just gastronomy.

A simple dish, matzah brei cannot be made with milk. With milk, it is like pastrami on white bread or chicken livers with mayonnaise. How could East European Jews, with only goose fat available for frying, include milk in matzah brei?

Perhaps the fascination with matzah brei is the ease of preparation. It consists of soaking matzah in water, squeezing very hard, and then frying in grease with or without an egg. It is served with sugar, honey, cinnamon, cinnamon-sugar, and even—by some iconoclasts—with catsup!

Jacob Licht, father of Rhode Island's former governor, Frank Licht, has been a master matzah brei maker all his life. This is his recipe.

3 matzot	2 tablespoons fat, *pareve*
2 large eggs	margarine, or butter for frying
Salt and freshly ground pepper to	Cinnamon, cinnamon-sugar,
taste	honey, maple syrup, etc.

1. Break the matzot and soak in boiling water for 15 minutes. Drain and squeeze dry.

2. Add the eggs and salt and pepper to taste.

3. Taking tablespoonsful of batter at a time, fry in the chicken fat, margarine, or butter, patting the center down a bit. (You may want larger matzah pancakes, in which case just add more batter each time.) When

brown on one side, turn and fry on the other. Serve with cinnamon, cinnamon-sugar, honey, maple syrup, or even catsup!

Serves 3–4. (M, P, or F)

"I've been making matzah brei all my life"—Jacob Licht (photo: Judith Licht)

MATZAH STUFFING

What Jewish holiday cookbook would be complete without a good recipe for Passover stuffing?

2 matzot
1 large onion
1 large potato
2 eggs
3 tablespoons matzah meal
2 stalks celery, finely diced

2 tablespoons chicken fat or
   pareve margarine
1 tablespoon chopped parsley
Salt and pepper to taste
Paprika to taste

1. Break the matzah in small pieces and soak in hot water. Drain thoroughly, and squeeze well.

2. Grate onion and potato. Drain off extra water.

3. Combine matzah, onion, and potato. Add remaining ingredients.

Makes 4 cups. (F or P)

HORSERADISH AND BEET SAUCE

And fresh matzo with strongly seasoned fish and fresh horseradish that tore your nostrils apart, and Passover borsht that tasted like something in Paradise, and other good things that man's evil spirit can summon...
                                    Sholom Aleichem, "Home for Passover"

Although horseradish per se is not mentioned in the Bible and was not native to the Middle East, *maror,* or bitter herbs, are cited in the Book of Exodus, with the pascal lamb and unleavened bread, as prescribed foods for the Passover feast. In the second century horseradish became—along with coriander, nettle, horehound, and romaine lettuce—one of the bitter herbs of the Passover.

Seventy-five percent of all horseradish production in the United States is done at Tulkoff's, located on Horseradish Lane in Baltimore. Harry and Lena Tulkoff, immigrants from Russia, started a fruit-and-produce market on Lombard Street, across from the present factory. So often would people ask the Tulkoffs to grate their horseradish that they decided it would be more profitable to produce packaged horseradish sauce. With the amount of corned beef consumed in Baltimore, it was a wise decision.

1 medium horseradish root (about ½ cup)
1 16-ounce can beets, drained
1 teaspoon salt
¼ teaspoon pepper
2 tablespoons sugar
¾ cup white vinegar

1. Peel horseradish and grate it by hand or with a food processor.

2. Grate the beets, adding them to the horseradish. Combine well.

3. Add the salt, pepper, and sugar gradually. Since the strength of the horseradish will vary according to age and the individual root, you should test as you add each ingredient.

4. Add all the vinegar the horseradish and beets will absorb. Adjust to taste. Mix well.

5. Store in the refrigerator in a tightly covered jar. Serve with gefilte fish or boiled beef.

Makes about 3 cups. (P)

MEAT BORSCHT

At one time fresh milk products and coffee were not made commercially for Passover. Other means had to be devised to make tasty meals for a people accustomed to the wide use of milk, cheese, sour cream, and farmers cheese. Passover borscht, for example, was thickened by being slowly poured over the beaten yolk of an egg.

Eva Lubetkin Cantor of New York remembers the making of Passover borscht at her home in New York City at the turn of the century. "Then there was the brewing of the russell which was genuine borscht, only it was beet brew. The beets were put in a large barrel covered with warm water and salt. It took three or four weeks to ferment and turn sour. Every day or so the fermentation and crust were skimmed off with a slotted ladle. When it didn't form any sediment on top, it was ready. Most delicious, clear beet juice. It was the basic ingredient for borscht. We just added to it water, sugar, eggs, sour cream, and for *fleishig* meatballs and hot plain boiled potatoes."

Originally a Ukrainian dish made with a pork base, this economical staple was varied by the Jews with a beef base and a meatless, sweeter version.

2	pounds lean beef, cubed	1–2	cloves garlic
1	cracked soup bone	1	teaspoon salt
2½	quarts water	2	tablespoons brown sugar
8	beets, grated	⅓	cup lemon juice, or to taste
2	onions, diced	2	eggs

1. In a large, heavy pot, simmer the meat and bone in the water, covered, about 1 hour.

2. Add the beets, onions, garlic, and salt. Simmer covered for another 1½ hours.

3. Add the brown sugar and lemon juice and correct seasonings.

4. In a separate bowl, beat the eggs. Gradually add a little hot soup to them, beating continuously to prevent curdling. Add the eggs to the large pot and blend in.

Serves 8. (F)

GNOCCHI DI SPINACI

In an Italian Jewish cookbook, *La Cucina nella Tradizione Ebraica*, published in 1970 in Padua, each holiday includes a menu in either the Ashkenazic, Sephardic, or Italian tradition. The following Venetian gnocchi di spinaci, from the Luzzatto family, comes from the third group.

2 cups cooked and squeezed spinach (4 bags fresh or 4 packages frozen chopped spinach)	1 egg
	3 tablespoons potato starch
	Nutmeg to taste
	Salt to taste
1 cup ricotta or farmers cheese*	3 quarts water
¾ cup freshly grated Parmesan cheese*	2 tablespoons butter

1. Combine the spinach, ricotta and Parmesan cheese, egg, potato starch, nutmeg, and salt.

2. Bring water to a rolling boil in a large pot. Add salt.

3. Wetting your hands first, form the spinach mixture into dumplings the size of walnuts and drop them, one by one, into the boiling water. They will drop to the bottom. When they rise to the surface, remove and drain.

4. Just before serving, preheat oven to 350°. Place the gnocchi in a buttered flat casserole. Sprinkle with Parmesan cheese or a light béchamel sauce. Heat for a few minutes in the oven. This is a delicious vegetable dish at Passover or any time during the year.

Makes about 24 large or 40–50 small gnocchi. (M)

MRS. FEINBERG'S VEGETABLE KUGEL

Try this Cincinnati vegetable kugel with your next roast, from the late Rosa Feinberg, wife of Rabbi Louis Feinberg.

*If these cheeses are not found in your area and are not kosher-for-Passover, substitute the closest ones available.

1 cup grated raw apple	1 teaspoon salt
1 cup grated raw sweet potato	1 teaspoon baking soda
1 cup grated raw carrot	1 teaspoon cinnamon
1 cup matzah cake meal	1 teaspoon nutmeg
1 scant cup *pareve* margarine	¾ cup sugar

1. Preheat oven to 325°. Grease a 10″ casserole or muffin tins.

2. Mix all the ingredients together well.

3. Pour into the baking dish. Cover with aluminum foil and bake for 45 minutes. If using muffin tins, bake for 30 minutes.

4. Raise oven to 350°, remove cover, and bake an additional 15 minutes. Slice and eat hot as a vegetable with meat.

Serves 6–8. (P)

Note: A food processor makes this recipe effortless. Yes, baking *soda*, a pure product and not a leavening agent, can be used at Passover.

VEGETABLES, FRENCH STYLE

There are Jewish restaurateurs, Jewish wine merchants, but who ever heard of a Jewish French chef? Michel Fitoussi, chef of the lavishly expensive Palace Restaurant in New York, is just that—and a prize-winning one. At the ripe old age of twenty-seven, Michel has won national French-cooking medals. His food sculptures, which he prepares out of mutton fat, bread, pastry, and icing, are superb. He presents, for example, a pompano baked in salt, on a tray decorated with a three-sailed bread-sculpture schooner.

Michel treats his work as a marvelous game and is extraordinarily creative. As chef of an haute cuisine restaurant in New York, he does not prepare Jewish holiday food. Most Jewish holiday food does not and cannot include the last-minute, rich sauces that make the preparation of French food such an art. Although he is familiar with traditional recipes at home and serves them for Passover, he would not give these recipes to me. If Michel calls a recipe his own, he tests it "at least one hundred times." He chose rather to give me two of his own creations: carrot, asparagus, and turnip bundles and a salad with leeks, particularly appropriate for the first Seder.

FAGOTS DE LÉGUMES
(Vegetable Bundles)

Quantities deliberately have been omitted for these colorful and engaging vegetable "bundles." Let your needs be your guide.

Carrots	Clarified butter or *pareve*
Asparagus	margarine
White turnips	Salt to taste
Trimmed green tops from very	
fresh scallions	

1. Peel carrots and cut lengthwise into ⅛" slices. Cut slices into large "matchsticks" 1" long. Briefly blanch in a large quantity of boiling water (they should remain firm and crisp) and refresh under cold running water.

2. Cut scallion greens into strips 10" long and ¼" wide. Blanch in boiling water for 5 seconds and immediately plunge into cold water.

3. Across centers of scallion greens, stack carrot sticks, 2 high and 3 across. Bring ends of scallion greens up over the carrot stacks, tie in simple bows, and trim as you would the ribbon of a gift package.

4. Repeat the procedure with the asparagus and turnips, leaving the asparagus whole.

5. Place vegetable bundles in a small pan with margarine or clarified butter and salt to taste. Cook, covered, over low heat just until tender. Remove carefully from margarine or butter and serve 1 bundle of each vegetable per person.

(M or P)

SALADE À MA FAÇON

3 bunches arugala or enough of	**Dressing:**
any hearty lettuce to serve 8	2 egg yolks
people	2 teaspoons Dijon mustard
1 bunch watercress	Juice of 1 large lemon
White part of 1 leek, julienned	1 cup olive or good vegetable oil
	Salt and pepper to taste

1. In a large salad bowl, mix greens and leek.

2. In a blender or food processor, whip egg yolks, mustard, and lemon juice.

3. Gradually add oil in a thin, steady stream, beating until thick. Season with salt and pepper. Add dressing to greens and toss.

Serves 8. (P)

"Is this an occupation for a Jewish boy?" asks Michel Fitoussi, chef of New York's Palace Restaurant (photo: Anthony Spinazzolla)

LITVAK MATZAH KUGEL

Kugels were described as casually as bread in writings from over eight hundred years ago in Germany. From there, the Sabbath pudding spread eastward. In 1500, for example, Polish writings describe farfel kugels.

    This unusual Litvak matzah-meal kugel comes from Helen Harrison of Baltimore through her son, Steve, our next-door neighbor in Cambridge. Steve looks forward to Passover to taste this kugel, which is made with leftover chicken or brisket. He felt my book would not be gastronomically complete without it!

9 eggs	2 cups water (approximately)
½ teaspoon salt	2 cups cooked and ground
2 tablespoons chicken fat or	chicken or brisket
pareve margarine	Grieben or onions left over from
3 cups matzah meal	rendering chicken fat

1. Beat the eggs until frothy.

2. Stir in the salt and chicken fat. Add the matzah meal slowly, alternating with water. Use enough water to make a medium, pastelike consistency.

3. Let stand in the refrigerator at least 1 hour to let the matzah meal expand.

4. Preheat oven to 350°. Grease a round 10″ soufflé casserole.

5. Combine the ground meat and the grieben or onions.

6. Alternating layers, place a layer of matzah-meal batter, half the meat, more batter, the rest of the meat, and a final layer of batter.

7. Bake 1 hour, or until puffy, brown, and firm. Cut into pie slices and serve as a side dish with meat or chicken soup.

Serves 6–8. (F)

TURKISH BAKED EGGPLANT WITH CHEESE

In the poor *shtetls* of East Europe, a meat meal did not necessarily mean that meat was served. Goose, chicken fat, or meat suet was all that was needed. It could be used for frying or spread on bread and served with potato soup or kasha as the main course. Thus, without bread at Passover, much frying was done and many meatless meat meals were eaten. The foods included potato latkes, matzah-meal pancakes, matzah brei, potato-starch blintzes, and so forth.

Sephardic Jews did not have this problem, however. Vegetable and olive oils were, for the most part, locally made and thus available even to the very poor. They, too, have fried meat dishes at Passover; they also have fried milk ones.

6 tablespoons vegetable oil	2 tablespoons fresh parsley
1 large eggplant	1 tablespoon fresh or 1 teaspoon
4 eggs	dried rosemary
1 cup grated Parmesan, cheddar,	1 tablespoon fresh or 1 teaspoon
or other sharp cheese	dried basil
1 cup cooked rice or 1 mashed	2 tomatoes, sliced
potato (about 1 cup)	Salt to taste

1. Preheat oven to 350°. Grease a 9″ × 6″ baking dish with vegetable oil.

2. Wash and slice the eggplant into ¼″ slices. Sauté in oil.

3. Place half the eggplant slices in the baking dish.

4. Beat 2 of the eggs well; add the cheese and potato or rice. Mix well and cover the eggplant slices with the mixture.

5. Place another layer of eggplant on top.

6. Cover with chopped, fresh mixed herbs and tomatoes. Beat the remaining eggs and pour on top of the tomato layer. Season with salt and the remaining oil.

7. Bake in oven for 45 minutes to 1 hour, until a custardlike crust forms.

Serves 4–6. (M)

SYRIAN STUFFED PRUNES

In Jerusalem there is a tiny restaurant called Cohen's, where only ten to fifteen people can eat comfortably at one time. If you ask Michel (Moussa) Cohen, the proprietor, to order for you, he will (depending on his mood) serve you an elegant array of memulaim, stuffed vegetables such as onions, carrots, eggplants, zucchini, tomatoes, and peppers. The grand finale might include stuffed prunes.

Although pomegranate syrup is extremely expensive in this country, it is the walnuts that make this a festive delicacy in Cohen's native Damascus.

12 ounces pitted prunes	1 cup sweet red wine
½ cup walnut halves	1 tablespoon pomegranate
2 tablespoons butter or *pareve*	syrup*
margarine	Juice of ½ lemon

1. Stuff the prunes with the walnut halves.

2. Sauté in butter or margarine for about 5 minutes, until tender.

3. Add the wine, pomegranate syrup, and lemon juice. Simmer, uncovered, over a low heat for about 20 minutes. Serve as an accompaniment to turkey, lamb, or veal with artichokes (p. 201), using the juice as a sauce.

Serves 6-8 as a side dish. (M or P)

LEEK PATTIES
(Kofta)

Leek patties, or kofta, are eaten at Passover by Greek Jews. According to Theonie Mark, author of *Greek Islands Cooking*, Greeks eat only braised leeks, and thus we can surmise that the Greek Jews brought this recipe with them from Spain. This Greek recipe from Boston includes potatoes. We can see from the potatoes that it is a late version. Leek patties with matzah crumbs, feta cheese, or meat is an extremely old Sephardic holiday recipe. How far back leek patties go is anybody's guess—perhaps to Egypt: "We remember the fish which we were wont to eat in Egypt for nought; the cucumbers, and the melons, and the leeks, and the onions, and the garlic," we read in Numbers 11:5.

*Available at Greek and Middle Eastern food stores.

2 pounds leeks	Salt and pepper to taste
2 large potatoes, peeled and boiled	½ cup grated Romano cheese
	Vegetable oil for frying
3 eggs	

1. Wash the leeks carefully. Dice the white base and part of the green leaves. Parboil in salted water for 5 minutes. Drain.

2. Using a potato masher or food processer, mash the potatoes. Add the leeks, blending them in well.

3. Add the eggs, salt and pepper to taste, and Romano cheese. Blend well.

4. Heat some oil in a heavy frying pan. When the oil is sizzling (375°), drop the leek patties in by tablespoonsful. Fry until golden brown on each side. Drain on paper towels.

Makes about 12. (M)

YOGHURT

Abraham drank it. Some authorities attribute Sarah's long reproductive cycle to it. Solomon's wisdom came from his consumption of it. Yoghurt, of course!

Legend has it that yoghurt was discovered some six thousand years ago. A camel merchant, traveling with his herd, concubines, and servants from Ur to Eridu, filled a leather bag made from the stomach of a sheep with milk. When the sun went down at the end of the day, he settled his herd and prepared to enjoy a cool drink. To his surprise, he found instead a custardy, slightly acid milk product. He further discovered that this drink, mixed with water, quenched his thirst.

Bacteria contained in the bags had combined with the milk as a result of the body warmth of the camel he was riding and the heat of the sun. At nightfall, when the desert temperature dropped dramatically, it cooled the milk and stopped the action of the bacteria. Whether or not this particular story is true is not important. This is more or less the way yoghurt was discovered somewhere in the Middle East or the Balkans. Soon the nomads learned that they could make yoghurt by inoculating fresh milk with a small amount of already-prepared yoghurt.

Americans are just now learning to eat yoghurt, which is so very easy to make. I merely boil milk, remove from heat at the boiling point, let sit 15 minutes, add 1 teaspoon of yoghurt culture per cup of milk, stir, pour into cup containers, cover, place in a warm oven, turn the oven off, and let sit overnight. That is all there is to it!

Persian Jews, however, have been eating yoghurt for centuries. At the end of Passover, they eat a special yoghurt dish, more like a thick soup, to break the abstention from bread.

To Persians, yoghurt is an essential food. But with no kosher dairies in the country, even the less observant Jews would abstain from milk, cheese, butter, and yoghurt products during Passover. Thus, on the evening of the last night of Passover, yoghurt would be served again.

Yashar Shirazi remembers how on this last night his father would place silver coins in a bowl of water. Whoever could put his thumb in the water and raise up the coin without touching the wall of the bowl would have good luck through the year. Flowers and green branches would adorn the table on this evening, as a wish for a green and fruitful life until next Passover.

CUCUMBER YOGHURT SALAD
(Mastva Khiar)

2 cups yoghurt	2 radishes, sliced thin
1 cup cold water	¼ cup white raisins
3 ice cubes	¼ cup chopped walnuts
2 small or 1 large cucumber, peeled and diced	1 tablespoon crushed, dried or 3 tablespoons fresh mint
1 small onion or the white part of 2 scallions, diced	Salt and freshly ground pepper to taste

1. Combine all the ingredients. Adjust mint, salt, and pepper to taste.

2. If possible, let sit overnight.

Serves 4-6. (M)

SPINACH SOUFFLÉ
(Fritada de Espinaca)

At Passover, some vegetables—such as corn, string beans, and peas—are not eaten by Ashkenazim but are by Sephardim. However, there remain the East European standbys: beets, cucumbers, and cabbage. In addition, asparagus, artichokes, and spinach are the major seasonal substitutes. For daily eating, spinach is one of the most popular vegetables at Passover, especially in Sephardic cultures. This Passover soufflé, in a less Americanized version, is served by Turkish Jews on Saturday morning after synagogue with coffee and burekas. Other versions include mashed potatoes and Romano cheese, rather than cream and cottage cheese.

10 ounces fresh or 1 package frozen spinach, defrosted	½ cup matzah meal
½ pound cream cheese	3 eggs, well beaten
1 pound cottage cheese	Salt and pepper to taste

1. Preheat oven to 350°. Grease a 1-quart soufflé dish.

2. Cook the spinach thoroughly and drain well. Melt the cream cheese over boiling water and add to the hot spinach. Add the cottage cheese and matzah meal and mix well.

3. Stir in the eggs, salt, and pepper.

4. Pour into the soufflé dish and bake for 40 minutes, or until light golden on top.

Serves 4–6. (M)

MINA DE ESPINACA CON CARNE
(Matzah, Spinach, and Meat Pie)

Mina, the classic vegetable or meat matzah pie, is a Sephardic favorite. Basically, it is a substantial matzah brei with spinach filling. Often prepared for brunch during Passover, when the men return from Sabbath morning services, it is served with brown hard-boiled eggs, fruit, and coffee. A meat mina is also used as one of the dishes for a Sephardic Seder or main-meal dish during Passover. This Turkish rendition is especially tasty.

4 matzot	2 tablespoons pignolia (optional)
1 pound fresh spinach	1 teaspoon salt, or to taste
1 medium onion, chopped	Pinch of allspice
6 tablespoons vegetable oil	1 cup mashed potatoes
1 pound chopped beef	3 eggs

1. Soak the unbroken matzot in cold water until soft (about 2 minutes). Drain very well on a cloth or paper towel. Squeeze out the water if necessary. This step is important; otherwise, the mina will be too soggy and not crunchy.

2. Wash the spinach, drain thoroughly, and dry. Then chop lightly.

3. Sauté the onion in 2 tablespoons oil. Add the meat and cook until the meat is brown. Just before it is done, add the pignolia. Season with salt and allspice. Degrease.

4. Cook the spinach briefly, until it just wilts. Drain and mix with the meat and potatoes.

5. Beat 2 eggs very well. Pour over the spinach–meat mixture and mix well.

6. Preheat oven to 400°. Grease a pie plate or square baking pan with 2 tablespoons oil.

7. Cover the bottom of the pan with 2 whole matzot. It they break up, you can patch them.

8. Spread the spinach–meat mixture on top. Cover with the remaining 2 matzot. Brush the top with the remaining 2 tablespoons oil. Beat the remaining egg and spread over all.

9. Bake 50 minutes, or until top is lightly browned.

Serves 4–6. (F)

LAMB

And they shall eat the flesh in that night, roast with fire, and unleavened bread; with bitter herbs they shall eat it.

Exodus 12:8

In American Jewish circles there is some confusion as to the use of lamb on Passover. Spring is the time of year when young lambs are most plentiful, and a time of thanksgiving to celebrate the herd's survival through the long winter. It was and still is logical that lambs be slaughtered to eat at springtime feasts. Indeed, roast lamb is the traditional spring food throughout the Middle East.

Until the destruction of the Second Temple, a one-year-old lamb was always sacrificed on the eve of Passover and eaten that same night, inaugurating the festival. It was eaten with bitter herbs and matzah. To this day, Samaritans roast lambs on Passover.

Some Jews, however, will not eat roast lamb or any roasted meat at Passover because of the bitter memory that the Temple sacrifices are no longer possible. Middle Eastern Jews will eat lamb, but never roasted. For other Jews, exactly the reverse is true: roasted lamb or other roasted food is served to commemorate the ancient sacrifices.

The following is my mother's roast lamb recipe. The baked lamb that follows is a standard main dish for a Sephardic Seder.

PASSOVER ROAST LAMB

1 7-pound shoulder of lamb*	½ cup shredded celery leaves
Salt and pepper to taste	⅓ cup cubed green pepper
1 clove garlic, minced	2 tablespoons catsup, or to taste

1. Preheat oven to 325°.

2. Rub the meat all over with salt and pepper. Place slivers of garlic in between the bone and the flesh. Place meat on a rack in a roasting pan, surrounded by celery leaves and green pepper.

3. Allowing 20 minutes per pound, roast in the oven. About 1 hour before it is done, smooth catsup over the top of the lamb. This will make a crusty skin and add to the flavor of the gravy.

4. To make the gravy, first drain off all the fat and remove lamb to a warm

---

*A leg of lamb is basically a kosher cut of meat, but it would be extremely laborious and costly for a butcher to cut the many veins in the hindlegs of the animal for the blood to run out. For this reason, kosher butchers prefer to sell the shoulder cut.

place. Add a little water to the gravy in the pan, leaving in the celery leaves and green pepper, and boil down on the top of the stove. Serve with asparagus, roast new potatoes, and mint jelly.

Serves 6–8. (F)

LAMB SHANKS IN LEMON SAUCE

4	(about 3 pounds) lamb shanks	1	tablespoon lemon juice
1	large onion, chopped fine	1	teaspoon salt
1	clove garlic, minced	1	bay leaf
1¼	cups water	1	tablespoon potato starch

1. Brown the lamb in a heavy casserole. Push to one side of the casserole. Add onion and garlic, and sauté until soft. Stir in 1 cup water, lemon juice, salt, and bay leaf. Cover.

2. Simmer 3 hours, or until very tender. Remove meat and keep hot.

3. Blend potato starch with the remaining ¼ cup water. Stir into the liquid in the pan. Cook, stirring constantly, until the gravy thickens and boils for 1 minute. Remove bay leaf.

Serves 4. (F)

GREEK EGG LEMON CHICKEN
(Agrastada)

This is a favorite Greek Passover dish.

1	2½-pound chicken	Juice of 1 lemon
	Salted water	Salt and pepper to taste
5	eggs	¼ cup *pareve* margarine

1. Place the chicken in a heavy pot. Cover with salted water and bring to a boil. Cover and simmer ½ hour, or until chicken is cooked. Remove to a separate plate and cool the chicken.

2. Preheat oven to 350°.

3. Bone the chicken and place all the meat and skin in an ovenproof low casserole.

4. Pour off all but ⅔ cup liquid from the original pot. Gradually beat in the eggs, lemon juice, salt, pepper, and margarine. Pour this sauce over the chicken.

5. Bake about 25 minutes, or until golden brown.

Serves 4–6. (F)

VEAL WITH ARTICHOKES

Veal with artichokes is served in Egyptian Jewish homes, often for the second night of Passover. I first tasted this particularly superb dish at the home of the Egyptian-born, Israeli-raised Harvard University Professor Nadav Safran.

9–12 artichokes, depending on size, or 2 14-ounce cans artichoke hearts	⅓ cup vegetable oil
	Salt and pepper to taste
	½ teaspoon turmeric
2 cups water	½ teaspoon cumin
2 lemons	2 tablespoons fresh parsley
3 pounds veal shanks with bones removed, cut in chunks	1–2 cloves garlic

1. Peel off the outer leaves of the artichokes and pull out the hairy center. cut out the heart. Divide each heart in quarters and drop into water to cover with 1 quartered lemon. If using canned artichoke hearts, merely quarter and place in water with 1 quartered lemon.

2. Sauté the meat in oil, leaving a few tablespoons of oil for later use with the artichokes. Add salt, pepper, turmeric, cumin, and parsley. When the meat is brown, lower flame and add ⅓ cup water. Cover and simmer over a low flame for 1 hour.

3. Meanwhile, place the artichoke hearts in ½ cup water with the remaining 3 tablespoons oil, garlic, salt, and the remaining 1 lemon, quartered. Bring to a boil and lower flame. Simmer, covered, for about 10–15 minutes until tender but not soft.

4. Add the artichokes and the sauce to the meat. Cover and let stew for another ½ hour. Serve with Syrian stuffed prunes and rice.

Serves 6–8. (F)

PASSOVER TSIMMES

Rose Siegel was born in a *shtetl* near Minsk, Russia, in 1900 and came to the United States in 1922. Her husband died and left her with three small children and little money. She ran a rooming house to make ends meet and later became a kosher caterer. Adhering to the Jewish dietary laws and preparing traditional fare, she was in demand for Orthodox bar mitzvahs, weddings, and other social occasions. A memorable event for her was the preparation of a kosher luncheon at the Supreme Court when an Orthodox group honored the late Chief Justice Earl Warren. "What a country America is to have a kosher caterer at the highest court in the land," commented Mrs. Siegel to the Chief Justice.

When Mrs. Siegel learned to cook as a child, there were no manufacturers of Passover products. Today most Jews buy specially prepared matzot, matzah-meal cake flour, and potato starch at their local markets. In Russia, everything was cooked from scratch after the regular dishes were exchanged for those used at Passover and the entire house cleaned of all leavening agents. Flour—watched over after milling lest it come in contact with water—was mixed at home with water to make the matzah. From that matzah, meal was ground by hand, to be used in such recipes as Mrs. Siegel's matzah-meal dumplings, tsimmes, or popovers (p. 182). Fine matzah-meal cake flour was not available. Potato starch was made from the sediment collected after potatoes were grated for potato pancakes. From the starch Mrs. Siegel makes, among other dishes, outstanding apple blintzes.

5 cups diced carrots	4 medium potatoes
1 pound top rib or flanken, cut into stewing pieces	1 medium onion
2 sweet potatoes, quartered	2 eggs
½ cup brown sugar	½ cup matzah meal
½ pound pitted prunes	Salt and pepper to taste

1. Boil the carrots in water to cover in a 3-quart covered pot until the carrots are soft (about ½ hour). Add the meat, sweet potatoes, brown sugar, and pitted prunes. Simmer, covered, until the potatoes are done (about 45 minutes).

2. Grate the potatoes, squeezing out the potato starch, and the onion on the small holes of a grater or in a food processor. Add the eggs and matzah meal. Season with salt and pepper to taste.

3. Preheat oven to 350°.

4. Shape the potato mixture in the center of the pot or any oblong casserole. Place the carrots and meat on each side and on top. Cover with the liquid and bake, covered, for ½ hour. Serve immediately from the casserole.

Serves 6–8. (F)

PASSOVER APPLE BLINTZES

Pancake Batter:
6 eggs
1 cup potato starch
2 cups water
Oil for frying

Apple Filling:
2 pounds apples, peeled, cored, and diced
¼ cup sugar
1 teaspoon cinnamon
½ teaspoon grated lemon rind
¼ cup chopped walnuts (optional)
½ cup raisins (optional)

1. Beat the eggs well. Slowly add the potato starch and water, beating well until the batter is pale, yellow, and foamy.

2. Lightly oil a 6″ skillet or crêpe pan and place over a medium-high flame (about 350°). (A teflon pan is especially good for this.)

3. Using a ladle, pour in the batter to coat the pan and drain off any excess batter. When the batter seems dry, shake the pancake out onto a cloth placed on a flat surface. Let cool. Continue making blintzes until all the batter is used up. When the blintzes are dry, you can pile them one on top of another.

4. Preheat oven to 400°. Grease a large low casserole.

5. To the chopped apples, add sugar, cinnamon, lemon rind, walnuts, and raisins. Mix well.

6. Taking a blintz, place a heaping tablespoon of apple filling in the center. Fold over each side and then roll up, jelly-roll fashion. Place seam side down on a greased cookie sheet. Continue until all blintzes are filled.

7. Brush the tops of each blintz with oil and heat in the casserole in the oven about 20 minutes, or until golden brown. Serve as is, or with sour cream.

Makes 20–22. (P or M)

If you wish to use a cheese filling, see p. 226.

ALMOND MACAROONS
(Maranchinos)

There are dry macaroons, chewy macaroons, tasty ones, and bland ones. Until I tasted the following crunchy-on-the-outside, chewy-on-the-inside maranchinos at the home of Greek Jews in Boston, my favorites had been those served in the dairy bar of the King David Hotel in Jerusalem, half coated with rich chocolate. Since most Jews make a coconut or almond version of macaroons, these cookies are probably an ancient Jewish *pareve* Passover sweet, which need no grease to cook. They are also a marvelous means of disposing of extra egg whites. If you have leftover yolks, use them in the dressing for the French salad on p. 190.

Making almond macaroons (photo: Edward Fitzgerald)

2½ cups blanched almonds	Matzah flour for dusting
2¼ cups sugar	¼ cup blanched almonds, split,
5 egg whites	for topping

1. Preheat oven to 350°.

2. Grind the almonds very fine in a food processor or other grinder.

3. Place the almonds in a bowl. Add the sugar and egg whites, one at a time, blending by hand or with a food processor until a paste is formed which can be manipulated with the hand. Refrigerate for 10 minutes. (The Greek style of separating eggs is to pierce a tiny hole in one end and then slowly let the white ooze out, preserving the yolk within the shell for later use.)

4. Dust a large cookie sheet with matzah flour.

5. Take a piece of dough the size of a plum. Roll between the palms to make a ball and pinch the top to shape like a pear. Place, wide side down, on the cookie sheet. Place half a blanched almond on top.

6. Bake 20–25 minutes, until the cookies rise and brown a little. Cool and separate with a spatula, taking care not to break them.

Makes about 24. (P)

KRIMSEL

On the table, the fresh crisp matzos *were also waiting, and in the oven a delicious Passover borsht was simmering, and hot* kneidlach *with chicken fat, and maybe even a potato pudding!...Such wonderful* chremzlach *that it would have been hard even for an epicure to tell if there was more honey in them or more chicken fat, because they were so sugary and so rich that they stuck to the gums and ran down his beard.*

Sholom Aleichem, "The Lottery Ticket"

When my parents married, my German father asked my American mother to learn how to make one dish—krimsel. Here is her American variation on a German theme. With leaven forbidden at Passover, krimsels are easy-to-make fritters with fruit. They can be made of matzah meal and filled with nuts and preserves; or, as in my family recipe, made from soaked matzah and nuts, with no jam filling. Either way, they are crispy and delicious!

3 matzot, soaked and squeezed very dry	1 tablespoon matzah meal
	¾ cup sugar
2 tablespoons seeded chopped raisins	Grated rind of 1 lemon
	1 tablespoon lemon juice
2 tablespoons chopped almonds	Vegetable oil for deep-frying
3 eggs, separated	

1. Mix the matzot, raisins, almonds, egg yolks, matzah meal, sugar, lemon rind, and lemon juice.

2. Beat the egg whites until stiff. Fold into the matzah mixture.

3. Heat the vegetable oil to 375°. Drop the mixture by tablespoons and brown on both sides. Drain well. Serve warm, with stewed prunes flavored with orange juice.

Serves 6–8. (P)

PASSOVER LEMON SPONGE CAKE

This Russian Passover lemon sponge cake is almost identical to the Greek pan de España de Pesah. According to Theonie Mark, author of *Greek Islands Cooking*, the pan de España was brought to Greece by Sephardic Jews at the time of the Inquisition.

The classic sponge cake includes neither butter nor leavening agents. For Jews, it is the perfect sweet *pareve* dish for any meal.

The trick to making a good sponge cake is to beat as much air as possible into the separated eggs before steaming the cake mixture in the oven. Given the fact that Jews checked eggs closely for blood and needed ways to experiment with rising agents acceptable at Passover, it may have been a pre-Inquisition Spanish or Portuguese Jew who discovered how to beat yolks until they are lemony and whites until stiff peaks form.

12 eggs, separated	½ cup chopped walnuts
1½ cups sugar	(optional)
½ cup orange juice	¼ cup potato flour
Grated rind of 1 lemon	1 cup matzah-meal cake flour
Grated rind of 1 orange	Pinch of salt

1. Preheat oven to 325°.

2. Using an electric mixer or food processor, beat the egg yolks until frothy and lemon-colored. Add sugar gradually. Add orange juice and grated lemon and orange rinds. Add nuts if desired.

3. Sift together the potato flour and the matzah-meal cake flour. Add to the mixture.

4. Beat the egg whites until frothy. Add a pinch of salt and beat until stiff and shiny but not dry. (A good sponge cake needs a great deal of air beaten into the eggs.)

5. Bake in an ungreased 10″ angel-food pan for 1 hour. Remove from pan immediately, inverting on another plate. Use a cake divider to cut.

Serves 8. (P)

MATZAH ALMOND TORTE

In my browsing of temple cookbooks, I see frequent references to *The Twentieth Century Cookbook*, by C. F. Moritz and Adelle Kahn, published in Montgomery, Alabama, in 1897. I tracked it down and found that Passover recipes often call for a combination of matzah meal and baking powder. At the Library of Congress, I discovered that in 1926 Miss Moritz wrote a second work, *Every Woman's Cookbook*. In both books, there are recipes for matzah almond tortes, and both include baking powder.

The use of baking powder in recipes for Passover is puzzling. Evidently Miss Moritz distinguished between baking powder—a leavening agent—and yeast, and thought the former appropriate for use with matzah meal at Passover. She probably used it as an economical and modern substitute for some of the eggs in a German torte; she also replaced expensive almonds with locally grown pecans.

Miss Moritz's non-kosher cookbooks are American in the sense of the contemporary *Settlement Cook Book*, so popular elsewhere in the United States at about the same time. Here is a moist Passover variation of her torte recipes—without the baking powder!

8 eggs, separated	¼ teaspoon salt
1½ cups sugar	1 tablespoon cold water
¼ cup sifted matzah meal	½ cup pecan meat, ground
½ tablespoon lemon juice	½ cup almonds, ground
Grated rind of ½ lemon	

1. Beat the egg yolks until light. Gradually add the sugar and continue beating until the eggs are lemon-colored.

2. Preheat oven to 325°. Grease and flour with matzah flour a 9″ spring-form pan.

3. Sift the matzah meal and add to the yolks.

4. Add the lemon juice and rind, salt, and water. Fold in the nuts.

5. Beat the egg whites until stiff. Fold into the mixture.

6. Transfer to the spring-form pan and bake 45–60 minutes, or until a toothpick comes out clean. Serve as is or with the following glaze.

Glaze:

1 egg yolk	Grated rind of ½ lemon
½ cup lemon juice	1 teaspoon butter or *pareve*
½ cup sugar	margarine

1. While the torte is still in the oven, beat together the egg yolk, lemon juice, sugar, and lemon rind. Place the mixture in a saucepan and boil it, stirring constantly until it thickens. Stir in the butter.

2. With a toothpick, poke holes in the top of the cake at 1″ intervals. When the cake has cooled slightly, still in the pan, pour the glaze over it. Let stand a few minutes so the glaze sinks in, and then remove from the pan.

Serves 8. (P or M)

CHOCOLATE SOUFFLÉ ROLL

When this recipe appeared in my column in the Boston *Globe* magazine, the newspaper received several calls from indignant readers: How could there be such a thing as a flourless chocolate soufflé roll? Well, there is! This particular recipe comes from the old Window Shop bakery on Brattle Street in Cambridge, started by Bostonians to help immigrant German refugees during World War II, and now called The Blacksmith House.

A similar soufflé roll was served at the Jewish Bake Shop in Cincinnati, also started by that city's German Jewish community for the new German refugees. Political film-maker Charles Guggenheim remembers the chocolate roll recipe prepared by his grandmother, Grace Stix, one of the prime movers behind the Cincinnati-based shop. The Cincinnati version was made by adding flour, filling with whipped cream, and covering with a chocolate icing. The following Boston version, which even Charles approves, can be served at Passover—and will be the hit of your Seder.

7 ounces dark, good-quality semi-sweet chocolate	7 eggs, separated
4 tablespoons strong coffee	¾ cup sugar
	2 tablespoons cocoa

1. Preheat oven to 350°. Grease a 10″×15″ jelly-roll pan. Cover with greased wax paper.

2. Melt chocolate and coffee over hot water in a double boiler and stir until chocolate is melted. Cool slightly.

3. Beat the egg yolks with ½ cup sugar until fluffy and pale yellow.

4. Add the chocolate and coffee to the yolks.

5. Beat the egg whites until soft peaks form. Add ¼ cup sugar, beating gradually until stiff peaks form.

6. Fold the egg whites into the chocolate mixture. Place batter in pan and bake 15-20 minutes, or until the roll is firm.

7. Remove and cool for 5 minutes. Then place a damp towel over the roll and cool completely at room temperature (this prevents the roll from drying out). Store in a cool place.

8. When ready to use (with the mocha filling, these steps can be done in advance), remove the towel from the roll and sprinkle with cocoa. Place an ungreased sheet of wax paper over the roll and turn the roll upside down. Remove the pan and the first piece of wax paper.

9. Spread the whipped cream or mocha filling over the flattened cake and roll up very carefully and quickly. Store in refrigerator.

Serves 8-10. (M or P)

Mocha Cream Filling:

9 tablespoons *pareve* margarine	2 eggs
¾ cup very fine sugar	Confectioners' sugar
3 ounces semi-sweet chocolate	Shaved chocolate for garnish
2 tablespoons strong coffee	

1. For the mocha filling, cream the margarine and sugar very well.

2. Melt the chocolate in coffee in a double boiler over hot water, stirring constantly. Cool slightly. Add to the margarine mixture and blend well. Add the eggs and continue beating until very smooth and light. Set aside in a cool place.

3. Sprinkle the top of the cake with confectioners' sugar and then shaved chocolate. Since the chocolate roll usually cracks a bit in rolling, the decoration will cover this.

Whipped Cream Filling:

1½ cups heavy cream	2 teaspoons confectioners' sugar
1 teaspoon vanilla or rum	Shaved chocolate for garnish

1. Just before serving, whip the cream with the vanilla or rum and confectioners' sugar.

2. You may wish to reserve some of the whipped cream and decorate the outside of the cake, using a pastry bag or a spatula. Sprinkle the top with shaved chocolate.

MATZAH APPLE SCHALET

In writing a cookbook like this, an author follows up on many leads. Perhaps one of the most fascinating for me was a visit to Bruno and Lisl Stern of New York's Washington Heights. Both from Wuerttemberg, they are truly keepers of tradition. In the 1930's Bruno had the foresight to take photographs of the everyday life of German Jews in his hometown of Niederstetten. The result is his audio-visual presentation, "Of Times Gone By—My Town, My House, My Family." He describes in the slide show and in a book published in Stuttgart, *Memories of My Youth in a Small Town in Wuerttemberg and of its Jewish Congregation,* Passover in a southern German town. Side by side with old photographs are interspersed pictures of the traditional holiday foods which his wife, Lisl, prepares so well.

Holiday foods were served on "Jews' porcelain." When a Jew married in the eighteenth century, he was obliged to buy a set of porcelain from the king's factory—thus the name!

Stern also has a collection of old cookbooks from the nineteenth and early twentieth centuries. The most interesting to me was the 1874 *Kochbuch* written in beautiful script by his grandmother, Rosa Muhlfelder Stern. Here is her matzah apple schalet recipe, which to this day Lisl Stern serves at Passover.

Rosa Muhlfelder's kosher cookbook, with 182 recipes, which she tried to have published in Frankfurt in 1874 (photo: Bruno Stern)

4 matzot	½ cup raisins
2 large eggs, separated	2–3 McIntosh apples, peeled,
¼ cup sugar	cored, and diced
½ teaspoon cinnamon	½ cup hazelnuts or almonds,
Rind and juice of 1 lemon	coarsely ground

1. Soak the matzot in cold water until soft. Then squeeze dry.

2. Preheat oven to 450°.

3. In a large bowl, mix the egg yolks, sugar, cinnamon, and lemon rind and juice. Add the raisins, apples, and nuts. Mix well. Combine with the matzot.

4. Beat the egg whites until stiff peaks form. Fold into the mixture.

5. Bake in a 9″ greased spring-form pan 1 hour, or until golden. Cool, and serve at room temperature.

Serves 6–8. (P)

PASSOVER WINE CAKE

This is one of those Passover nut cakes which originated in Russia and, because of its moist texture, has had great success in this country.

9 large eggs, separated	½ teaspoon ginger
1½ cups sugar	Pinch of salt
⅔ cup matzah cake meal	¾ cup ground walnuts
⅓ cup potato starch	¼ cup sweet red wine
1 teaspoon cinnamon	

1. Preheat oven to 350°.

2. Beat the egg whites until they form stiff peaks but are not dry.

3. Beat the egg yolks until they are foamy, gradually adding the sugar.

4. Sift together the matzah cake meal, potato starch, cinnamon, ginger, and salt. Add gradually to the egg yolks.

5. Place the ground walnuts in a cup and add enough sweet wine to fill the cup. Fold into the cake mixture.

6. Fold in the egg whites.

7. Grease and flour a 10″ tube pan. Bake 50–60 minutes.

Serves 8. (P)

BEET EINGEMACHTS
(Beet Preserves)

Eva Lubetkin Cantor was the youngest of thirteen children growing up in New York City at the turn of the century. Her father, who was born in Lithuania, was the first to introduce machine-made matzot; he later went into the wholesale flour business.

In a family oral history, Eva has recaptured the past. Passover was "like preparing for a wedding." In those days, everything was homemade—no Manischewitz or Goodman's products to make life easier. "My mother prepared gallons of beet eingemachts." These beet preserves were eaten with a spoon and drunk with tea (in a glass, of course). Eingemachts could also be made from radishes and carrots. "I can still see the maids scraping the beets and getting their faces and arms all speckled with red dots. We kids used to get a bang out of that. When it was time to prepare the almonds, they had to be shelled. The most fun was when my mother poured boiling water over the nuts and we had to get the brown covering off. They were slippery, and we would shoot them at each other. When the preserves were finished, they were put into ten-gallon crocks."

Eva continues this Lubetkin tradition to this day. During Passover, members of her family gather together, sip tea, and eat her beet eingemachts, which Eva makes in quarts rather than gallons.

¾ cup water	2 medium lemons
2 cups sugar	1 tablespoon ground ginger
2 pounds beets	1 cup sliced blanched almonds

1. Pour water over sugar. Mix well in a large enamel saucepan. Bring to a boil slowly and let simmer, uncovered, while you prepare beets.

2. Peel and cut the beets in half, then into thin strips. Cut the unpeeled lemons in half and then into thin strips. (If you have a food processor, the grating blade is perfect for this step.)

3. Add beet and lemon strips to the sugar mixture. Cover and let simmer slowly about 1½ hours, stirring occasionally. Do not let stick.

4. Uncover and add ginger. Simmer about another ½ hour, or until you test it with a spoon to see if it is thick enough. Turn off heat, and let cool overnight.

5. Next day, toast almonds and fold into the cold preserves. Seal.

Makes about 2 pints. (P)

SHAVUOT

SHAVUOT

Honey and milk are under thy tongue.

Song of Songs 4:11

A mountain of God is the mountain of Bashan;
A mountain of peaks is the mountain of Bashan.
Why look ye askance, ye mountains of peaks,
At the mountain which God hath desired for His abode?
Yea, the Lord will dwell therein for ever.

Psalm 68:16–17

Shavuot, or the Feast of Weeks, comes seven weeks after Passover and was originally the celebration of the completion of the barley harvest with the sacrificial offering of the first fruits at the Temple. Later, it came to commemorate the giving of the Ten Commandments on Mount Sinai.

It is customary to eat dairy food at Shavuot. How do dairy dishes fit into a barley harvest festival? At this time of year, late May or early June, such foods are eaten because of the large amount of cheese produced. Churning and cheesemaking are common features of spring harvest festivals the world over, when goats, sheep, and cows begin to graze more and thus produce more milk.

As if a pastoral explanation were not enough, Jewish scholars have discovered additional ones. In the above psalm, for example, Mount Sinai, on which the Ten Commandments were given, is called by six different names— mountain of God, mountain of Bashan, and mountain of peaks *(har gavnunim)* are mentioned in the psalm. *"Gavnunim"* means "gibbous, many peaked," but the word has the same root as *gevinah,* Hebrew for cheese. Thus it could also be called Cheese Mountain, a common folk image. Accordingly, the eating of cheese at this season is a reminder of the giving of the Law. In addition, the Torah is likened to milk and honey in the Song of Songs.

Another explanation for cheese eating is that by the time the Israelites had returned to their camp after receiving the Ten Commandments, so much time had elapsed that their milk had turned sour—the first step in making cheese.

According to another rabbinic source, the Israelites fasted while they went to receive the Ten Commandments and returned so hungry that they drank milk immediately rather than go through the long process of preparing a meat meal. To this day, some Jews have first a milk meat at Shavuot, followed by a meat one.

At the celebration of the barley harvest, two loaves of bread were offered in the Temple. They were often shaped in long loaves with four corners to symbolize the four methods of interpreting the scriptural text: the simple, the esoteric, the homiletical, and the allegorical meanings. The Torah is also likened to bread; thus the long Shavuot loaf symbolizes the length and breadth of the Law.

MENUS

Cold Sour-Cherry Soup★
Rachal (Fish with Sour Cream and Potatoes)★
Green Salad
Palacsinta★ Filled with Cheese or Apricot Preserves

Borscht★
Gefilte Fish★ or Pickled Carp
Bread
Cheese Blintzes★

Palestinian Fruit Soup★
Cheese Knishes★
Herring in Sour Cream★
Cheesecake★

Cold Spicy Fish★
Spinach Soufflé★
Carrot Salad★
Yoghurt★ with Sugar

COLD SOUR-CHERRY SOUP

When my Hungarian-born grandfather, Henry Gluck, was in his nineties, I used to go with him to Tik Tak, a marvelous Hungarian restaurant on Second Avenue in New York. One of my favorite dishes was a cold sour-cherry soup. Ava Ehrlich, who emigrated from Budapest to Bethesda, Maryland, shared this recipe with me. The addition of wine makes it a sweet alternative to Bloody Marys for a Sunday brunch.

2 20-ounce cans or 2 pounds fresh pitted sour cherries	1 cinnamon stick
1 cup sugar, or to taste	1 cup sour cream
	1 cup dry red wine (optional)

1. Drain the cherries, retaining the juice in a saucepan. Set the cherries aside. Add enough water to the juice to make 3 cups. Add sugar and the cinnamon stick. Bring to a boil, stirring to dissolve the sugar, and add the cherries. Partially cover and simmer over low heat for 10–15 minutes.

2. Remove cinnamon stick and blend until smooth.

3. Return to heat and bring to a boil. Then cool the soup a bit and add the sour cream, letting it dissolve. Chill.

4. Before serving, add the wine. Additional sour cream can be served in a side dish or as a dollop in each bowl.

Serves 6–8. (M)

PALESTINIAN FRUIT SOUP

Every synagogue cookbook needs at least one or two prime movers to complete the always-more-tedious-than-expected project. Cleveland's Rebecca Brickner, wife of the late Rabbi Barnett Brickner and mother of Rabbi Balfour Brickner of New York, is just such a person. It was she who chaired the Fairmont Cookbook Committee in 1957. *The Fairmont Cookbook* is, to my mind, one of the finest of the many synagogue cookbooks.

Mrs. Brickner learned to make the fruit soup recipe featured in the book as a student in Palestine in 1931–32. Fruit soups have become extremely popular in Israel; they originated with German Jews who began making them while summering on the shores of the Baltic.

2 oranges, peeled	1 cup brown sugar or honey
2 stalks rhubarb, cut in pieces	½ teaspoon salt
4 slices fresh pineapple	½ teaspoon cinnamon
1 cup strawberries	2 tablespoons lemon juice
1 cup pitted cherries	1 cup sour cream
6 cups water	

1. Combine all the ingredients except the sour cream. Adjust to taste.

2. Simmer, covered, about 20 minutes, or until the fruit is tender.

3. Purée or force through a sieve.

4. Chill and add sour cream before serving.

Serves 6. (M)

Note: Other fruits may be substituted, but make sure there is a combination of tart and sweet.

WOLFIE'S BORSCHT

The epithet "Borscht Belt" was coined in an article in *Variety* when a journalist described the Catskills as the place where so many vaudeville actors got their start. Since then, borscht, originally a Ukrainian dish, has been associated with Jews.

The following cold borscht recipe comes from Wolfie's Restaurant, the Sardi's and Lindy's of Miami Beach. It is another fresh hot-weather drink.

2½ pounds beets, peeled and diced (or quartered)	1 tablespoon sour salt or lemon juice
1 onion, sliced	Salt to taste
1 stalk celery, chopped	6 eggs
2½ quarts water	Sour cream
½–1 cup sugar	Dill (optional)

1. Simmer the beets, onion, and celery in the water, covered, for about 40 minutes, or until the beets are tender.

2. Add the sugar and sour salt. Strain or place in a blender and purée. Add salt to taste. The strained beet juice will keep several days in the refrigerator.

3. Simmer again. Add 1 cup of soup to the eggs, then slowly beat the eggs into the rest of the soup. Let cool before serving with sour cream. Sprinkle with dill if desired.

Serves 10. (M)

RADISHES IN SOUR CREAM

Black radishes were eaten as snacks, sliced with onion on black bread, and turned into eingemachts (preserves) in the poor *shtetls* of East Europe. The wide use of sour cream, too, came from this area. Served generously over vegetables, it makes a popular main dish for a milk meal. It is also poured over cottage cheese, used as a dressing for blintzes, and served on radishes.

Poor Jews would only include one salad in a main milk meal, but for the rich a radish salad might be one of many fish and vegetable appetizers on the zakuska, or hors d'oeuvres table, which began each meal.

1 bunch red radishes	1 teaspoon vinegar
½ teaspoon salt	Sprinkling of black pepper
3 tablespoons sour cream	

1. Rinse and dry the radishes. Slice thin, but not paper-thin. Place in a shallow dish and sprinkle with salt. Put a weight on top. After ½ hour, drain off the excess water.

2. Stir in the sour cream and vinegar, and sprinkle with pepper. Serve chilled.

Serves 6. (M)

MARK TALISMAN'S BAGELS

You take a hole, and you put some dough around it.
Old Yiddish recipe for bagels

What is more Jewish—and American—than the bagel? Of all the foods handed down from our East European forebears, who ate these buns as snacks in the afternoon, bagels have probably become the most universally popular.

Bagels, lox, and cream cheese with tomatoes and onions are not only Shavuot, circumcision, and even Sunday-brunch Jewish favorites, they are standard fare for all American brunches. Green bagels are served on St. Patrick's Day, and this bread with a hole is served in first-class delicatessen lunches on airplanes. At least one university served the bagel, lox, and cream cheese triumvirate for its annual board meeting. Twenty-four–hour bagel factories operate in many cities.

Symbolic of the endless circle of life, bagels were mentioned as early as 1610 in the community regulations of Cracow. These bagels were given to women in childbirth. (Today, doctors prescribe day-old bagels for teething infants.) The origin of bagels is, however, clouded in mystery. One theory traces them to 1683 Vienna, where bakers created stirrup-shaped buns in honor of their deliverance from the Turks by the King of Poland, who was a riding buff; *buegal* is the Austrian word for stirrup. Another theory is that "bagel" is a Yiddish corruption of Middle High German *bougel* or *beugel*, meaning a twisted or curved ring or bracelet. A third theory is that bagels were invented as an economical food for poor people because the hole saved material!

Mark Talisman, the bagel man (photo: Allan Gerson)

A true bagel is made from white-wheat, high-gluten flour and is perfectly plain. The secret is to boil it in water to reduce the starch content as well as to give it an outer sheen and hard crust. There were also milk and egg bagels. Today there is an endless variety of rye, pumpernickel, wholewheat, onion, poppy-seed, raisin, or even pizza bagels. But give me plain water bagels anytime. Mark Talisman agrees—for more about him, see pp. 65–66.

2 tablespoons margarine
1 cup milk, scalded
2 tablespoons (2 packages) dry
  yeast
Pinch of sugar
1 cup warm water
8 cups (about) unbleached all-
  purpose flour

1 tablespoon salt
3 quarts water
2 tablespoons kosher salt
Sesame, poppy, and/or caraway
  seeds

1. Melt the margarine in the scalded milk.

2. Proof the yeast with a pinch of sugar in the warm water.

3. Combine the two liquid mixtures and gradually blend in the flour and the salt until a soft, sticky dough is formed. (A food processor is fine to start this.) Knead well and place in a greased bowl. Cover and let rise in a warm place until doubled in bulk (about 1 hour).

4. Preheat oven to 400°. Boil about 3 quarts water with 2 tablespoons kosher salt.

5. Knead dough again on a floured board. Break off a piece about the size of a plum and roll out into a 5½"-long snakelike shape, tapering the dough at the extremities. Twist into a circle and press the ends together. Place on a floured board. Continue until all the dough is used up. Let stand, uncovered, until the dough begins to rise (about 10 minutes).

6. Drop the bagels one by one into the boiling salted water, boiling a few at a time. Cover and wait until the water boils again. With a slotted spoon, turn the bagels, cover again, and wait until the water boils (about 2 minutes). (The water gives the bagels a crunchy crust.) Remove to a greased cookie sheet.

7. Sprinkle with sesame, poppy, or caraway seeds and bake about 30 minutes, or until golden. These bagels freeze well.

Makes 20–24. (M)

Note: These will not be as hard as commercial bagels because no preservatives are used. They are deliciously crunchy on the outside and chewy inside.

LOX

The Jewish people have always liked salty foods. What was offered to God or His emissaries had to be pure. No sourness or rottenness, no food in a state of decay, fermentation, or dissolution would be appropriate. Perhaps this is the original reason Jews honor salt, a pure mineral. All sacrifices were strewn with it. The Dead Sea healed and purified because of its salt content. Newborn children were rubbed with it. Coarse salt is issued for clearing the blood out of meat, poultry, and even fish. A table is not ready for a meal without salt, a reminder of the Tabernacle.

Herring and lox are both salty fish greatly liked by Jews. Today, with freshly cut belly lox so expensive, many people buy precut lox. Salt is added as a preservative. Nova Scotia salmon is the more expensive, less salted variety.

The American addiction to bagels and lox comes from the dairy cafeteria, which draws on traditional East European dairy and fish cuisine. It has crossed over to delicatessens and to such gourmet emporia as New York's Zabar's, which carries smoked whitefish, sable, salmon, chub, and of course all kinds of pickled herring. Of all, however, lox is the most popular.

LOX, SOUR CREAM, AND CAVIAR MOLD

1 tablespoon (1 envelope) unflavored kosher gelatin	2 tablespoons freeze-dried or fresh chopped chives
¼ cup cold water	1 teaspoon lemon juice
½ cup heavy cream	1 tablespoon chopped parsley
8 ounces cream cheese	1 tablespoon horseradish
1 cup sour cream	½ pound smoked salmon (lox), coarsely chopped
1 tablespoon Worcestershire sauce	4 ounces red salmon caviar
Dash of Tabasco sauce	

1. Soak the gelatin in cold water. Add the heavy cream.

2. Combine the cream cheese and sour cream in a food processor or electric mixer.

3. Add the gelatin mixture, Worcestershire sauce, Tabasco, chives, lemon juice, parsley, and horseradish to the cream-cheese mixture and combine well.

4. Blend in the lox and the caviar.

5. Rinse a 1-quart mold with cold water. Dry, then rub some vegetable oil inside. Fill with the mixture and chill at least 12 hours.

6. When ready to serve, insert a sharp knife around the mold, wrap the mold with a damp towel, place a plate on top, reverse the plate, and unmold. Serve with sliced black bread.

Makes a bit less than 1 quart. (M)

LOX BRUNCH SPREAD

½ cup finely minced onion	3 teaspoons chopped dill
½ pound lox (smoked salmon), shredded	4 teaspoons prepared horseradish
	¾ cup sour cream

Mix all ingredients well, adjusting to taste. Let stand, covered, a few hours for tastes to blend. Serve on thick slices of pumpernickel or bagels.

Makes 1½ cups. (M)

THOMAS JEFFERSON'S FRIED FISH, JEWISH FASHION

Thomas Jefferson was a remarkable man. Among his many talents, he was this country's first well-known gourmet! It was he who had the foresight to import to the United States the first macaroni, Parmesan cheese, figs, raisins, almonds, mustard, good vinegar, oil, anchovies, and vanilla.

At Monticello he built a small outdoor fish pond adjacent to the house. Local fish were caught in nets in nearby streams and lakes and then placed in his pool, whereby he could have fresh fish whenever he wished.

It seems that one of his favorite recipes was fried fish, Jewish fashion. This we know from a collection of favorite recipes assembled by his granddaughter, Virginia Randolph, who grew up in her grandfather's home. Without her grandfather's original, she searched and found a written recipe for the dish in *A Shilling Cookery Book for the People*, written in 1855 by Alexis Soyer, the noted chef of London's exclusive Reform Club.

To this day, English Jews eat fried fish on Friday night, having the cold leftovers the following day. Brought to England by Dutch Jews originally from Spain and Portugal, the dish was possibly tasted by Jefferson during his sojourn in Europe or later at the home of a Virginia or Georgia Jew.

Here is what Soyer had to say about Fried Fish, Jewish Fashion:

> *Here is another excellent way of frying fish, which is constantly in use by the children of Israel, and I cannot recommend it too highly; so much so, that various kinds of fish which many people despise, are excellent cooked by this process; in eating them many persons are deceived, and would suppose them to be the most expensive of fish. The process is at once simple, effective, and*

economical; not that I would recommend it for invalids, as the process imbibes some of the fat, which, however palatable, would not do for the dyspeptic or invalid.

Proceed thus:—Cut one or two pounds of halibut in one piece, lay it in a dish, cover the top with a little salt, put some water in the dish, but not to cover the fish; let it remain thus for one hour. The water being below, causes the salt to penetrate into the fish. Take it out and dry it; cut out the bone, and the fins off; it is then in two pieces. Lay the pieces on the side, and divide them into slices half an inch thick; put into a frying pan, with a quarter of a pound of fat, lard, or dripping (the Jews use oil); then put two ounces of flour into a soup-plate, or basin, which mix with water, to form a smooth batter, not too thick. Dip the fish in it, that the pieces are well covered, then have the fat, not too hot, put the pieces in it, and fry till a nice colour, turning them over. When done, take it out with a slice, let it drain, dish up, and serve. Any kind of sauce that is liked may be used with it; but plain, with a little salt and lemon, is excellent. This fish is often only threepence to fourpence per pound; it containing but little bone renders it very economical. It is excellent cold, and can be eaten with oil, vinegar, and cucumbers, in summer time, and is exceedingly cooling. An egg is an improvement in the batter.

The same fish as before mentioned as fit for frying, may be fried in this manner. Eels are excellent done so; the batter absorbs the oil which is in them.

Flounders may also be done in this way. A little salt should be sprinkled over before serving.

In some Jewish families all this kind of fish is fried in oil, and dipped in batter, as described below. In some families they dip the fish first in flour, and then in egg, and fry in oil. This plan is superior to that fried in fat or dripping, but more expensive.

Many of the above-mentioned families have stated days on which they fry, or stew their fish, which will keep good several days in summer, and I may almost say, weeks in winter; and being generally eaten cold, it saves them a deal of cooking. Still, I must say that there is nothing like a hot dinner.

And here is Thomas Jefferson's recipe made more modern in the late Marie Kimball's compilation of *Thomas Jefferson's Cook Book.*

FRIED FISH, JEWISH FASHION

Take a pound piece of halibut, lay in a dish. Sprinkle salt on the top and put some water in the dish, about half way up the fish. Let stand one hour. Take it out, dry it, cut out the bones. It is then in two pieces. Lay the pieces on their side and cut in slices one-half inch thick. Put ¼ pound of any desired fat in a frying pan. Mix four tablespoonfuls of flour with one egg and a little water to form a smooth batter, not too thick. Dip the fish in this, until well covered, drop in the hot fat and fry to a golden brown. Drain in brown paper, put on platter and serve. Any desired sauce may be used, but plain, with salt and lemon is usual. Other fish may be done in this way.

RACHAL
(Fish with Sour Cream and Potatoes)

Rachal is a delicious Hungarian fish dish which Jews prepare on the Friday night of Shavuot. The Jews replaced the bacon of the original recipe with butter.

6 medium potatoes
¼–½ pound butter
Salt to taste
Paprika to taste
3 pounds carp, rockfish, or
   haddock (½ of a 6-pound fish
   with head removed, bones
   intact, and cut in 6 steaks)

1 tablespoon breadcrumbs
1 tablespoon fresh dill
1 cup sour cream

1. Boil the potatoes in their skins and peel. Slice thin.

2. Butter liberally a baking–serving casserole, such as an oblong gratin dish. Fill the bottom with potato slices. Sprinkle with salt and paprika. Continue until all the potatoes are placed in the casserole.

3. Place the fish on top. Sprinkle the fish with about 1 tablespoon paprika, 1 teaspoon salt, breadcrumbs, and dill. Dot with butter. Cover with the sour cream and bake for ½ hour, or until fish flakes easily with a fork. This dish can also be made with green pepper and tomato slices.

Serves 6. (M)

GROSSINGER'S BLINTZES

Golde appeared with the blintzes piled high on a platter, plump and juicy, and "sweet as the life-giving manna from heaven."

Sholom Aleichem, "Schprintze"

Blinchiki, the ancestors of blintzes, were brought to other parts of Russia and Poland, as well as to the United States, by Jews from the Ukraine. Unlike the Russian blini, they are not yeast-risen. Blintzes are filled with blueberries, strawberries, or more usually a combination of cream cheese and eggs, and then baked or fried. Spread with cinnamon or sugar or sour cream, they are delicious.

The following recipe comes from that haven of mammoth meals, Grossinger's. Grossinger's opened in 1914 as a boarding house in the healthy Catskills for poor sweatshop workers who needed a place in the country. It advertised three healthy, well-balanced meals and fresh air for congested lungs. The word spread quickly, and trainloads of people came up to the Catskills.

To this day, the menus at Grossinger's include endless choices, although my husband insists the portions have decreased since his days as a waiter in the Catskills. A *milchig* lunch might include such items as cold borscht with a boiled potato; their famous pickled herring in cream; marinated carp; heavy sour cream with bananas, peaches, or fresh strawberries; and, of course, Grossinger's famous blintzes with blueberries and sour cream.

Batter:

3 eggs	2 tablespoons salad oil
1 cup milk or water	3/4 cup sifted flour
1/2 teaspoon salt	Butter or oil for frying

1. Beat the eggs, milk, salt, and salad oil together. Stir in the flour.

2. Heat a little butter or oil in a 6" skillet. Pour about 2 tablespoons of the batter into it, tilting the pan to coat the bottom. Use just enough batter to make a very thin pancake. Let the bottom brown, then carefully turn out onto a napkin, browned side up. Make the rest of the pancakes.

3. Spread 1 heaping tablespoon of cheese filling, blueberry preserve, or apple jelly along one side of the pancake. Turn opposite sides in and roll up like a jelly roll.

4. You can fry the blintzes in butter or oil or bake them in a 425° oven until brown. Serve dairy blintzes with sour cream.

Makes about 18. (P or M)

Sour-Cream Batter:

1 egg	⅛ teaspoon salt
¼ cup milk	1 cup sifted flour
¾ cup sour cream	Butter for frying

1. Beat together the egg, milk, sour cream, and salt. Stir in the flour, mixing until smooth.

2. Heat some butter in a 7″ skillet. Pour about 2 tablespoons of the batter into it, tilting the pan to spread the batter evenly. Fry until browned and turn to brown other side.

3. Preheat oven to 450°.

4. Place a heaping tablespoon of cheese filling on each pancake. Tuck in the opposite sides and roll up like a jelly roll. Arrange in a buttered baking dish and bake 10 minutes. This batter makes a rich pancake, and is suitable for fruit fillings.

Makes about 16. (M)

Cheese Filling:

2 cups farmers cheese	2 tablespoons sugar (optional)
1 egg yolk	1 teaspoon lemon juice
½ teaspoon salt	½ teaspoon vanilla
1 tablespoon butter	

In a small bowl, mash the farmers cheese. Stir in the egg yolk, salt, butter, sugar, lemon juice, and vanilla. (If you use cottage cheese instead of farmers cheese, it must be drained through cheesecloth or a sieve or the filling will be too loose.) If you don't wish the blintzes to be sweet, leave the sugar out of the filling.

(M)

Blueberry Filling:

1½ cups blueberries	1 tablespoon cornstarch
3 tablespoons sugar	⅛ teaspoon nutmeg

Toss all the ingredients together. For another sweet filling, see p. 203.

(M)

Note: Blintzes can be filled, then frozen, without losing taste or texture. Do *not* thaw them before frying or baking—just cook longer.

HUNGARIAN CHERRY EVEN-WEIGHT CAKE
(Egyensuly)

This "even-weight" cake is literally a pound cake, which often includes a pound or thereabouts of eggs weighed in their shells. Flour, butter, and sugar are then added to equal the weight of the eggs. This recipe calls for about ¾ pound of each ingredient.

¾ pound (1½ cups) unsalted butter
¾ pound (1½ cups) sugar
¾ pound (about 6) large eggs
¾ pound (3 cups) sifted all-purpose flour

Pinch of salt
Grated rind of 1 lemon
1 pound sweet or sour pitted cherries or sliced peaches

1. Preheat oven to 350°. Grease and flour a 9" spring-form, bundt, or loaf pan.

2. Cream the butter and sugar extremely well with an electric mixer or food processor.

3. Add each egg separately, beating after each addition.

4. Sift the flour with the pinch of salt four times through a sifter held high in the air. This adds more air to the cake, making it lighter.

5. Add the flour, gradually, and the lemon rind to the batter. Mix well, being sure to scrape the sides of the mixture.

6. Fold in the cherries or peaches.

7. Bake for 1 hour, or until the cake springs back when touched and pulls away from the sides of the pan. Cool on a rack and turn out.

Serves 8. (M)

VIENNESE TORTES

"I wasn't educated for anything," states Alice Broch, the original Viennese baker behind Cambridge's celebrated Window Shop bakery on Brattle Street. "In the Vienna of Franz Liszt, Gustav Mahler, and Johann Strauss, a proper young girl's education included music, languages, and cooking: to play lilting waltzes on the piano, to speak the languages of the countries near Vienna, and to prepare the delicacies for the food-conscious Viennese."

When in the 1930's Mrs. Broch felt the growing horror of Hitler's policies toward the Jews, she realized she would have to prepare for a new life elsewhere. Deciding to bring with her the secrets of Viennese pastry, she sat down each day with her cook, Maria, and copied the recipes for all the marvelous meringues, tortes, and rich creams of her youth. "I knew that my musical talents would not be sufficient to help me get by in the United States, but I did think that there might be a demand for Viennese pastry."

How right Mrs. Broch was! When she arrived in Boston with her husband, two sons, and Maria's cookbook, she was practically penniless. The reception she and other formerly well-to-do, educated Jewish and non-Jewish refugees received from the Cambridge community proved, however, a wonderful surprise. Shortly after arriving, Mrs. Broch met the directors of the already existing Window Shop, which then specialized in handicrafts made by refugees. One board member said to her, "You are Viennese and all Viennese are good cooks." Urging Mrs. Broch to start a bakery, she handed her a check for $300. Before she knew it, Mrs. Broch and two immigrant friends were shifting Maria's Viennese recipes to fit the proportions of American ingredients.

As Mrs. Broch tells it, the Window Shop success story was not without its measure of hard work. "My day began at 5 A.M." In the early years, she had to experiment with Maria's recipes, adjusting them to the new measurements, flours, sugars, chocolate, etc. First, she had to transfer grams to pounds and ounces and then to convert Viennese flour to our pastry, bread, and cake flour. Whereas in Vienna there was one kind of sugar, we use three—granulated, superfine, and confectioners'. When a recipe in Maria's book called for *vier Tafeln Schokolade*—four tablets of chocolate—Mrs. Broch had to figure out the exact weight of an Austrian tablet.

At first she had to make fondant, an elaborately prepared sugar icing used in Austrian tortes, herself—first boiling sugar and water to the soft-ball stage, cooling to tepid, kneading, and finally mixing with chocolate and butter—until she learned she could buy fifty-pound cans of it ready made.

While we in this country normally use dry yeast, Mrs. Broch was accustomed to wet yeast. Then there was the absence of European baking tins, which after some time she was able to locate in New York. To give one example, Mrs. Broch experimented eleven times with the famous Linzertorte until she reached today's formula.

Viennese pastry is rarely from Vienna. Vienna was the crossroads of Central Europe, located so close to Italy, France, and Germany that the cooking was always influenced by its neighbors, keeping the best of each. Streusel cakes, sponge cakes topped with fruit, and a butter, flour, and sugar crumb mixture are Czech. Linzertorte is from the Austrian town of Linz, and Dobos torte is a rich chocolate layered wonder from the Hungarian town of Dobos.

Regardless of the origin of a particular Viennese pastry, one thing is certain: only the best quality sweet butter, chocolate, almonds, hazelnuts, flour, eggs, and sugar serve as the ingredients, with delicate hand decorations as the finishing touch. Vienna is especially well known for its tortes, round cakes with either ground nuts or flour and sometimes a combination of both.

Here are two recipes adapted from Maria's handwritten book.

BLITZ MERINGUE TORTE

Cream Filling:
1 egg
3 tablespoons sugar
1 tablespoon cornstarch
1 cup sour cream
Rind and a few drops of juice
   from 1 lemon

Torte:
¼ cup unsalted butter
⅓ cup sugar
3 egg yolks

1 cup all-purpose flour
½ tablespoon baking powder
¼ cup light cream

Meringue:
3 egg whites
¼ teaspoon cream of tartar
¾ cup sugar
1 teaspoon almond extract
¾ cup slivered almonds
Whipped cream or jam

1. Preheat oven to 275°.

2. Stir and cook the egg, sugar, cornstarch, and sour cream of the filling over a double boiler until thick (about 5 minutes).

3. Cool. Add the lemon rind and juice and set aside in the refrigerator.

4. Cream together the butter, sugar, and egg yolks.

5. Sift the flour with the baking powder and add, alternating with the light cream, to the butter mixture. Blend very well.

6. Grease and flour two 8″ round pans and divide the batter between them. Don't be surprised if the batter is heavy and there is very little of it.

7. Beat the egg whites with the cream of tartar until soft peaks form. Then gradually add the sugar and the almond extract, all the time whipping the egg whites until stiff.

8. Top the batter in the cake pans with the meringue mixture, sprinkling one with some of the almonds.

9. Bake 30 minutes, or until the top is firm and slightly golden. Cool in pans until lukewarm. Turn out tortes and cool on a cake rack so that the meringue is facing up.

10. When cool, spread the sour-cream filling over the bottom layer and place the almond-coated one on top.

11. To add a final decorative (and delicious) touch, use a spatula to spread the sides with whipped cream or jam. With your hand, spread the remaining almonds on the cream or jam. Store in a cool place.

Serves 8. (M)

BLUEBERRY STREUSEL TORTE

Streusel:
3 tablespoons unsalted butter
⅓ cup confectioners' sugar
½ cup all-purpose flour
1 teaspoon cinnamon
¼ cup grated almonds or·walnuts
   (optional)

Torte:
5 tablespoons unsalted butter, margarine, or vegetable shortening

½ cup sugar
Rind and juice of 1 lemon
2 eggs, separated
1⅓ cups all-purpose flour
½ teaspoon baking powder
3 tablespoons milk
2 cups frozen or fresh blueberries

1. Preheat oven to 350°. Grease and flour a 9″ spring-form pan.

2. Mix the streusel ingredients with your hands and set aside.

3. Cream the butter, sugar, and lemon rind and juice until fluffy. Add the egg yolks, and cream well until light yellow in color.

4. Sift the flour and baking powder. Add alternately with the milk to the egg-yolk mixture. Beat just until the flour is incorporated. The dough will be very stiff.

5. Beat the egg whites until stiff. Fold into the flour mixture.

6. Spread the torte batter over the spring-form pan, add the blueberries, and cover with the streusel.

7. Bake 50–60 minutes, until the top is light brown. This torte is delicious warm for brunch, or served with ice cream.

Serves 8. (M)

RASPBERRY MELBA TORTE

Delicious red raspberries can grow like weeds. If you know the right places to find them, or have bushes in your yard, you do not have to pay the premium asked in local supermarkets. In Europe, raspberries were available at the time of Shavuot and later in the summer merely by picking the wild berries off bushes.

This exquisite torte recipe has had a long journey. Originating in pre-war Warsaw, it traveled through Russia and then Australia before moving, one generation later, to London and then Brookline, Massachusetts, where Irene Pletka now lives. Her mother, visiting from Australia, shared it with me. Needless to say, it is only prepared for very special occasions. The original recipe calls for 2–3 pints of fresh raspberries. I have reduced the amount of raspberries and added peaches.

Crust:

¼ pound unsalted butter or *pareve* margarine
10 tablespoons sugar
Pinch of salt
Rind of 1 lemon
Juice of ½ lemon
½ teaspoon vanilla

1½ cups all-purpose flour
½ teaspoon baking powder

Filling:

2 tablespoons raspberry jam
2 pints fresh raspberries, or 1 pint raspberries and 5 freestone peaches
Confectioners' sugar

1. Whip together the butter or margarine and sugar. Add the salt, lemon rind, lemon juice, and vanilla.

2. Work the flour and baking powder into the above ingredients with a food processor, mixer, or your hands. Wrap in waxed paper and let stand in the refrigerator overnight.

3. When ready to bake, preheat oven to 375°.

4. Take one-third of the dough and press it into the bottom of a 9″ spring-form pan. Bake 15 minutes. Remove from the oven.

5. Press one-third of the dough onto the sides of the pan. Brush the bottom with raspberry jam.

6. Spread all the raspberries over the bottom of the crust. (If using the peach–raspberry combination, peel the peaches and slice in crescent shapes. Arrange in the pan. Cover with the raspberries.)

7. Cover the fruit with a lattice crust, and then, with the remaining dough, make a snake around the edge, attaching the lattice top to the sides.

8. Return to oven and bake 45 minutes, until golden. Remove from oven and sprinkle with confectioners' sugar. When cool, remove from pan and serve.

Serves 6–8. (M or P)

CHEESECAKE

It has been rumored that Lindy's restaurant in New York City invented its famous cheesecake. Not so. The chef may have perfected this heavy, velvety, lemony cheesecake of cheesecakes, but the genre has a much longer history. It probably originated with the first ovens, after the early peoples of the Middle East learned to place soured cream in a bag, hang it up, and allow it to drain. To the curd that formed, they added honey, lemon peel, and egg yolks, as well as some more soured cream; they then baked the cakes, which were probably rather lumpy. In any event, Judith ate cheesecake in the court of Holofernes. The Crusaders carried the recipes to Europe; the Mongols brought curd to Russia; and the Jews carried cheesecake recipes to all the places of their wanderings. In Poland, for example, a cheesecake eaten at Shavuot consisted of farmers cheese and sugar. The French have a main-course quiche Lorraine, a Genoise cake base with pastry up the sides and a rich filling of cream cheese and pot cheese, or a simple cream-cheese tart. Hungarians serve strudel filled with cottage cheese and raisins.

The most intricate and perhaps the granddaddy of all Western cheesecakes, however, is the Russian Easter paskha. Beginning days in advance, cottage cheese is made from raw milk. Using a fine sieve, the whey is removed from the curd. When the cottage cheese reaches the desired consistency after several days of hanging, it is mixed with sugar, eggs, sour cream, butter, and chopped nuts. Then it is cooked briefly. A special wooden mold is filled with this mixture, covered with cheesecloth, and set in a cool place for twenty hours to allow the liquid to drain out. When it is ready, the mold is inverted and the paskha can be decorated with spring flowers or candied fruits.

Less difficult than the Russian paskha, and more like Lindy's famous cheesecake, is the following recipe. It comes from Gisella Warburg Wyzanski, of the famous Warburg banking family of Hamburg. Gisella came to this country in 1939 and knew how to cook "absolutely nothing," since at the Warburg home cooking was left entirely to the servants. She learned to cook in Cambridge and was one of the prime movers behind the Window Shop bakery.

6	tablespoons unsalted butter	1	cup sugar
1	cup graham-cracker crumbs		Juice of ½ lemon
6	eggs, separated	1	teaspoon vanilla
1	pound cream cheese	2	tablespoons flour
1	pound sour cream		

1. Preheat oven to 300°. Grease the sides of a 9″ spring-form pan.

2. Melt the butter and combine with the graham-cracker crumbs. Press the crumbs into the bottom of the pan. Save some crackers.

3. Combine the egg yolks, cream cheese, sour cream, sugar, lemon juice, vanilla, and flour. Beat very well until light and fluffy.

4. Beat the egg whites until stiff peaks form. Fold into cream-cheese mixture. Pour the batter into the pan and sprinkle with the remaining graham-cracker crumbs.

5. Bake 1 hour. Turn off oven and leave cake in the oven for 1 additional hour. Then leave the oven door ajar for 30 minutes more.

Serves 8. (M)

The
MINOR HOLIDAYS

THE MINOR HOLIDAYS

God increase our worldly goods,
And guard us soon and late,
And multiply our bliss like seeds
Of pomegranate.
For our Redeemer do we wait
All the long night through,
To bring a dawn as roseate
As Apple's hue.
Sin, like a stubborn shell and hard,
Is wrapped around our soul;
Lord, break the husk and let the Nut
Come out whole!

God give us many friends, renew
Our old prosperity,
And be our foemen shrivell'd up
Like Carobs dry.

Behold, from hour to hour we wait
The dayspring yet to be
While all our hearts are dark and black
As Mulberry.

Judah Kala'i, FRUIT OF THE GOODLY TREE

Within the seasonal cycle are major and minor festivals. Two minor ones are of special interest.

Tu Bi-Shevat, the New Year of Trees, is one of the four natural new years mentioned in the Mishnah. At about Shevat 15, in early February, the sap begins to rise in the fruit trees of Israel. To celebrate this event, it is customary to eat up to fifteen different kinds of fruits and nuts. Some people stay up the night before, reciting the passages of the Bible referring to fruits or the earth's fertility. Under the influence of the American Arbor Day, Israelis go out and plant saplings. In the United States, Tu Bi-Shevat is the time to collect funds for reforestation in Israel.

Sephardim chant the Judah Kala'i poem above and eat traditional fruits and nuts. The apple represents the glowing splendor of God. Hard, medium, and soft nuts depict the three different characters of Jews. The almond stands for the swiftness of divine retribution, since it blooms before any other tree. The pomegranate is a sign of fertility, peace, and prosperity. The carob, the food of the poor, represents humility, a necessary element of penitence.

Thirty-three days in the counting of the *omer* comes the festival of Lag Ba-Omer. Since ancient times there have been no feasts or special occasions such as weddings (or, for the very religious, haircuts) between Passover and Shavuot seven weeks later, when two loaves of bread were once offered at the Tabernacle. This may come from an ancient superstition of observing semi-mourning to insure a good wheat harvest for the coming year. On Lag Ba-Omer, however, feasting is permitted. Not a sacred occasion, it is a time for picnicking in the forest and countryside.

MENUS

Tu Bi-Shevat

Baked White Fish★

Fesenjan (Pomegranate Walnut Chicken)★

Chelou (Crunchy Persian Rice)★

Stuffed Prunes★

Baklava★

Sweet-and-Sour Carp★

Cheese Knishes★

Yoghurt Salad★

Carob Brownies★

Figs Stuffed with Walnuts★

Lag Ba-Omer Picnic

Gefilte Fishballs★

Roast Chicken★

Eggplant Salad★

Potato Salad★

Carrot Salad★

Fresh Fruit

Aunt Eva's Cookies★

Herring in Sour Cream★

Cheese Knishes★

Cold Sour-Cherry Soup★

Jaffa Salad★

Fresh Fruit

Rugelach (Cream-Cheese Cookies)★

SPEISEN-FOLGE.

Königin-Suppe

Forellen
Sauce Hollandaise
Sauce Mayonnaise

Geräucherte Zungen
Pflückerbsen

Kalbskopf en tortue

Sorbet d'Ananas

Entenbraten
Salat und Compot

Stangenspargel

Gefrorenes

Nachtisch.

GETRÄNKE.

1911er
Brauneberger Bürgerslay

1904er
Deidesheimer Kieselberg

1900er
Chateau Lafite

Heidsiek Monopole

Fiftieth anniversary menu of the author's great-grandparents. Would that we could serve those wines today!

The
LIFE CYCLE

THE LIFE CYCLE

The river of life...flows from birth toward death. Day follows day with wearisome monotony. Only the holidays twine themselves together to form the circle of the year. Only through the holidays does life experience the eternity of the river that returns to its source. Then life becomes eternal.

Franz Rosenzweig

This little child, ____, may he become great. Even as he has entered into the Covenant, so may he enter into the Torah, the nuptial canopy, and into good deeds.

Circumcision blessing

Blessed art Thou, O Lord our God, King of the Universe, who hath created joy and gladness, bridegroom and bride, mirth and exultation, pleasure and delight, love and brotherhood, and peace and friendship. O Lord our God, may there be heard in the cities of Judah and in the streets of Jerusalem the voice of joy and the voice of gladness, the voice of the bridegroom and the voice of the bride, the jubilant voice of the bridegrooms from their canopies and of youths from their feasts of song. Blessed art Thou, O Lord, who maketh the bridegroom to rejoice with the bride.

Last of the seven wedding benedictions, based on Jeremiah 33:10-11

The family gatherings at circumcision, bar mitzvah, marriage, and death differ greatly from those of the seasonal holidays. While the latter events take place for everyone, year after year, the former can happen at any time within the year and affect each individual in a different way. Yet the celebration surrounding each event is more than a family affair. Through these bonds, all Jews show their responsibility for one another. The individual or couple reinforces its position as a member of the Jewish religious community. A festive communal gathering becomes a means of celebrating the wish for health, wealth, happiness, children, wisdom, and good deeds.

People are never left unaccompanied at what we may call life-cycle events. The woman about to give birth is closely watched; the newborn baby is never left alone until after the circumcision; the bride and groom are surrounded by family and friends for sometimes as many as seven days prior to the wedding; the mourner has family and friends around him. And if this natural accompaniment were not enough, a *minyan* is needed to perform circumcisions, bar mitzvahs, weddings, and funerals. These are all means of binding the individual to the covenant of Judaism.

Wine, symbol of joy, is present at all these events.

Bread—made from the seven grains of Israel—has also become a catalyst for symbols at such events. The mother in childbirth was allowed to eat only a piece of *afikomen* or the blossom end of the etrog, presumably

240

symbols of good luck. "One more child—one more loaf of bread" came to be a Jewish folk saying. At the bar mitzvah and wedding feasts, a bread blessing is recited and hallah eaten before the meal begins. A loaf of bread is the traditional gift to someone with a new home. A loaf of bread was to be set beside a dying man to straighten his limbs and ease his final moments.

Although we like to think of the Jewish religion as enlightened, it is surprising how many superstitions originating in ancient times have carried over to this day. Foods were often a means of showing magical or symbolic power. On the one hand, people hoped for many children, happiness, peace, wisdom, etc. But they were also fearful that the evil eye, Lilith, or other demons would harm them or their family. So means were devised to combat these evil forces. Chickens, fish, circles, and the lucky number seven all have magical significance. A woman in childbirth, for example, might have a chicken swung around her head seven times to ward off evil spirits. Seven benedictions were and are still read at the marriage ceremony.

Circular symbolism is carried over to the table. Circular foods, available the year around, were used since the events of our lives have no seasons. Beans, eggs, lentils, and peas were round and abundant; they were used whenever the mystery of life had to be explained.

Rich foods took on a special significance, to show the wealth of the family performing the wedding or the bar mitzvah. They were also used to wish for wealth and fertility, as in the goldene yoikh—the golden chicken soup with rich rings of fat—eaten by the bridal couple immediately after the ceremony.

Fish, too, symbolize wealth and fertility. In some countries the bride will jump over a fish presented by the bridegroom before the wedding to symbolize the wish for many children. As far back as talmudic times, it was customary to strew fish, wine, oil, parched corn, nuts, and meats before the bridal pair. In the Middle Ages, grains of wheat were strewn; today it is rice.

Meals for such events usually take on the tone of the country in which the family resides. But despite the dispersals, the symbolic foods remain pretty much the same.

MENUS

Brit Milah (Morning)

Herring in Sour Cream★

Bagels★

Cream Cheese

Lox★

Honey Cake★ or Kugelhopf★

Coffee and Wine

Brit Milah (Lunchtime)

Cold Cuts
Potato Salad★
Cole Slaw
Honey Cake★ or Anise Cookies★
Wine Punch
Coffee

Bar Mitzvah

Gravlaks (Pickled Salmon)★
Mustard Sauce
Whitefish Roulade
Marinated Vegetables
Cold Rice Salad
Bagels★
Cream Cheese
Chocolate Fudge Cake★

Bar Mitzvah

Finger Appetizers
Salad
Cornish Hen
Green Beans Almandine
Baked Kishke with Prunes★
Parfaits

Bar Mitzvah or Wedding

Yaprak (Stuffed Grape Leaves
with Apricots)★
Lahmajoun*
Kibbes*
Sambusak★
Tahina*
Eggplant Salad★
Fruits

My Wedding Menu

Finger Appetizers
Hummus*
Tahina*
Pita Bread
Honey Orange Chicken★
Rice
Eggplant Kugel*
Green Salad
Chocolate Wedding Cake with
White Icing

East European Wedding

Schnapps
Gefilte Fish★
Goldene Yoikh (Chicken Soup)★
Roast Chicken★
Lokshen Kugel★ or Potato Kugel★
Hot Fruit Compote★
Honey Cake★
Mead and Wine

Mourners' Meal

Huevos Haminadav (Hard-boiled
Eggs)★
Mujeddrah (Rice with Lentils)★
Bagels★
Cream Cheese
Lox★

*In Nathan and Goldman, *The Flavor of Jerusalem.*

KNISHES

"Ron's getting married!" Julie screamed at me when I came through the door.
"Ron's getting married!!...This afternoon he told us. They spoke long
distance for forty minutes last night. She's flying here next week, and there's
going to be a huge wedding. My parents are flittering all over the place.
They've got to arrange everything in about a day or two."

Philip Roth, GOODBYE, COLUMBUS

The movie "Goodbye, Columbus" has probably done more than anything else to immortalize the American Jewish wedding. Jewish caterers have also played their part. Not only have they preserved East European culinary customs, but they have also transformed what was once a simple occasion into a considerably more elaborate one. Former caterer Rose Siegel recalls that in her native town of Minsk, a *brit milah* or a bar mitzvah was celebrated with a little bit of honey cake and some wine or brandy. For a wedding, a woman was hired by the family to make meals for visiting guests and to bake enough honey cake for all those assembled at the ceremony. A wedding meal included gefilte fish, goldene yoikh, noodle or potato kugel, compote, and mead and wine. There were no American wedding cakes.

Today a veritable feast is prepared. Knishes, tiny frankfurters, or stuffed mushrooms—only a few of the hors d'oeuvres—are followed by an elaborate seated meal, ending with a huge buffet of rich Viennese pastries.

Pastries such as Russian pirogi or knishes (of Slovakian origin) stuffed with cheese or potatoes for Shavuot, cabbage for Sukkot, kasha for Hanukkah, and chicken liver for Rosh Hashanah were once served with potato or beet soup. That was the whole meal. In this country, their form has become daintier. They are now standard Jewish finger hors d'oeuvres for the parties attending weddings and bar mitzvahs.

This particular recipe for knishes comes from Heidi Wortzel, one of Boston's finest cooks and a former French cooking instructor who studied at Paris' Cordon Bleu Cooking School. At a bar mitzvah, Heidi tasted marvelous knishes filled with potatoes and cracked pepper. At home, she experimented until satisfied she had achieved the original taste. Here it is.

Pastry:

4 cups sifted all-purpose flour	6 tablespoons vegetable shortening
1 teaspoon salt	10–13 tablespoons ice water
1 cup butter or *pareve* margarine	1 egg yolk

1. Sift the flour and salt into a large bowl. Add the butter or margarine, cut in small pieces, and the shortening. Blend with a pastry blender until the mixture resembles coarse flakes of oatmeal. Add the ice water and blend, with the cupped palm of your hand, until a single mass is formed.

2. Divide the dough in half. Place one portion on a lightly floured surface. Quickly push the dough away from you, taking small amounts at a time, to blend the flour and shortening. Gather it up in a ball, dust with flour, wrap in plastic wrap, and refrigerate overnight. Repeat the process with the second ball of dough.

3. Preheat oven to 425°.

4. Taking the balls of dough one at a time, roll them out on a lightly floured surface into a rectangle. Cut the rectangle into strips about 8″ long and 3″ wide. Place a strip of filling down the center of the strip of pastry and fold over the sides to completely enclose the filling. Cut the pastry into 2″ lengths and round the ends with your hands.

5. Place on an ungreased baking sheet and brush with a mixture of 1 egg yolk mixed with 1 tablespoon water.

6. Bake for 20 minutes, or until the knishes are golden brown.

Makes about 70. (P or M)

Note: These knishes can be baked, cooled, then frozen. Reheat on a cookie sheet in a 375° oven for 12–15 minutes. The fillings can be made a day ahead and refrigerated.

Potato Filling:

3 large baking potatoes, peeled and quartered	2 large onions, chopped
	¼ cup chopped parsley
3 tablespoons butter or *pareve* margarine	Salt to taste
	Cracked pepper to taste
3 tablespoons oil	2 eggs, lightly beaten

1. Place the potatoes in a 2-quart saucepan. Cover with cold water, bring to a boil, and cook until the potatoes are very tender (about 25 minutes).

2. While the potatoes are cooking, melt the butter or margarine and oil together in a skillet. Add the chopped onions and fry until golden brown but not quite crisp.

3. Drain the potatoes and mash with a ricer or masher until smooth. Stir in the sautéed onions, chopped parsley, salt, pepper, and eggs. The filling should have a slightly peppery taste, which can be obtained by using cracked pepper instead of ground.

(P or M)

Cheese Filling:

1 pound farmers cheese	2 tablespoons chopped parsley
4 tablespoons butter or margarine	2 tablespoons sour cream
1 cup chopped scallions, some green included	Salt and freshly ground pepper to taste
1 egg, beaten	

1. In a mixing bowl, mash the farmers cheese until smooth.

2. In a skillet, melt the butter or margarine. Add the scallions and sauté until they are limp but not brown. Scrape them into the mixing bowl. Add the egg, parsley, sour cream, salt, and pepper.

(M)

Sauerkraut Filling:

1 16-ounce can sauerkraut	1 large onion, chopped
3 tablespoons butter or *pareve* margarine	Salt and cracked pepper to taste
	Pinch of sugar

1. Rinse the sauerkraut thoroughly under cold water. Drain and pat dry. Chop the drained sauerkraut and set aside.

2. In a skillet, melt the butter or margarine and add the chopped onion. Sauté over low heat for 5 minutes. Add the drained sauerkraut and sauté 3 minutes longer. Add the salt, pepper, and sugar. Let cool.

(P or M)

YAPRAK

(Stuffed Grape Leaves with Apricots)

Yaprak—stuffed grape leaves with apricots—are, like Hungarian stuffed cabbage, symbols of plenty and usually served at Sukkot. They are easily adaptable as finger food and are traditionally served at Sephardic life-cycle functions. The following recipe is often served in the Brooklyn, New York, and Deal, New Jersey, Syrian communities.

½ pound grape leaves, fresh, frozen, or bottled
1 pound ground meat
½ cup uncooked rice which has been washed in cold water
2 tablespoons water
1 teaspoon salt
¼ teaspoon allspice

Dash of white pepper
Dash of turmeric (optional)
½ tablespoon dried mint
15–30 apricot halves
⅓ cup prune juice or ¾ cup tamarind syrup
Juice of 1 large lemon
¾ cup hot water
1 tablespoon sugar, or to taste

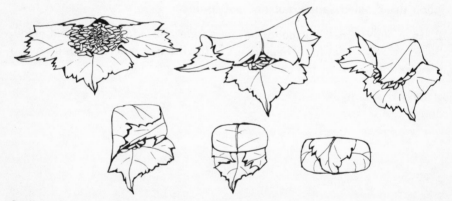

Stuffing the grape leaves (drawing: Debbie Insetta)

1. Thaw frozen grape leaves in lukewarm water 1 hour before starting. Soak bottled leaves in cold water for just a few minutes.

2. Mix the meat with the rice, water, salt, allspice, pepper, turmeric, and mint.

3. Scatter the bottom of a heavy pot with some of the apricot halves.

4. Place a leaf, dull side up and stem removed, on a flat surface, with the stem end away from you. Place a tablespoon of filling on the leaf near the stem end; flatten out to the width of the leaf. Fold the stem end over the filling.

Press the filling firmly underneath the leaf. Fold the sides in and roll from the top toward you. Place the stuffed grape leaves and the apricots in alternate layers in the pot.

5. Cover with a plate to keep the yaprak down, and then place a regular cover on the pot. Steam the grape leaves over a very low flame for about 20 minutes.

6. Combine the prune juice or tamarind syrup, lemon juice, ¾ cup hot water, and sugar. Simmer for about ½ hour and adjust seasoning to taste.

7. Cover the yaprak with the sauce. Bring to a boil and simmer for 1 hour.

8. Allow to cool in the pot and then chill.

Makes about 36. (F)

MEAT PASTELS

Just as the Ashkenazic caterers have transformed knishes into finger food, Sephardim have learned to make tiny torpedo-shaped kibbes, burekas (triangular pastries filled with spinach, eggplant, or cheese), sambusaks, and pastels. Sambusaks are made by Iraqi and Syrian Jews, and burekas by Turkish and Balkan Jews. Perhaps the grandmother of them all is the pastel, a fancy Friday night pastry, supposedly brought from Spain to Turkey. The dough can be made like that for sambusak (p. 160), from fillo, or from egg-roll wrappers, as in this Moroccan recipe from Casablanca.

100 fine egg-roll wrappers	1 teaspoon nutmeg
2 pounds lean ground meat	½ teaspoon allspice
½ cup fresh chopped parsley	½ teaspoon salt
1 cup grated onions	2 cups water
1 teaspoon mace	Vegetable oil for deep-frying

1. One hour before beginning, remove egg-roll wrappers from freezer. Sauté the ground meat over low heat, stirring occasionally. Add the parsley, onions, and seasonings. Blend well and gradually add the water. Cover and simmer, stirring occasionally, until the water evaporates and the meat is very soft (about 1 hour).

2. Grind the meat in a food processor or meat grinder until it is smooth.

3. Cut an egg-roll wrapper in half, then fold lengthwise.

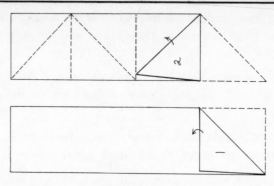

Folding the pastels (drawing: Debbie Insetta)

4. Take 1 heaping teaspoon of filling and place at one corner of the wrapper. Fold the corner over into a triangle and fold up like a flag. The bottom corner is folded last. Repeat until all the wrappers are filled.

5. Freeze for later use, or finish cooking immediately.

6. Heat 4″ of oil in a heavy-bottomed pan to 375°. Deep-fry a few pastels at a time, turning when golden. Drain. Cut each pastel in half. Before serving, place in a warm oven to heat through.

Makes 200 pastels—allow about 3 per person. (F)

BAR MITZVAH GRAVLAKS
(Pickled Salmon)

One of the most delicious bar mitzvah meals I have ever tasted was that of Joseph Richman, son of Phyllis Richman, restaurant critic of the Washington *Post*. For this Sunday morning feast (it was Rosh Hodesh), the Richmans decided to have a spring *milchig* brunch-luncheon at the auditorium of their Conservative Tifereth Israel Synagogue in Washington. Potted geraniums bought at a garden show decorated the tables, and the entire menu for over two hundred guests reflected the springtime availability of fresh foods. A cold rice mold with spots of green was surrounded by blanched, crisp, fresh string beans and asparagus spears. Whitefish soufflé rolls, marinated vegetables, and mock lox—or gravlaks—were eaten with miniature bagels and cream cheese. Red and white wine was the only drink, and a chocolate praline cake modeled after the gâteau marjolaine of Les Pyramides restaurant in Vienne, France, the only dessert. Friends helped cook everything in the synagogue's kosher kitchen.

Not wanting to spend the prohibitive price for fresh lox, Phyllis decided to make her own. She marinated gravlaks in the kitchen for three days. Although she actually served a plateful at each table, she suggests having an entire fish elegantly carved on a long buffet table.

3 parts kosher salt to 1 part sugar	Cracked pepper
1 whole salmon or sea bass, cleaned (or 1 side of salmon cut into 2 equal pieces), split, with bones removed	Fresh dill

1. Mix the salt and sugar. Rub them over the fish. Place one half of the fish, skin side down, on a stainless-steel dish or glass platter. Sprinkle the top with cracked pepper and then spread on a layer of dill.

2. Place the other half of the fish, skin side up, on top of the first. Wrap the fish in tinfoil or plastic wrap. Top with a plate weighted down with a couple of bricks for even pressure.

3. Refrigerate for 2–3 days. Every 12 hours, turn the fish and, if you like, baste with the liquid from the fish.

4. After 3 days, scrape away the dill and cracked pepper and then drain the salmon. Transfer the fish to a board and with a very sharp knife slice thinly at an angle almost parallel to the board. Serve with horseradish, mustard sauce, or alone. The gravlaks will keep refrigerated after curing for at least one week.

Serves approximately 8 people per pound of fish. (P)

HUEVOS HAMINADAV
(Hard-boiled Eggs, Sephardic Style)

The spirit of God broods over the silent waters of creation like a great bird tending its nest.

Rashi's commentary on Genesis 1:2

As the bride went forth from her father's home, an egg was broken above her head. Preceded by fife and drum, she arrived at her home as though deaf and dumb, as she pretended to be while being decked out, then under the canopy, until she went forth and lay on her bed, a statue of stone.

Traveler's description of a wedding in Tangiers

A legend in the Talmud describes God taking up two halves of an egg, which fertilize each other and then result in the creation of the world. The round, perfect egg has always been associated with the mysteries of life and death, of fertility and immortality. Thus, the egg on the veil of the Moroccan bride insures the abundance of the hen, good luck, and many children.

In Judaism, as in most religions, superstitions abound surrounding the egg. Moroccan girls, for example, step over fish roe to increase their fertility. Barrenness in a Jewish woman is cured by eating a double-yoked egg. In circumcision rites, an egg insures the sexual capacity of the young boy. Two eggs are often brought for luck on the first visit to a newborn boy; one to a girl. It is said that an egg thief brings seven years' bad luck and often death. The body of such a thief rolls around the grave and is never still.

At Passover the roasted egg, or *betzah*, has various meanings. The most usual is that it represents the burnt offering brought to the Temple on Passover eve.

Mourning eggs are eaten by all Jews. They represent the roundness of the world and the mourning that comes to us all.

For many centuries, Sephardim have been eating huevos haminadav. These dark-brown creamy-tasting eggs are colored with onion peel or coffee grounds and gently simmered or baked for many hours, sometimes overnight. Cooked in the Saturday dafina, or long-simmering stew, they are also eaten alone as part of the Saturday morning Desayuno, or breakfast, with burekas and coffee.

Water	1 teaspoon salt
Outer skins of 6–10 brown onions	1 teaspoon freshly ground pepper
Coffee grounds (optional)	12 eggs
¼ cup olive or vegetable oil	

Place the water (enough to cover the eggs), onions skins, coffee grounds, oil, salt, and pepper in a large casserole. Carefully add the eggs. Bring the water to a boil. Cover and cook over a very low heat for 6 hours or overnight. The eggs can also be placed in a 225° oven overnight.

(P)

GOLDENE YOIKH
(Chicken Soup)

And God blessed them, saying: "Be fruitful, and multiply, and fill the waters in the seas, and let fowl multiply in the earth."

Genesis 1:22

Chickens have always been one of the symbols of fertility and prosperity for the Jewish people. For poor people, where meat in general was scarce and chickens a luxury, chickens and particularly hens, with their mystical egg, excited the imagination.

In early Israel, a cock and a hen were carried in front of the bridal pair as they were escorted under the canopy. This talmudic custom was transmuted in the Middle Ages to flying a pair of fowl over the heads of the bride and groom. In fifteenth-century Mainz, the bride and groom broke their pre-wedding fast by eating an egg and a hen after the ceremony.

For the New Year and for weddings, it was customary in East Europe to serve goldene yoikh, or the fattest chicken soup possible. To poor people, wanting in substantial food, the goldene yoikh evoked images of wealth and success. Today, in affluent America, the yellow rings of chicken fat are not necessary. Backs of chickens can be substituted for the whole chicken and provide leaner soup.

1 4–5 pound soup chicken	1 onion, quartered
2 large celery stalks with leaves, sliced	3 sprigs parsley
	Salt to taste
2 large carrots, scraped and sliced in 2″ strips	White pepper to taste

1. Place cleaned and washed chicken in a large pot and cover with water. Bring to a boil and skim broth thoroughly.

2. Add the vegetables and seasoning. Cover and simmer slowly about 3 hours. When done, strain the soup.

Serves 8–10. (F)

MUJEDDRAH
(Rice with Lentils, Esau Style)

And Jacob sod pottage; and Esau came in from the field, and he was faint. And Esau said to Jacob: "Let me swallow, I pray thee, some of this red, red pottage; for I am faint."...And Jacob said: "Swear to me first"; and he swore unto him; and he sold his birthright unto Jacob. And Jacob gave Esau bread and pottage of lentils; and he did eat and drink, and rose up, and went his way.

Genesis 25:29–34

After the death of Abraham, Jacob prepared lentils for his father. A dish of lentils was the prominent food served at the mourners' meal following a funeral during biblical times. Later it was replaced by eggs as the main dish.

Circular legumes symbolize immortality and are a magical means of keeping away evil spirits. Thus, it is natural that these round natural foods should have a place at events when keeping life is important. On the Friday night preceding a *brit milah* and on the Watch Night before the *brit*, cooked beans (fava beans) and peas (chick-peas) are eaten. The Watch Night meal is to help the child's lucky star. The legumes were considered by Jews, as well as by many other people, a sort of offering to appease the demons. The rounded lentil was also used to combat the evil influence of Lilith, who was feared as a threat to lying-in women and their offspring.

Contrary to popular belief, Esau's pottage was not lentil soup but rather mujeddrah, a delicious combination of lentils, onions, and rice traditionally stewed in olive oil. I have decreased the amount of oil in the following recipe and it is still tasty.

1 cup brown lentils	2 large onions, sliced in rings
2 teaspoons salt	2 tablespoons vegetable or olive
1 cup long-grain rice	oil
2 cups water	

1. Pick over the lentils; wash and drain. Boil in water with 1 teaspoon salt for about 30 minutes, or until tender.

2. In another pan, bring water to a boil. Add the rice and the remaining 1 teaspoon salt. Turn off the heat and let sit until the lentils are ready.

3. Drain and rinse the lentils and rice. Combine. Bring about 1½ cups water to a boil. Put in the lentils and rice, cover, and simmer slowly about 20 minutes, or until the rice is cooked.

4. Sauté the onions in oil until golden. Add to the cooked rice and lentils. This dish goes well with egg-lemon chicken (p. 200) and a salad.

Serves 6–8. (P)

PASTILLA
(Chicken and Almond Pie)

This extraordinary crunchy pie can be served as an hors d'oeuvre or main dish for a special occasion. Ordinarily prepared with pigeons in Morocco, it is used there by Jews for weddings, bar mitzvahs, or *brits*. Typically Arab, it is usually made with dough similar to that of egg-roll wrappers and cooked brushed with butter (Jews use vegetable oil).

1 3-pound chicken	1 teaspoon ground ginger
Salt and pepper to taste	Pinch of saffron in ½ cup warm
1 cup vegetable oil or *pareve*	water
margarine, melted	½ teaspoon allspice
3 onions, finely chopped	1 cup (or more) water
1 large bunch parsley, finely	12 ounces blanched almonds
chopped	2 tablespoons sugar
1 tablespoon fresh coriander,	6–8 eggs, beaten
finely chopped, or 1 teaspoon	12–15 sheets fillo dough
dry coriander	Confectioners' sugar and
¼ teaspoon turmeric	cinnamon for garnish
1¼ teaspoons cinnamon	

1. About 2 hours before starting, remove the fillo from the freezer, but keep tightly covered.

2. Salt and pepper the chicken. Brown in its own juices in a heavy skillet. Remove to a plate. Add the onions and parsley to the skillet. Sauté in 2 tablespoons vegetable oil or margarine until golden, stirring frequently.

3. Return chicken to the skillet and add coriander, turmeric, 1 teaspoon of the cinnamon, ginger, saffron in water, allspice, and 1 cup of water (or more if you think it is needed). Bring to a slow boil. Cover and simmer for about 45 minutes, or until the chicken is done.

4. Meanwhile, sauté the almonds in 4 tablespoons oil until brown. Remove to dry on paper towels. When cool and dry, chop coarsely and combine with the sugar and the remaining ¼ teaspoon cinnamon.

5. If you are going to cook the pastilla immediately, preheat oven to 375°.

6. When chicken is done, remove from pot and let cool.

7. If you wish, skim off some of the fat from the sauce and leave sauce over a small flame to reduce the stock.

8. When the chicken is cool, debone it and, using your fingers, break it into small chunks, about ¼″ each. (Except for very fatty parts, use the entire chicken.) Place on a plate.

9. When the sauce is reduced, slowly add the beaten eggs and stir for a minute or two until eggs become custardlike. Do not let the sauce become too dry.

10. You can assemble the pie several ways, using either a round quiche pan or a 9″× 13″ Pyrex pan. Brush oil on the bottom of either pan you use.

11: Rectangular method: Place 1 fillo sheet in the pan and brush with oil. Repeat with 5 more sheets. Over them, spread ½ the nuts, ½ the egg mixture, all the chicken, the remaining egg mixture, and the remaining nuts. Cover with 5–6 sheets of fillo, again brushing with oil each time. Fold over any loose ends and brush the tops with oil. Take a last leaf of fillo, fold under so that it neatly covers the pie, and brush with oil. (You can also layer the fillo between the different foods.)

12. Circular method: Place 1 sheet of fillo in the middle of the quiche pan. Brush with oil and then repeat with 5 more fillo sheets, moving the pan a bit so that the fillo fans the entire pan. Fold 2 pieces of fillo and place in center. In a circle 9″ in diameter, sprinkle ½ the almonds on top, then ½ the egg mixture, all the chicken, the remaining egg mixture, and finally the remaining almonds. Cover with the extended edges of the 6 fillo sheets, brushing the edges first. Seal down, then place 2 more sheets of fillo on top; fold over and seal underneath, so that an enclosed circular crust is formed.

13. Bake the pie 30–45 minutes, until top is evenly browned. When ready to serve, sprinkle the top with confectioners' sugar and cinnamon, almonds, or both, in crisscross fashion over the entire pastilla.

Serves 6–8 as a main dish and 12–15 as an hors d'oeuvre. (F)

Note: If preparing in advance, do Steps 1–12, cover with aluminum foil, and freeze. Remove a few hours before cooking and cook as normal (perhaps baking a bit longer).

BAKED KISHKE WITH PRUNES

Kishke (stuffed derma or intestine), ganef (stuffed gooseback), or helzel (stuffed goose or chicken neck) is eaten by Jews at the Sabbath noon meal. In East Europe, the dish is usually made from flour or breadcrumbs, spices, egg, fat, and minced onion stuffed in a casing or the neck.

The Sephardim make theirs differently. In Syria, for example, Jews make it from pine nuts, meat, green peppers, and spices. Once the filling is stuffed into the cleaned intestine of a goat or cow, it is sewn up at the open end and either cooked together with the cholent (as on pp. 47–49) or roasted separately. Today a thin plastic casing is used for the stuffing.

American Jewish caterers have given kishke, known here as stuffed derma, a new gastronomic life. It is now served as a starch at weddings and bar mitzvahs. The following Berger family kishke with prunes was served at a recent bar mitzvah in Chevy Chase, Maryland.

12 ounces pitted prunes	1 length (about 1 pound) kishke*
1 cup water	

1. Boil prunes in the water, simmering until the prunes are soft (about 20 minutes).

2. Mash all except 8–10 prunes with a potato masher. Slice kishke into ¾″ slices.

3. Preheat oven to 325°.

4. Layer the bottom of a 9″ pie plate with mashed prunes. Top with kishke rounds and then another layer of mashed prunes. Add another layer of kishke and top with a whole prune in the center of each round. Add water up to 1″.

5. Bake, uncovered, about 1 hour.

Serves 8–10. (F)

---

*Available at kosher delicatessens.

CHOCOLATE FUDGE CAKE

The only birthday mentioned in the entire Bible is that of Pharaoh. Which is not to say that Jews do not celebrate birthdays today; they are merely not a written part of Jewish custom. Historically, in the cycle of life, it is rather the *Yahrzeit*, the anniversary of someone's death, that is remembered. Living in Christian cultures where birthdays and often saint's days are celebrated, Jews have adapted the birthday party as their own.

What is more American and more perfect for a birthday than an old-fashioned, homemade, rich chocolate fudge cake. Rosalyn Talisman of Cleveland learned to make the following recipe over forty years ago from her neighbor, Elinor Lee. Thirty-five years later Elinor tasted the cake at Rosalyn's and liked it so well she asked for the recipe!

½ cup cocoa	**Frosting:**
1 cup boiling water	2½ cups confectioners' sugar
½ cup butter	4 ounces (½ cup) cream cheese
2 cups sifted all-purpose flour	½ cup cocoa (more if you want
2 cups sugar	a darker frosting)
1½ teaspoons baking soda	1 teaspoon vanilla
1 teaspoon salt	2 tablespoons sour cream (more
2 eggs	for a thinner frosting)
½ cup sour cream	
1 teaspoon vanilla	

1. Preheat oven to 350°. Grease and flour a tube pan.

2. Mix the cocoa, boiling water, and butter until dissolved. Let cool.

3. Combine the flour, sugar, baking soda, and salt.

4. Slowly mix the dry ingredients into the cooled cocoa mixture. Add the eggs, one at a time, beating well after each addition. Add the sour cream and vanilla.

5. Bake in the tube pan 35–40 minutes, or until a toothpick comes out clean.

6. When the cake is cool, combine the frosting ingredients, blending very well. Spread over the cake.

Serves 8–10. (M)

SACHER TORTE

Invented in 1832 by Viennese chef Franz Sacher for the renowned statesman Prince Klemens von Metternich, the Sacher torte is a rich chocolate cake with apricot jam and a chocolate glaze. My grandmother made her own version, which she served on special occasions in Bavaria. As long as I can remember, the Sacher torte has meant birthdays, since my father always requests one for his. The advent of *pareve* margarine at the turn of the century enabled German and Austrian Jews who kept kosher homes to eat this chocolate temptation at a meat meal.

¼ pound unsalted butter or *pareve* margarine, at room temperature	6 eggs, separated
	1 cup unbleached all-purpose flour
½ cup sugar	3 tablespoons potato flour
6 ounces semi-sweet chocolate	Pinch of salt
1 teaspoon vanilla	½ cup apricot preserves
2 tablespoons strong coffee	

1. Preheat oven to 325°. Grease and flour a 9″ spring-form pan.

2. Cream the butter or margarine. Add the sugar and cream the mixture until fluffy.

3. Melt the chocolate with the vanilla and coffee in a double boiler. Add to the butter–sugar mixture. Blend well.

4. Add the egg yolks, one at a time, mixing well after each addition.

5. Sift the flour with the potato flour and the salt. Add to the chocolate mixture.

6. Beat the egg whites until stiff but not dry, and fold gently into the batter, which will be very heavy.

7. Turn the batter into the spring-form pan and bake 1 hour, or until a toothpick stuck into the center comes out clean. Cool the torte on a cake rack, right side up. The torte will fall somewhat.

8. When cool, cover the torte with apricot preserves and chocolate glaze.

Chocolate Glaze:

½ pound semi-sweet chocolate	½ cup water
½ cup sugar	

1. Simmer the chocolate with sugar and water in a saucepan over direct heat, stirring constantly until the chocolate melts. Then simmer over low heat for about 10 minutes.

2. Set the cake rack on a piece of waxed paper and, holding the saucepan about 2″ from the cake, pour the glaze over it evenly. Smooth the glaze with a metal spatula. Let the cake stand until the glaze stops dripping. Then, using 2 metal spatulas or a cake trowel, transfer to a plate and refrigerate for 3 hours to harden the glaze. Remove from the refrigerator ½ hour before serving. Serve alone or with whipped cream (*schlag*).

Serves 8. (M or P)

LINZERTORTE

The Austrian Linzertorte is a single-layer almond crust filled with raspberry preserves and covered with lattice work. It is the choice for birthdays of my French-born, German-descended cousin Eveline Moos Weyl.

1 cup all-purpose unbleached flour	2 egg yolks
Dash of cloves	1 cup unsalted butter, softened
Dash of cinnamon	½–1 cup thick raspberry or currant jam
2 cups finely ground almonds	1 egg white
½ cup sugar	Confectioners' sugar

1. Sift together the flour, cloves, and cinnamon. Add the almonds, sugar, and egg yolks.

2. With a wooden spoon or food processor, work in the butter to make a smooth dough. Refrigerate at least 30 minutes, or until firm.

3. Preheat oven to 300°.

4. Roll out about half of the dough to a thickness of ½″. Line the bottom and sides of a shallow 9″ cake or spring-form pan.

5. Spread jam on top. Roll out the remaining dough and, using a pastry cutter or sharp knife, cut into strips ½″ wide. Put on top of the torte in a dainty lattice. Brush with the egg white.

6. Bake about 1 hour, or until it is lightly browned. Let cool for 5 minutes and then sprinkle with confectioners' sugar.

Serves 8. (M)

PALACSINTA
(Hungarian Crêpes)

A combination of Hungarian crêpes, apricot preserves, and chocolate would make a stunningly appropriate birthday cake to bake for someone of Hungarian descent!

1½ cups sifted all-purpose flour	Butter or *pareve* margarine for
2 whole eggs	frying
1½ cups soda water	

1. Combine the flour and the eggs. Add ½ cup soda water and mix into a paste. Using a wooden spoon, beat until all the lumps disappear. Stirring constantly, slowly add the remaining water.

2. Into a small frying pan or crêpe pan over a medium flame, put about ¼ teaspoon of butter or margarine. Swoosh it around. Add batter with a small soup ladle, moving the pan around until it is thinly and evenly coated. Let it heat awhile, until bubbly and dry. Then slide a knife, dipped into the butter, underneath the edge of the pancake. When ready, turn it over for about 30 seconds. Remove to a plate. Repeat process, adding butter each time. These crêpes freeze well.

Makes 12. (M or P)

Palacsintas can be used as is for blintzes (see pp. 203 and 226 for fillings) or served Hungarian-style with a filling of apricot preserves and sprinkled with confectioners' sugar. The following layered crêpes are a Hungarian dessert for special occasions.

PALACSINTATORTE
(Chocolate Apricot Crêpe Cake)

12 *pareve* crepes (recipe above)	¼ cup chopped walnuts
1 cup apricot preserves	1 tablespoon raisins
1 tablespoon cocoa	2 egg whites
4 teaspoons sugar	

1. Preheat oven to 300°.

2. Place 1 crêpe on a round, greased, ovenproof plate. Top with a thin layer of apricot preserves. Cover with another crêpe. Sprinkle with cocoa and sugar. Cover with a crêpe. Sprinkle with some nuts and raisins. Continue in alternating layers until all the crêpes are used up. (You may want to use more or less cocoa mixture or apricot preserves, according to taste.)

3. Mix the egg whites with 1 teaspoon of the apricot preserves and about 1 teaspoon sugar. Beat until shiny. Pour over the top crêpe.

4. Bake until meringue is brown (about 10–15 minutes). Serve immediately.

Serves 6–8. (P)

GESUNDHEITSKUCHEN
("Good Health" Cake)

The gesundheitskuchen is my aunt Lisl's "good health" cake, which she brought with her from Germany. It is served at birthdays and can be given to people who are ill.

3 eggs	2½ cups sifted flour
1 cup sugar	1 heaping tablespoon baking
1 cup vegetable shortening,	powder
melted and cooled	1 cup milk
1 teaspoon vanilla	Grated rind of 1 lemon
½ teaspoon salt	Confectioners' sugar

1. Preheat oven to 350°. Grease a tube pan.

2. Beat eggs well. Add sugar, again beating well. Add cooled shortening and vanilla, and mix. Add the remaining ingredients, except the confectioners' sugar, and mix until smooth.

3. Pour into tube pan and bake for 45 minutes. Cool in the pan for 10 minutes; then turn out and cool completely. Sprinkle top with confectioners' sugar.

Serves 8–10. (M)

ANISE COOKIES

In Germany my grandmother gave this easily digestible cookie to nursing mothers.

4 eggs	½ teaspoon baking powder
1 cup sugar	½ teaspoon vanilla
2 cups all-purpose flour	Grated rind of ½ lemon
½ teaspoon salt	1 teaspoon anise seed

1. Preheat oven to 325°.

2. Beat eggs and sugar together.

3. Sift flour with salt and baking powder. Add to the egg mixture. Blend in the vanilla, lemon rind, and anise seed.

4. Spoon into a greased long (about 12″) poundcake tin. Bake about 45 minutes, until light brown.

5. Slice while warm into ⅓″ pieces. Place on a large cookie sheet and toast in the oven until golden. Turn over and toast other side.

Makes about 20. (P)

WEDDING CAKE

On the wedding day, immediately after the marriage ceremony, there was a collation of all kinds of the finest sweetmeats, foreign wines and out-of-season fruits. . . . After the ceremony all the guests were led into a great hall, the walls of which were lined with gilded leather. A long table crowded with regal delicacies stood in the center, and each guest was served in order of rank.
                    Glückel of Hameln, 1672, description of her daughter's
                                        wedding in Amsterdam

My wedding was at a time of many shortages after a lost war and a revolution. My mother had a most difficult time getting a festival together. In fact, we had two meals, dinner and supper, for between forty and fifty guests. The ceremony took place in our lovely synagogue in Augsburg, but afterward we drove home by horse and buggy where a beautiful table had been set. I don't remember the menu exactly, but usually a wedding meal consisted of many courses, including soup, fish, chicken, a roast, with cakes and ices for dessert.

In the evening, cold cuts with various salads were served. As a special treat, we had Vollbeer—beer with full alcohol content, a luxury at this difficult time. I don't think we had a wedding cake; it was not customary. The one good Jewish restaurant in our town catered the meals at my wedding. There was a piano player for entertainment, but the very nice thing was that our friends wrote plays and songs which they performed and which contained episodes of our lives.

Recollections of my aunt Lisl's wedding in Augsburg, Germany, 1920

Probably more than any other event, the wedding meal is influenced by wealth and the food customs of the country in which the bridal couple resides.

The wealthy Dutch of the seventeenth century ate sweetmeats at their weddings. My middle-class aunt in post–World War I Germany had a less elaborate meal. Although she does not recall her menu, it may have been similar to that of her parents' wedding in 1897. Theirs included queen soup; salmon and trout with Hollandaise sauce; potatoes; carrots and peas with warm tongue; young roast goose with salad and various fruit sauces; chocolate pudding, cold sherbets, tortes, and petits fours. The evening meal featured cold cuts with salad.

Wedding cake as we know it does not appear until the end of the nineteenth century. Here is the first American Jewish recipe for wedding cake, from Esther Levy's *Jewish Cookery Book*, published in 1871.

A FINE COWLEDGE, OR WEDDING CAKE

Wash two and a half pounds of fresh butter in spring water first, then in rose water, beat the butter to a cream; beat twenty eggs, yolks and whites separately, half an hour; have ready two pounds and a half of the finest flour, well dried and kept hot, a pound and a half of sifted sugar, one ounce of spices, in fine powder, three pounds of currants, nicely cleaned and dry, half a pound of blanched almonds, three-quarters of a pound of citron mixed with orange and lemon; let all be kept by the fire; mix all the dry ingredients in by degrees; beat them thoroughly; then add a half pound of stoned raisins, chopped as fine as possible, so that there are no lumps, and a teacupful of orange flower water; beat it all together for one hour; have a good sized cake tin; it should not be more than three parts full, as there must be space allowed for rising. It will take from three to four hours' baking.

THE BAKLAVA STORY

A Christian, a Jew, and a Moslem went to Istanbul to try their luck. Time passed, and they wanted to sleep. It was very cold, and each of them was keen to sleep in the middle, as it was warmer there between the others.

The Jew said, "It is written in the Holy Torah that I must sleep in the middle."

The Christian and Moslem wondered.

"Look," continued the Jew. "You, Suleiman, celebrate your Sabbath on Friday. You, George, celebrate yours on Sunday, but mine is in the middle, on Saturday. As my feast day is in the middle, my place to sleep must also be in the middle."

The other two agreed to this, and the Jew snuggled up to sleep between the two of them.

When they reached Istanbul, they found a golden coin in the street and started to discuss what to do with it. The Jew kept quiet. The Christian and Moslem decided after a long quarrel and much talking that with the money they could buy a baklava, a sweet Turkish cake, and the one who dreamed the most beautiful dream would eat it in the morning.

In the night the Jew woke up and felt very hungry. He tasted the cake. He tried to awaken his friends, but they were sound asleep and did not hear him. The Jew went to sleep for an hour; again he woke up and ate another piece of the cake. He tried again to awaken his friends, but again he was unsuccessful. So he continued to nibble at the cake all night, until not a morsel remained.

In the morning the three friends went to a cafe in the market. Many people were assembled there; Moslems, Christians, and Jews. Suleiman told them what had happened—how they had found a golden coin in the street and spent it on a baklava. Now they wanted the people to judge who had dreamed the most beautiful dream.

The Christian told his dream first. "I dreamed that Jesus himself came to me and carried me on his wings to the Garden of Eden. When we arrived there, he pointed out to me all the saints sitting around and entertaining each other."

Then it was Suleiman's turn. "I dreamed that Mohammed himself appeared before me and took me to have a look at the Garden of Eden. Is there any dream more beautiful than that?" he asked the people.

When the Jew's turn came, he said, "My dream was different from yours. Unfortunately, I was not lucky enough to visit the Garden of Eden as both of you did. But Moses, our lawgiver, came to me and said, 'Suleiman is with his master, Mohammed, in Mecca; George is with his master, Jesus, in Nazareth. Who knows if either of them will return or not?' And he advised me to eat the baklava."

"Did you eat it?" they asked eagerly.

> *"Of course,"* came the answer. *"Do you think that I disobey our lawgiver's advice!"*
>
> Isaac Al-Bahri, recorded by Elisheva Schoenfeld, FOLKTALES OF ISRAEL

Baklava, the dream bread in this tale of a Turkish Jew, is a very old sweet, ideal for large functions. Originally a Turkish many-layered fillo pastry filled with nuts and syrup of honey or sugar and water, it is made in variations throughout the Middle East. This Lebanese version is contributed by Annie Totah (see p. 50). Kadaif is the shredded-dough version.

LEBANESE-STYLE BAKLAVA

2 pounds fillo dough	1½ pounds unsalted butter or
Vegetable shortening	*pareve* margarine
3 cups walnuts, or 1 cup	1½ cups water
unsalted pistachio nuts and 2	1 tablespoon honey
cups walnuts or almonds	1 tablespoon lemon juice
2 teaspoons cinnamon	1 tablespoon rose or orange-
3¼ cups sugar	blossom water (optional)

1. Be sure fillo is at room temperature before beginning. Preheat oven to 400°. Grease an 11″ × 18″ × 2″ pan with vegetable shortening. Chop the nuts coarsely and mix with the cinnamon and ¼ cup sugar. Set aside.

2. Melt and clarify the butter or margarine. Taking 1 fillo sheet at a time, place loosely in pan and brush with butter. Continue placing the fillo and brushing with the butter until half the sheets are used.

3. Spread the nut filling evenly over the fillo, covering with the remaining fillo sheets, brushed with butter, as above, until all the sheets are used.

4. Cut into diamond-shaped pieces—first vertical lines every 2″, and then diagonal lines—to make 40–50 pieces. (At this point the baklava can be frozen and baked later, if so desired.)

5. Bake for 10 minutes. Reduce oven to 350° and bake another 15 minutes. Reduce oven once more to 300° and bake 15 minutes more, or until golden brown. Let stand 10 minutes, tilting the pan slightly (this way any excess butter can be removed).

6. Boil together the remaining 3 cups sugar, water, honey, lemon juice, and rose or orange-blossom water. Simmer for 10 minutes. Remove from heat and let stand for 10 minutes. Pour the hot syrup all over the surface of the baklava, using a tablespoon to spread it. Leave uncovered until syrup is absorbed. If you keep the baklava covered and in a cool place, it will last for several weeks.

Makes 40–50. (M or P)

KADAIF

2 pounds shredded kadaif
  dough*
Vegetable shortening
3 cups ground walnuts, or 1 cup
  ground unsalted pistachio nuts
  and 2 cups ground walnuts
2 teaspoons cinnamon

3¼ cups sugar
2 tablespoons honey
1 pound unsalted butter or
  unsalted *pareve* margarine
1½ cups water
1 tablespoon lemon juice

1. Have kadaif at room temperature. Preheat oven to 400°. Grease an 11″ × 18″ × 2″ pan with vegetable shortening.

2. Mix together the nuts, cinnamon, ¼ cup sugar, and 1 tablespoon honey. Set aside.

3. Melt and clarify the butter or margarine.

4. Spread the kadaif on a table or place it in a large bowl. Pour the butter over and, with your fingers, separate the shredded dough until all is well buttered. Divide the kadaif into 2 equal halves. Spread half on the bottom of the pan and gently press with your fingers to cover the surface completely. Spread the nut filling evenly over the dough and cover with the remaining kadaif.

5. Bake 20–30 minutes, until golden brown. Cool in the pan for about 10 minutes.

6. Boil together the remaining 3 cups sugar, water, the remaining 1 tablespoon honey, and the lemon juice. Simmer for 15 minutes. Let stand for 10 minutes.

7. Using a tablespoon, ladle the hot syrup over the warm kadaif. Let stand about 15 minutes, covered. Cut into squares.

Makes 40–50. (P or M)

---

*Kadaif can be purchased at Greek or Middle East specialty stores.

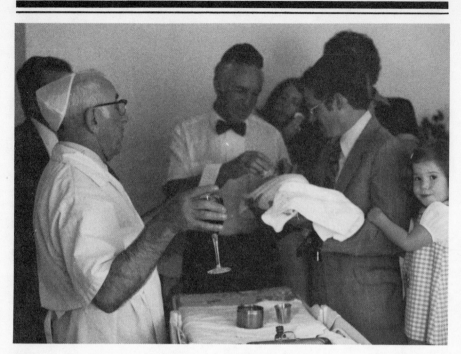

Wine at the circumcision (photo: Marvin Rogul)

WINE

WINE
A Note on Wine

And Noah the husbandman began, and planted a vineyard. And he drank of the wine, and was drunken.

Genesis 9:20–21

Ever since Noah descended from the ark and planted his vineyard, Jews have had a special attachment to wine. The connection has been largely religious and sacramental. Before drinking, a special benediction is recited over it. At the circumcision rite a baby's lips are brushed with wine; at a meal of consolation, mourners drink up to ten cups. Among Conservative and Reform Jews, it is customary that a bar mitzvah boy say his first *kiddush* on the pulpit. At wedding ceremonies, a glass of wine is sipped by the bride and groom. At least four cups are drunk at the Passover Seder. At Purim and Simhat Torah, drinking and even drunkenness are tolerated. The Friday night and Sabbath noon meals are preceded by a blessing over wine.

Wine has always been considered good medicine. *Lehayyim*—To life!—is the standard Jewish toast.

One should note that wine drunk during a meal will not intoxicate, but wine taken afterward will. The Jewish custom of drinking wine before the start of a meal has the effect of inducing the appetite while at the same time adding a certain formality to the proceedings that follow.

From earliest times, wine played an important role in the economy. By the time of the First Temple, taxes were payable in olive oil and wine. Wine was obligatory at public religious functions and for domestic ceremonial occasions. It was a symbol of the hospitality and prosperity of the city-dweller or of the peasant settled on his own land. (In shepherds' tents, only water or milk was drunk.)

Although early wine came from grapes, pomegranates, raisins, figs, and dates, only grape wine was used for sacramental purposes. In fact, throughout the Bible the vineyard is often a metaphor for the people of Israel.

In Deuteronomy 32:38 it is stated: "Who did eat the fat of their sacrifices, And drank the wine of their drink-offering? Let him rise up and help you, Let him be your protection." From this rabbis deduced that the only kosher wines or wine productions were those made and handled by Jews under religious supervision. This prohibition originated in the days when the ancient Israelites lived among pagan peoples who used wine as a libation to their gods. Thus, almost from the beginning Jews have been vintners.

Kosher wine means that the grapes have been touched only by Jews from the time they are pressed until the wine is bottled and poured. It bears the *hecksher*—the rabbi's certificate of approval—on the label. This does not apply to other grain and potato alcoholic beverages. For example, vermouth, arak, champagne, and brandy must comply to the above to be kosher. Beer, vodka, and gin have no wine in them and do not have to be made kosher. The only problem with grain alcohol comes at Passover: if it is made from grain, it cannot be used. Blended whiskey that contains no form of wine is permissible to all Jews.

The custom of drinking only kosher wine has continued to this day, although the reasons the rabbis gave changed in the sixteenth century. Since Christians could not be considered pagans—but there was always the fear of social intercourse, leading to intermarriage—the halakhic authorities thought it best for Jews to drink wine processed and bottled only by Jews. This prohibition often ran into problems. What to do with champagne, for example? If a kosher caterer employs non-Jewish waiters to pour champagne at a wedding, the Orthodox Jew will not touch it. To overcome this problem, wine companies boil their wine just before bottling. By so pasteurizing it, it is considered still kosher even if it is touched by gentile hands.

An interesting sidelight of kosher wine is that certain manufacturers of non-kosher wine will cleanse their factory every few years and work with rabbis to produce a certain amount of kosher stock. Asti Spumante and Yago Sangria are two.

Until the eighth century, Jews produced wine in Palestine. With the Moslem conquest, it was prohibited for Moslem religious reasons. It was not until the 1880's, when Edmond de Rothschild established wineries at Rishon-le-Zion and Zichron-Jacob, that production began again in earnest. These wineries produce three-fourths of Israel's wine today. Most of the thirteen thousand acres of wine-grape vineyards are planted with common French red and white grapes. Seventy percent of Israel's wine exports go to the United States, mostly under the label of Carmel wine.

As the Jews dispersed throughout the world, they needed to produce their own wine for religious purposes. Thus, wherever they lived in the Diaspora, Jews were found in the wine business. At one point in some towns in Russia and Poland in the eighteenth and nineteenth centuries, as much as eighty-five percent of the Jewish population was somehow involved in wine or liquor production or distribution. With all the limits put on Jews, alcohol was one of the few trades they could easily enter (although they paid a high tax to the government). They were even tavern-keepers in East Europe. This profession has carried over to the United States, where most wine or liquor concerns started as Ma-and-Pa grocery stores and spread outward.

During Prohibition, wine was considered an alcoholic beverage. But Catholic and Jewish wines were permitted for religious purposes. Shortly after Prohibition, Manischewitz, owned by the Monarch Wine Corporation of Brooklyn, New York, began producing kosher wine. Later on came Kedem and Schapiro. Other companies include Mogen David (now a subsidiary of

Coca-Cola) and Star. Their vineyards are in upstate New York.

So drink *Lehayyim* and, if you are enterprising, try to make your own. Here is an old recipe for Concord grape wine from—where else?—Concord, Massachusetts.

CONCORD GRAPE WINE

18 quarts Concord grapes
15 pounds sugar

1. Either pick or buy the grapes. Wash. After draining all the water from the grapes, put them in a 5-gallon earthenware crock.

2. Add the sugar, shaking the crock gently to distribute evenly. Cover tightly. Bind with cloth over the cover to seal securely.

3. Keep in a warm place about 3 weeks. After the first 3–4 days, uncover and stir with a large, long-handled spoon to dissolve the sugar. Cover tightly and seal with a cloth as before. Do this every few days. If the fruit ferments too much, move to a slightly cooler place.

4. After 3 weeks in a warm place, remove to a cool place. Let stand 2–3 weeks more, until the fruit settles. Strain through a strainer and a cloth.

5. Bottle in jugs, jars, or bottles. Put away in a cold place. When ready to use, the sediment will have settled to the bottom and the wine at the top should be clear and bright.

BOMBAY KIDDUSH WINE

Jewish table customs are often connected with wine. In nineteenth-century Turkey, for example, after saying the *kiddush* on Friday evening, it was the custom to take a cup of wine and drop some of its contents on the floor of every room in the house, saying: "Elijah the Prophet, Elijah the Prophet, come quickly to us with the Messiah, son of David." Elijah the Prophet was always considered the precursor of the Messiah, and the Messiah is to come on Passover. We all know that Elijah is expected in each Jewish home at the Seder meal, and so a silver cup is placed on the table filled with wine for his arrival.

Whatever the custom, the *kiddush* opens the meal. Today most Jews merely buy their wine from Jewish wine merchants. They probably once traded a goose or other commodity raised or produced at home for their *kiddush* wine. Nevertheless, some Jews did and do make their own.

Pearl Sofaer, born in Bombay and now living in Sausalito, California, was the first-born daughter in her family. It was her task to make the *kiddush* wine each Thursday evening from large black currants, for it is permissible to use a common national drink in place of true wine. Any leftover wine was put in large olive casks from Baghdad and eventually turned into vinegar.

CURRANT WINE FOR KIDDUSH

1 cup large black currants*
2 cups water

1. On Thursday evening the eldest daughter of the family should wash and pit the currants and place them in a bottle with 2 cups water.

2. Cover and keep in a room with the temperature about 90° (obviously, this must be made in the summer).

3. On Friday night pour, say the *kiddush* over the wine, and drink.

Makes about 3 cups.

Note: Any leftover wine can be stored in a large cask. In six months you will have delicious vinegar.

CHAMPAGNE

It is common knowledge among champagne connoisseurs that the monk Dom Perignon discovered champagne. What is less well known is the fact that a Portuguese Jewish wine merchant named Dom Isaac Levy, whose family fled to France during the Inquisition, inadvertently invented the sparkling wine in a case of wine from Dom Perignon's cellar! As a vintner, Dom Levy had thought it a good idea to use Portuguese cork in aged wine to prevent the fermentation gases from escaping. He sent some corks to the Duke of Bedford at Woburn Abbey, England. Instead of letting the casked wine age before transferring it, and then corking it, the wine was corked without the aging process. Six weeks later, corks flew in the wine cellar as the gas that had accumulated in the bottles shot out with tremendous force.

*Large currants are available at some Greek and Mediterranean specialty-food stores.

Champagne was born. When the Duke requested more of this same wine, Dom Levy contacted Dom Perignon and the latter tested different wines to come up with the real champagne.

Now, all that was needed was for the cork to be kept down. Simon Benvenisti, a Jewish wine merchant from Amsterdam, came up with the thin, strong wire which is looped around the cork and twisted around the bottle.

The following is my father's family's champagne punch recipe, which he brought with him from Germany.

DAD'S CHAMPAGNE PUNCH

2 bottles Chablis, chilled
2 bottles champagne, chilled
2 20-ounce cans pineapple chunks

1. Six hours before serving, marinate the Chablis with the pineapple chunks and pineapple juice.

2. Just before serving, add the champagne.

Serves 20.

GLOSSARY OF JEWISH HOLIDAY AND FESTIVAL FOOD TERMS

ADAFINA Sephardic long-simmering stew (hamim), similar to cholent, made with meat, potatoes, chick-peas, vegetables, and rice.

AFIKOMEN Piece of matzah broken off from middle of three matzot used at the Passover Seder and set aside—and often hidden—to be eaten at the end of the meal.

APFELBUWELE Bavarian Jewish apple dessert in a crust, usually baked in a heavy iron pot.

ASHKENAZIM Central and East European, including Yiddish-speaking, Jews and their descendants.

BAR MITZVAH Jewish boy who has reached his thirteenth birthday and attained the age of religious duty and responsibilities.

BAT MITZVAH Jewish girl who at twelve years assumes religious duties and responsibilities.

BERCHES German and Central European hallah made from potatoes, tasting somewhat like sourdough bread.

BLINTZ A thin pancake with a filling, usually of cream or cottage cheese.

BORSCHT A soup having fermented or fresh red beet juice as the foundation, with sour cream or sour milk added when the soup is served.

BRIT MILAH Ceremony of circumcision performed on a male child on the eighth day after birth.

BUREKAS Turnovers of Turkish origin.

CHELOU Persian steamed rice.

CHOLENT Sabbath stew of slow-baked meat and vegetables.

COCIDO Spanish stew thought to be akin to adafina.

DAFINA See ADAFINA.

DESAYUNO Sephardic Sabbath breakfast.

EINGEMACHTS Jam or preserves made from beets, radishes, carrots, cherries, or lemons and walnuts, eaten (usually at Passover) with a spoon and served with tea.

ETROG Fruit of the citron, used with the *lulav* in celebrating Sukkot.

EGYENSULY Hungarian cherry pound cake.

FARFEL Noodle dough or matzah in the form of small pellets or granules.

FASSOULIA A stew of green beans and meat.

FESENJAN A stew of pomegranate and chicken.

FIDELLOS Hair-thin pasta.

FIJUELAS Moroccan deep-fried pastry.

FILLO Paper-thin dough.

FLEISHIG Made of, prepared with, or used for meat or meat products.

GEFILTE FISH Stewed or baked fish, stuffed with a mixture of the fish flesh, bread or matzah crumbs, eggs, and seasonings, or prepared as balls or oval cakes boiled in a fish stock.

GOLDENE YOIKH Rich, golden chicken soup, traditionally served at weddings.

GRIEBEN Cracklings from goose fat, usually salted.

HALLAH Loaf of white bread often baked in braided or twisted form and served especially at the Friday evening meal inaugurating the Sabbath.

HAMANTASH Triangular-shaped Purim cookie, filled with prunes, poppy-seeds, and/or nuts.

HAMETZ Leavened products.

HAMIM Long-simmering stew served by Sephardim on the Sabbath.

HANUKKAH Festival of Lights celebrating the Maccabean victory over the Seleucids in 164 B.C.E.

HAROSET Paste-like mixture of fruit, nuts, cinnamon, and wine eaten during the Passover Seder and symbolic of the mortar the Israelites used in building during the Egyptian slavery.

HAVDALAH Ceremony marking the close of Sabbath or of holidays and consisting of a recital by the head of the household of the appropriate benediction over a cup of wine, a spice box, and a newly lighted special candle.

HUEVOS HAMINADAV Long-cooked eggs served by Sephardic Jews on the Sabbath and other holidays.

KAPPAROT Symbolic ceremony on the eve of Yom Kippur in which a cock, hen, or coin is swung around the head and offered as ransom in atonement for one's sins.

KARPAS Piece of parsley, celery, or lettuce, placed on the Seder plate as a symbol of spring or hope, and dipped in salt water in remembrance of the hyssop and blood of the Passover in Egypt.

KASHA Mush made from coarse, cracked buckwheat, barley, millet, or wheat; or the grain before it is cooked.

KIDDUSH Ceremony proclaiming the holiness of the incoming Sabbath or festival; it consists of a benediction pronounced customarily before the evening meal over a cup of wine and usually two loaves of hallah.

KINDLI Hungarian cookies for Purim.

KISHKE Stuffed derma. Beef or fowl casing stuffed with a savory filling (as of matzah flour, chicken fat, and onion) and roasted.

KNEYDLAKH Soup dumplings made from matzah meal, eggs, chicken fat, and sometimes ground almonds.

KNISH Round or square of rich baking-powder dough, folded over a savory meat, cheese, or potato filling and baked or fried.

KOFTA Meatball or fried patty generally.

KOSHER Sanctioned by Jewish law, ritually fit, clean, or prepared for use according to Jewish law.

KREPLAKH Triangular pockets of noodle dough filled with chopped meat or cheese, boiled and eaten with soup or fried and eaten as a side dish.

KRIMSEL Deep-fried fritter made from matzot or matzah meal.

KUGEL Pudding made of noodles, potatoes, or bread, sometimes with raisins added.

KUGELHOPF Semi-sweet cake of Alsatian origin, usually of yeast-leavened dough containing raisins, citron, and nuts, baked in a fluted tube pan.

LAG BA'OMER Holiday falling on the thirty-third day of the counting of the *omer* between Passover and Shavuot.

LATKE Pancake usually made from grated raw potatoes.

LEKAKH Honey cake.

LOKSHEN Egg noodles.

LOX Smoked salmon.

LULAV Traditional festive palm branch carried and waved during Sukkot.

MAROR Bitter herbs eaten at Passover in remembrance of the bitterness of slavery.

MATZAH Unleavened bread of affliction and freedom.

MEGILLAH Narration of the Book of Esther read at Purim.

MENORAH Originally the holy Temple candelabra, with seven branches; today, usually the nine-candle *hanukkiah* used at Hanukkah.

MILCHIG Made of, or derived from, milk or dairy products.

MOHN Poppy seeds.

MOHRRÜBEN Carrots.

OMER Offering of barley, representing the first reaping of the grain harvest and presented to the priest in a Temple ceremony on the second day of Passover.

OZNE HAMAN Haman's ears; known as Hamansooren in the Netherlands, orechie de Aman in Italy, and hojuelo de Haman in Ladino. Deep-fried pastry, served with sugar at Purim.

PAN DE ESPAÑA Lemon sponge cake.

PAREVE Made without milk, meat, or their derivatives.

PASSOVER Festival of freedom celebrating the Exodus from Egypt.

PASTEL Turnover filled with meat, vegetables, or cheese.

PETCHA Calves' foot jelly.

PIROGI Small pastry turnovers stuffed with savory filling.

PRACHES Stuffed cabbage.

PURIM Festival celebrating the deliverance of the Jews from the machinations of Haman described in the Book of Esther.

ROSH HASHANAH Jewish New Year.

SCHALET Dessert pudding often made with apples.

SEDER Home or community service and ceremonial dinner on the eve of Passover, commemorating the Exodus from Egypt.

SEPHARDIM   Jews who settled in Spain and Portugal at an early date and later spread to Greece, the Levant, England, the Netherlands, and the Americas, and their descendants.

SEUDAT PURIM   Meal eaten on Purim.

SHABBAT   Sabbath.

SHALAH MANOT   Food portions consisting of at least one fruit and one sweet made from flour, given at Purim.

SHAVUOT   Feast of Weeks, commemorating the revelation of the Law on Mount Sinai; a wheat festival in biblical times.

SHOHET   Person officially licensed by rabbinic authority as a slaughterer for food in accordance with Jewish dietary laws.

SHTETL   Jewish small town in East Europe.

SHULHAN ARUKH   Code of Jewish Law.

SUFGANIYOT   Doughnut served at Hanukkah.

SUKKOT   Thanksgiving festival, originating as an autumn harvest festival.

TEYGLAKH   Small pieces of dough boiled in honey.

TISHA BE-AV   Fast day observed on Av 9, in commemoration of the destruction of the First and Second Temples in Jerusalem.

TREF   Ritually unfit.

TSIMMES   Sweetened, baked combination of vegetables or meat and vegetables, often with dried fruits.

TU BI-SHEVAT   New Year of Trees.

VARNISHKES   Noodles, often square or shaped like a bowtie.

YAPRAK   Stuffed grape leaves.

YOM KIPPUR   Day of Atonement, a solemn Jewish fast day.

BIBLIOGRAPHY

Many sources were consulted in the writing of this book. The following is a list of those books that were exceptionally helpful. (Works listed at the end of each quotation are not included here.)

Abrahams, Israel. *Jewish Life in the Middle Ages*. London, 1896.

Appel, Gersion. *The Concise Code of Jewish Law*. New York, 1977.

Baron, Salo W., et al. *Economic History of the Jews*. New York, 1976.

Douglas, Mary. *Purity and Danger: An Analysis of Concepts of Pollution and Taboo*. New York, 1966.

Encyclopedia Judaica. Jerusalem, 1971.

Gaster, Theodor H. *Customs and Folkways of Jewish Life*. New York, 1955.

―――. *Festivals of the Jewish Year*. New York, 1953.

―――. *The Holy and the Profane*. New York, 1955.

Ginzberg, Louis. *Legends of the Jews*. 7 vols. Philadelphia, 1909–38.

Jacob, H.E. *Six Thousand Years of Bread*. New York, 1944.

Schauss, Hayim. *The Jewish Festivals*. Cincinnati, 1938.

―――. *The Lifetime of a Jew*. Cincinnati, 1950.

Sperling, Abraham I. *Reasons for Jewish Customs and Traditions*. New York, 1975.

Trachtenberg, Joshua. *Jewish Magic and Superstition*. New York, 1939.

Universal Jewish Encyclopedia. New York, 1939/40–43.

INDEX